SHIPPING DEVELOPMENTS IN FAR EAST ASIA

Dedicated to my respected teachers

Shipping Developments in Far East Asia

The Korean Experience

TAE-WOO LEE
Department of Shipping Management
Korea Maritime University

Ashgate

Aldershot • Brookfield USA • Singapore • Sydney

Published by
Ashgate Publishing Limited
Gower House
Croft Road
Aldershot
Hants GU11 3HR
England

Ashgate Publishing Company
Old Post Road
Brookfield
Vermont 05036
USA

Reprinted 1999

Ashgate website:http://www.ashgate.com

British Library Cataloguing in Publication Data
Lee, Tae-Woo
        Shipping developments in Far East Asia; the Korean
        experience. - (Plymouth studies in contemporary shipping)
        1. Shipping - Korea - History - 20th century
        I. Title
        387.5'09519

Library of Congress Catalog Card Number :96-86686

ISBN 1 85972 493 0

Printed in Great Britain by Biddles Limited,
Guildford and King's Lynn

Contents

Section One: The causes of Korean shipping growth, 1962-81

Section Two: Dynamic shipping movements in Far East Asia

Figures and tables

Appendices

Foreword

This text represents the output from the extended applied academic collaboration between Korea Maritime University, Pusan, Korea, and the Institute of Marine Studies at the University of Plymouth, and in particular the Centre for International Shipping & Transport. Korea Maritime University, Pusan, and the Centre for International Shipping & Transport, Plymouth, are the most prestigious and largest maritime teaching and research institutions in the Far East and Western Europe respectively. Both provide courses from degree to doctoral level and both work actively with governments and industry in consultancy and research.

Collaboration between the two institutions has been going on since it first developed in 1991 when I was fortunate enough to visit Korea and spend two weeks based at KMU travelling from there to various institutions including Seoul National University, Korea Ocean Research Development Institute (KORDI), Korea Maritime Institute (KMI), Korea Maritime and Port Administration (KMPA), Mokpo Marine Polytechnic and Korea Transport Institute (KTI). It was during this visit that I had the pleasure of spending a considerable period of time working with Dr Tae-Woo Lee and it is from this collaboration that the links between the two institutions have continued to grow and prosper. By 1996 there was a steady flow of researchers moving between the two universities and KMU was providing a notable number of students for UK masters and doctoral programmes in the Centre. In addition there is now a regular movement of first degree students between the two groups, sponsored by the Korean shipping industry and Hanjin Shipping Company Limited in particular.

The most significant development however, was the year spent by Dr Lee at the centre in 1995 from which this volume has emerged. Texts covering the area of Far Eastern shipping are few despite the dramatic growth of the industry in the region to the point that ship operation, shipbuilding and in some cases ship management is now concentrated in the region. Korea is the leading maritime player and KMU has been actively involved in this development. Meanwhile, the United Kingdom remains the centre for ship finance and legal issues and thus the collaboration between the UK and Korean universities matches the industry's moves.

This book covers a wide range of issues in the maritime sector of the region. The early chapters derive from the work of Dr Lee focusing on the development of Korean shipping policy over the last three decades and its influence in the growth of the Korean shipping industry. This theme is continued in an analysis of the use of the Gerschenkron model in the shipping sector. Finally in this sector the role of ideology is examined in the emergence of a dominant maritime position.

The text then moves on to look at specific issues concentrating on an analysis of maritime transport in the Asia Pacific region within the context of regional economic co-operation. Case studies are presented examining the relationships between Korean, Chinese and Russian sectors. The issue of open registration is also examined before the text moves on to a wider discussion of the full international implications of developments. Examples from the cruise and ferry industries are then used to analyse the detailed market developments before the text concludes with a discussion of flagging strategies in the Korean context.

Much of the co-operation between the two institutes has been funded by the British Council and grateful thanks are due to the Seoul representatives of that institution. In addition both universities have provided support in terms of time and resources. It is hoped that this text will be of interest to academics, potential investors, the wider shipping industry, shippers and trade associations, the port industry and financial institutions with an interest in the region and helps to contribute to the debate on the role of Far Eastern shipping activities, providing the basis for further developments in research between the UK and institutions in that region.

Finally, it is with the greatest of thanks to Tae-Woo Lee for all the entertaining times we have spent together and particularly for the supply of vodka, to Marie Bendell at the Institute of Marine Studies for endless secretarial support and patience, and to Neal Toy at the Centre for International Shipping & Transport without whom this text would never have emerged.

Michael Roe
Centre for International Shipping & Transport
University of Plymouth

Preface

The idea for this book arose in conversation with very good friends Professor Michael Roe and Dr Richard Gray at the Centre for International Shipping and Transport, University of Plymouth, where I stayed as a visiting professor in 1995. What they wanted was something which would provide undergraduate students on the Maritime Business and Transport courses with a picture of the shipping developments in the Asia Pacific Rim and of where it stands in the world shipping market. There are a great number of books, many of them very good, which describe shipping developments in the world, or tell the story of particular periods in the development of shipping in traditional maritime countries. However, while I was preparing my lecture papers, I realised that, other than those dealing with Japan, there was a lack of publications directly related to the shipping industry in Far East Asia.

This book is an attempt to fill such a gap. Its object is to analyse the causes of Korean shipping growth over the period of 1962-81; to describe in a broad nature, the recent story of shipping developments between Korea, China and Far East Russia; and to say something of Asian cruise and ferry markets.

This volume contains some chapters taken directly from my PhD thesis which was submitted to the University of Wales, Cardiff in the United Kingdom in 1989 and papers presented at international conferences, examples of which are the World Conference on Transport Research in Lyon; International Association of Maritime Economists Conferences in Seoul and Boston; Asia Pacific Sea Transport Conferences in Singapore and Hangzhou in China; Japanese Society of East Asian Studies Conferences in Fukuoka of Japan and Tianjin of China. Chapter 3 was taken from the journal of *Marine Policy*. The whole chapter was restructured and rewritten for this publication. I especially give many thanks to Mr Andrew O. Coggins, Jr. and Mr Dong-Wook Song for their contribution to Chapter 12. My thanks also go to Mr Sam-Hyun Cho for his contribution to Chapter 7. Chapter 13 can be regarded as an epilogue of Section One, which addresses the recent situation in Korean shipping policy.

The methodology of this study included such techniques as library research, questionnaires and personal interviews. In addition to the statistical data provided through library research, it became, in particular, more evident that the literature was very limited in its dealing with recent Russian shipping matters after the disintegration of the former USSR and with regard to Chinese shipping circles. Since the executives of shipping companies are active participants in managerial planning, control, decision making and joint venturing, it would seem sensible and logical to know their thoughts, opinions and attitudes about various aspects of management. Personal interviews with top executives have provided a more complete understanding of the operations and details within the management of Russian and Korean shipping companies. This empirical approach has also contributed to the revealing of information concerning the practical side of the various problems.

It is hoped that this work will serve as an adequate text for readers interested in the history of Korean shipping in the period of 1962-81; and at the same time that it will provide an informative background for those who work in the field of shipping business and may become, or are already, involved in joint operations with Chinese and Russian shipping companies, in order to enable them to understand shipping developments in Far East Asia. Further, this book will be used as supplementary reading in advanced shipping business courses at postgraduate level.

With this publication, I have been extremely fortunate in being able to call upon the services of experienced and highly regarded individuals, shipping companies and organisations, here and abroad, to provide me with data, information, materials and comments on their respective management activities. Special thanks are extended to the following individuals and organisations (in alphabetical order):

Black Sea Shipping Company (Mr Alexei Yatsenko)
Dongnama Shipping Company Limited (President Geel-Yong Yang)
Dong Jin Shipping Company Limited (Chairman Young-Chan Kim)
Far Eastern Shipping Company
Hanjin Shipping Company Limited (Mr Kwang-Hee Lee)
Hyundai Merchant Marine Company Limited
Keoyang Shipping Company Limited (Captain Hak-Kyun Oh)
Korea Marine Transport Policy Foundation (Professor Yong-Sub Park)
Korea Maritime Research Institute (Dr Hyon-Kyu Park)
Korea Shipowners' Association
Korea Ship Management Companies' Association
Korea Maritime Port and Administration
Lena River Shipping Company
Shin Sung Shipping Company Limited (President Young-Kyu Park and
    Mr Min-Ho Seo)
Soyuzmorniiproekt (Dr Felix Arakelov and Dr Vitali Serebriakov)
Sungwon Shipping Company Limited (President Dong-Chul Jeon and
    Captain Hyun-Chae Lee)

Zinsung Shipping Corporation (President Hoon Rhee)

The old boys from the Advanced Management Programme (AMP, President Hong-Yang Kim) at the KMU have also been vital in enabling me to collect valuable information in shipping management as well as encouraging me to keep this work going.
  In spite of all the help received, including that expressed in the acknowledgement, deficiencies undoubtedly remain. I am solely responsible for the views expressed and for any errors and omissions and welcome readers to call them to my attention at the following address.

Tae-Woo Lee
Department of Shipping Management
Korea Maritime University
1 Dongsam-dong, Yeongdo-ku
Pusan 606-791, Korea

Acknowledgements

This book is the final product of the efforts of many people and of help from many organisations. First of all, I would like to express my sincere gratitude to my supervisors, Emeritus Professor Tae-Hyon Sohn at the Korea Maritime University (KMU), Professor Richard O. Goss and Professor John King at the Department of Maritime Studies and International Transport of the University of Wales, Cardiff, Emeritus Professor Ik-Soon Im at the Yonsei University, Emeritus Professor Kyu-Sang Park and Professor Kyu-Sung Shin at the Dong-A University for their constructive suggestions, invaluable comments and incisive criticism throughout the period of my studies. I am in particular indebted to the works and teachings of Professors Sohn and Goss. I should confess that whatever thanks I express would be insufficient to repay their supervision.

A one year stay in Plymouth gave me the opportunity to publish this book. For this my acknowledgements are due to the Centre for International Shipping and Transport, University of Plymouth and the British Council in Seoul. I benefited from the provision of very good research facilities and generous grants from them respectively. In particular, my profound and special thanks to Professor Michael Roe at the Centre. He wrote the preface for this book and his encouragement and support enabled me to start and finish the publication of the book. Special thanks are extended to Dr Anthony Redfern, Head of the Institute of Marine Studies and his colleagues. I am also indebted to the KMU, which allowed me to have one-year academic travel to the UK.

I am especially grateful to Mr Neal Toy, Miss Marie Bendell, Mr Kimmo Kosunen and Mr Dong-Wook Song, who laboured patiently typing and proof reading this book. The writing of this book would not have been possible without linguistic help from Neal and Kimmo. In particular, despite the fact that Neal and Dong-Wook are at the moment on their respective doctoral courses, their conscious efforts have been made to this book. I do hope that they achieve great academic success at the Centre in due course. Also my sincere thanks to the editorial staff at Avebury. In particular, Ms Sarah Markham. The final responsibility for any errors or omissions, whether of fact or interpretation is wholly mine.

I have the pleasant duty of expressing my thanks to Emeritus Professor Hiojung Jeon, Emeritus Professor Joon-Soo Lee, Professor Si-Kwon Young, Professor Joon-Soo Jon, members of the 'Beom-Woo' Scholarship Foundation (President Captain Sam S H Park), Dr Young-Ho Lee, Mr Jin-Haeng Jo, Mr Dae-Yong Gee, Dr Cheol-Soo Kim, Dr Gil-Soo Kim, Dr Seong-Hyeok Moon, Dr Seong-Cheol Cho and Dr Jae-Bong Kim for their warm encouragement and support paid to me prior to this publication, whenever I needed their helping hands. Also many thanks to my senior and junior colleagues, my assistants Mr Hyun-Duk Kim and Mr Kuy-Bum Yeom for their support during my absence at the KMU.

My mother and brothers, my wife Jin-Hwa, my lovely daughter Hannah, and my son Sang-Jeong had to pay the inevitable price of being rather neglected during my study. When I needed them, they were always with me. On the contrary, when they needed me, I was not always with them. They have certainly paid this price willingly. Last but by no means least, I wish to thank them for their forebearance and kind words of encouragement.

Section One

The causes of Korean shipping growth, 1962-81

1 Introduction

At the end of the Second World War, international shipping was controlled almost exclusively by a few advanced maritime countries. International trade was also dominated mainly by these countries. Thus, several nations which emerged from colonial or semi-colonial status after 1945 began to pay increasing attention to shipping and the allied trade problems and evolve their own policies. As a consequence, shipping matters were brought up in the regional commissions of the United Nations, especially the Economic and Social Council, Economic Commission for Asia and the Far East, Economic Commission for Africa and Economic Commission for Latin America (ECLA).

However, the first global effort to formulate a common approach to shipping and related matters, from the point of view of developing countries, was not made until the first meeting of the United Nations Conference on Trade and Development (UNCTAD I), held in Geneva in 1964.[1] UNCTAD has had a great impact in two distinct but closely interrelated functions: the initiation of new ideas, new concepts and new approaches to the problems of trade and development; and the negotiation of international agreements or conventions on specific issues. Prebisch's original analysis,[2] as presented to UNCTAD I in 1964, identified the main constraints on the development process as arising from the linkage of economies of developing, with those of developed countries, particularly the secular tendency of the terms of trade of developing countries to deteriorate. Through the work of ECLA and UNCTAD, he had a strong political and economic influence in developing countries. As a consequence, a comprehensive response to shipping questions crystallised at the Algiers conference of developing countries held in 1967.

Within UNCTAD, many arguments have been developed which deal with the motives and reasons for developing countries entering the shipping industry. Arguments about the effects of the industry on the countries and whether or not the investment in shipping was economic have also been developed. They may be largely classified into two main streams: one, largely the traditional maritime country's viewpoint, based mainly on the comparative advantage theory leading to a laissez-faire doctrine, and the other, largely the developing country's viewpoint,

3

on economic development and often non-economic factors, e.g. national prestige and defence.

From the latter's point of view, it is generally assumed that a national fleet can contribute to national welfare by:[3]

- creating income;
- effecting a country's industrialisation;
- reducing economic dependence;
- influencing the decisions of shipping conferences;
- contributing to national defence;
- diversifying employment;
- improving the balance of payments;
- facilitating trade;
- contributing to economic integration within the country and with neighbouring countries;
- stimulating industries with forward and backward linkages to the shipping industry.

The importance of shipping to developing countries, therefore, is perceived as multi-dimensional.

Shipping in most developed countries had, for several preceding decades, been governed by a laissez-faire philosophy which implied the minimum of international or national interference in its commercial operation and, in effect, the maintenance of the status quo. However, once it was decided to include shipping in the field of competence of UNCTAD, developed countries tried hard to refute the views of developing countries on shipping problems and to keep the terms of reference of the UNCTAD Committee on Shipping to a minimum.

Traditional maritime countries argued that the interest of international trade would best be served by maintaining the freedom of the seas,[4] by minimising government and international intervention, and by improving ports in developing countries. They also argued that the developing countries' desire to improve their balance of payments by setting up shipping fleets was misplaced and that their scarce resources could be better employed in other sectors.[5] They therefore recommended to developing countries that, prior to any investment decision, the main question to be answered should be to what extent the funds to be applied would contribute to value added and thereby help to raise the standard of living. In the long term, even politically motivated decisions must not violate economic principles; investments in uneconomic operations will always be at the expense of the State budget, which represents the sum total of all dues, duties and taxes levied on citizens. However, developed countries were not against developing countries setting up their own shipping fleets, but they insisted that this be done on the basis of sound economic criteria.[6] While developed countries maintained that this meant decision-making on shipping investment, from the point of view of the profitability of individual projects, developing countries rejected such a narrow

4

view, insisting that the definition be extended to indirect effects on shipping investment, e.g. its externalities.

Moreover, developing countries retorted that they had no say in the running of an industry of vital importance to them and especially so in the liner sector which was usually controlled by conferences; that they were convinced that the balance of payments impact of establishing their own fleets would often be favourable; and that liner conferences were not insensitive and charged freight rates which were high, discriminatory and anomalous, pointing out that freight cost relative to commodity value is higher for exports than for imports for developing countries.

Table 1.1
Growth of shipping tonnage in Korea and the world (1962-81)

Year	Gross tonnage (in thousands)		Changes in the growth rate (%)	
	Korea	World	Korea	World
1962	104	139,980	-	-
1963	108	145,863	3.8	4.2
1964	122	153,000	13.0	4.9 (1)
1965	129	160,392	5.7	4.8
1966	193	171,130	49.6	6.7
1967	306	182,100	58.5	6.4
1968	474	194,152	54.9	6.6
1969	767	211,661	61.8	9.0 (2)
1970	849	227,490	10.7	7.5
1971	940	247,203	10.7	8.7
1972	1,057	268,340	12.4	8.6
1973	1,104	289,927	4.4	8.0
1974	1,226	311,323	11.1	7.4 (3)
1975	1,624	342,162	32.5	9.9
1976	1,796	372,000	10.6	8.7
1977	2,495	393,678	38.9	5.8
1978	2,975	406,002	19.2	3.1
1979	3,953	413,021	32.9	1.7 (4)
1980	4,334	419,911	9.6	1.7
1981	5,142	420,835	18.6	0.2

Notes: (1) *The First Five Year Economic Development Plan, 1962-66.*
(2) *The Second Five Year Economic Development Plan, 1967-71.*
(3) *The Third Five Year Economic Development Plan, 1972-76.*
(4) *The Fourth Five Year Economic Development Plan, 1977-81.*

Source: *Lloyd's Register of Shipping Statistical Tables* (1987).

Developing countries claimed that they had the right to protect their fleets to establish their merchant fleet and enable their shipping industries to grow.[7] It seems that both parties marshalled arguments to support their own particular points of view without a systematic and comprehensive theoretical review.

Since the implementation of the First Five Year Economic Development Plan in 1962, Korea, in a very backward situation, expanded its merchant fleet rapidly between 1962 and 1981, rising from 104,000 gross tons (grt.) to 5.1 million grt., as shown in Table 1.1.

From the level of change in growth rate of gross tonnage, periods for Korea in Table 1.1 may be divided into five phases:

- the 1962-65 stagnant growth phase;
- the 1966-69 accelerated growth phase;
- the 1970-73 recession phase;
- the 1974-76 recovery phase;
- the 1977-81 high growth phase.

Table 1.1 shows that, except for 1973, the changes in the growth rate of Korean shipping tonnage exceeded those of world tonnage throughout the period 1962-81. While Taiwan and Brazil, as developing maritime countries, played an active role in expanding their merchant fleets in the 1960s and 1970s,[8] Japan, as an emerging developed maritime country, considerably expanded its shipping tonnage in the same period, and her national fleet increased to 40.8 million grt. in 1981 from 8.9 million grt. in 1962. Its share of the total world gross tonnage amounted to 9.7 per cent in 1981. It is interesting to compare the index of shipping tonnage in Korea with the indices of the above countries in terms of grt., based on 1962 = 100. Table 1.2 shows such indices.

While in 1981 the Taiwanese index had 388, Brazilian 426 and Japanese 460, the Korean index of shipping tonnage had more than 4,900. It can be seen from the table that the Korean growth rate of shipping tonnage during the period 1962-81 is higher than that in any other country. Figure 1.1, which is drawn on the basis of Table 1.1, presents the speed of growth of merchant marines of the above four countries and the world during the period 1962-81. The lines in the figure enable the different characters of growth in different countries to be seen. World tonnage has increased in a fairly regular fashion over the whole period. Reasonably regular growth curves, such as those of Taiwan, Brazil and Japan can be seen, each displaying a slightly different growth rate. There is a country displaying very rapid growth over a limited period; Korea between 1974 and 1981. From the figure it can be seen that among the above countries, Korean shipping experienced the highest growth rate in the whole period of 1962-81.

6

Table 1.2

Indices of shipping tonnage in Korea, Taiwan, Brazil, Japan and the world[+]

(1962-81)

Year	Korea	Taiwan	Brazil	Japan	World
1962	100	100	100	100	100
1963	104	107	102	112	104
1964	117	121	106	122	109
1965	124	131	104	135	115
1966	186	158	106	166	122
1967	294	159	108	190	130
1968	456	157	107	221	138
1969	738	198	115	270	151
1970	816	240	143	304	163
1971	904	272	144	344	177
1972	1,016	308	157	394	192
1973	1,062	302	175	415	207
1974	1,083	291	202	436	222
1975	1,562	298	224	448	244
1976	1,727	305	257	470	266
1977	2,399	321	277	451	281
1978	2,861	333	307	442	290
1979	3,861	414	333	451	295
1980	4,167	420	377	462	300
1981	4,944	388	426	460	301

(1962 = 100)

Note: +   *In terms of gross tonnage.*

Source: Calculated from Table 1.1 and *Lloyd's Register of Shipping Statistical Tables* (1987).

The purpose of the first part of this book is: to introduce the Gerschenkron model[9] and show that the model is applicable for analysing the past rapid growth of the Korean shipping industry in the period 1962-81; taking the case of Korea, to test the hypotheses based on the model and conclude that the Korean shipping industry had the advantage of relative backwardness and substituted some missing prerequisites[10] for shipping development in the context of the Gerschenkron model; and to suggest that the model would be a useful tool to judge the validity of establishing merchant marines in developing countries from comprehensive and historical points of view. In so doing, will be discussed some special features of the Korean shipping industry in the course of its establishment or expansion.

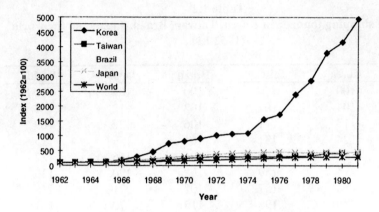

Figure 1.1 **Growth trends of shipping tonnage in Korea, Taiwan, Brazil, Japan and the world (1962-81)**

Gerschenkron developed a theory of industrialisation in his essay Economic Backwardness in Historical Perspective.[11] He maintained that in a number of important historical instances, industrialisation processes, when launched in a backward country, showed considerable differences, as compared with more advanced countries, not only with regard to the speed of the development or the rate of industrial growth but also with regard to the productive and organisational structures of industry which emerged. Furthermore, these differences in the speed and character of industrial development were, to a considerable extent, the result of the application of institutional instruments, i.e. the State and banks, for which there was little or no counterpart in an established industrial country. In addition, he observed that the intellectual climate within which industrialisation proceeded, i.e. its ideology, differed considerably among advanced and backward countries.

According to the Gerschenkron model, the reasons why industrialisation in backward countries was generally more rapid than in advanced ones were; firstly, an advanced country must for itself develop and accumulate the technology and capital for growth at the expense of risk and the high cost of trial and error. By contrast, a backward country can import the technology, capital and skilled labour from the advanced country, lessen such risk and cost, and shorten the period of industrialisation. Of course, the process may be a costly one. Secondly, technology imported into a backward country is modern and mainly related to, e.g. iron and steel and the shipbuilding industries, which are capital intensive. This is because the backward country is not likely to quickly overtake the mechanical engineering industries of advanced countries given their long history of develop-ment and high skills. On the other hand, the productivity of heavy and chemical industries depends partly on the average life of its equipment. Thus, once it has imported and established such modern plant, the backward country can enjoy superiority while the advanced country is not willing to renew its equipment

8

because of high sunk capital and high exit costs. Therefore, it is, Gerschenkron concluded, natural that the backward country has a discontinuous spurt at the initial stage of growth.[12]

Thirdly, the term "backward country" normally implies that there is an absence of institutions and organisations capable of employing and arranging resources. In order to implement industrialisation, an organisation capable of mobilising and employing resources efficiently and effectively is required by the backward nation. Generally speaking, this is the State or government. For instance, in pre-Revolutionary Russia, the State was the primary agent propelling economic progress in the country. Through multifarious devices, such as the State budget, preferential orders to domestic producers of railroad materials, high prices, subsidies, credits and profit guarantees to new industrial enterprises, the Russian government succeeded in keeping a high and increasing rate of growth of industrialisation until the end of the nineteenth century, substituting for some missing prerequisites.[13] A study in which the Gerschenkron model was applied to Japan showed that, in the Meiji era, the Japanese government played the main role in implementing industrialisation.[14]

Fourthly, to break through the barriers of stagnation in a backward country, to ignite the imagination of men and to place their energies in the service of economic development, an ideology or ethos (as it was called by Weber[15]), is strongly needed. The promise of better allocation of resources is not sufficient alone. For example, List's nationalism in Germany[16] and Saint-Simonism in France[17] contributed to the ideological climate within which industrialisation emerged in those countries.

From historical examples in Western countries, Gerschenkron discussed the causes of acceleration in the course of industrialisation of backward countries like those above. He proved his propositions by extensive historical research on Europe in the nineteenth century.[18] One of them is that the more backward a country's economy, the more likely was its industrialisation to start discontinuously as a sudden great spurt leading to a relatively high rate of growth. Thus, it is to some extent because the backward country enjoys some advantages of backwardness in the process of industrialisation that the backward country, once having entered into the initial stage of industrialisation, may make rapid progress.

In this book the Korean shipping industry is put into the Gerschenkron model by analysing its rapid growth in the period 1962-81. Four historical hypotheses in the Korean shipping industry are established on the basis of the Gerschenkron model. They are mainly concerned with the roles of institutional instruments, i.e. the State and banks, and of ideology, raising the following question: in what way and through what devices did a backward country, i.e. Korea, substitute for the missing prerequisites in the shipping sector?

The significance of the application of the Gerschenkron model to shipping may be expected, firstly, to enable developing countries to review new and important aspects of the problems concerned as well as to explore and define sound economic criteria for establishing or expanding their national fleets. Secondly, when the model is applied to the shipping field, shipping policies toward backward countries are unlikely to be successful if they ignore the basic characteristics of economic backwardness in the field of shipping, or unless they substitute missing pre-requisites in the shipping sector. Thirdly, the Gerschenkron model may be expected to highlight some aspects which economic theories, related to the establishment or expansion of merchant marines in developing countries, could not fully explain from the historical point of view.

For some parts of the period (1962-81) covered by this book, consistent data concerned with the Korean shipping sector was not available. One reason for this is that the sector has been controlled under various departments of the Korean government. For example, the Ministry of Construction is in charge of building industrial ports, while the Korea Maritime and Port Administration (KMPA) is responsible for building commercial ports. On the other hand, the Ministry of Trade and Industry takes charge of planned shipbuilding for the expansion of shipping, while the KMPA controls the import of second-hand ships. Thus, shipping data is dispersed and often inconsistent. Another reason is that the KMPA was only established in 1976. However, it is believed that the data used in this study, which applies the Gerschenkron model to the Korean shipping industry, is sufficient to develop the logic of the argument and to draw conclusions.

The second part of this book is concerned with the current issues in the Korean shipping circle. Such matters include the rise of other maritime powers in the Asia-Pacific region, the need for co-operation with those powers in the context of disparate social, economic and political backgrounds, the need to overcome regional bottlenecks in infrastructure, the development of instruments to optimise Korea's international shipping competitiveness and, the evolution of completely new markets in the region. These chapters have been based upon papers arising from a number of contemporary studies carried out by the author.

The outline of this book is as follows. It consists of six chapters in Section 1 and seven chapters in Section 2. Chapter 1 is an introduction to this book. In preparation for clarifying the causes of the establishment and expansion of the merchant fleet in Korea, the Gerschenkron model is introduced in Chapter 2. After exploring its applicability to Korean shipping, some hypotheses will be made in terms of the State, the banking system and an ideology following the model. Chapters 3, 4 and 5 include empirical tests on the hypotheses established in Chapter 2. In so doing the following question will be answered: in what way and through what devices did Korea substitute for the missing prerequisites in the shipping sector? Chapter 6 concentrates on summarising the results of the hypotheses tested and drawing out the peculiarities which have emerged in the process of examining Korean shipping growth.

Chapter 7 is the first chapter in Section 2 and focuses on the implications for maritime transport in the Asia-Pacific region within the context of regional economic co-operation. The case studies utilised here concern the development of relationships between the Korean enterprises and their Chinese and Russian partners. Chapter 8 highlights the fact that the development of other maritime

10

nations can also impose competitive threats to the Korean shipping industry by analysing how the shortsea market in the Asian-Pacific area has been affected by both the growth of the Far East Russian fleet and the increasing influence of open registers. Chapter 9 provides the reader with an insight into the challenges that have been brought upon one such Russian shipping company, the Far Eastern Shipping Company, during the time of fundamental political and economic transformation in that country. The major objective of Chapter 10 is to outline the problems which have occurred in formalising joint agreements between Russia and Korea. It seeks to examine joint ventures and joint operations from a global perspective, namely to identify the problems unique to joint ventures and joint operations between these two specific countries and which are merely replicas of similar obstacles encountered in joint ventures world-wide.

The competitiveness of the Korean fleet in a geographically and economically wider international sphere is addressed in Chapter 11. The advantages to be gained by the adoption of a quality management system are discussed in general and then are related to Korean shipping companies specifically. A conceptual prototype, relating expressly to the quality of seafaring labour as part of a more extensive total quality management system, is then suggested.

The potential for passenger shipping in the Asia-Pacific area is considerable. Chapter 12 examines the Asian cruise and ferry markets from a macro and micro viewpoint. The macro viewpoint regards the characteristics and causes of growth in the markets, their market segments and development stages. The micro viewpoint examines the operators, the fleets and the market structure of the ferry services between Korea, China and Far East Russia; potential prospects for the ferry lines in the region; and analyses the possibilities for co-operation between operators in the ferry business.

The competitive advantages to be gained by utilising either second or open registers have been well documented and Chapter 13, the final chapter of the book, examines the implications of utilising such registers from the Korean viewpoint and suggests that regulatory restrictions should be loosened to allow Korean companies to be able to compete more evenly on the world market. As ship management is closely interrelated to flagging strategies, this chapter also discusses the possible areas for co-operation between Korean shipping or ship management companies and advanced foreign ship management companies.

The use of Korean literature sources always complicates a system of citation. In the first complete reference to any work, we have supplied the full title in transliterated Korean, followed by a translation in brackets. Subsequent references also give the name of the author or the title in transliterated Korean with the translation.

Notes and references

1   On the history of UNCTAD activities in the field of shipping, see UNCTAD (1985), *The History of UNCTAD 1964-1984*, UNCTAD/ OSG/286, pp. 130-57, United Nations, New York.

2   Prebisch, R. (1964), *Towards a New Trade Policy for Development*, E/CONF.46/3, UN Sales No. 64.II.B.4, UNCTAD, New York.

3   Behnam, A. (1976), 'Political Factors and the Evolution of National Fleets in Developing Countries', *Maritime Studies and Management*, Vol. 3, p. 131; Wijnolst, N. (1975), 'Developing Countries and Shipping', *Norwegian Shipping News*, No. 17D, pp. 147-50; Arnold, B. (1969), 'Shipping Policies of Young Nations', *Intereconomics*, No. 8, pp. 216-7; UNCTAD (1968), *Establishment or Expansion of Merchant Marines in Developing Countries*, TD/26/Rev.1, pp. 5-12.

4   The 'freedom of the seas' has a wide meaning for developed countries; it includes not only freedom of navigation on high seas, but also the freedom to trade between any two countries.   On historical development of the freedom of the seas and its concept, see Gold, E. (1981), *Maritime Transport: The Evolution of International Marine Policy and Shipping*, Lexington Books, Lexington; Farthing, B. (1987), *International Shipping: An introduction to the policies, politics and institutions of the maritime world*, pp. 1-12, Lloyds of London Press, London.

5   Haji, I. (1972), 'UNCTAD and Shipping', *Journal of World Trade Law*, Vol. 6, No. 1, p. 61.

6   The term 'sound economic criteria' was used in the context of the 'Common Measure of Understanding'.   A number of controversies surrounding its definition have developed between developing and developed countries.   From the developing countries' point of view, this subject was discussed in Rajwar, L. M. S., et al., (1971), *Shipping and Developing Countries*, The Carnegie Endowment for International Peace, pp. 33-4, New York.   This term was also discussed by Goss. See Goss, R. O. (1988), 'The Role of Merchant Shipping for Developing Countries', a paper for the SOBENA Congress, Rio de Janeiro.

7   Economic Intelligence Unit (1964), *Ocean Shipping and Developing Countries*, E/CONF.46/27, pp. 49 and 187, UNCTAD, Geneva.

8   On the expansion of Taiwanese shipping, see Lee, M. and Pearson, R. (1987), 'Expansion of China's Fleet', *Marine Policy*, Vol. 11; Lee, M. and

Pearson, R. (1988), 'The Expansion of the National Fleet of the Republic of China on Taiwan 1960-1985: the Policies Adopted and Conflicts Created', *Maritime Policy and Management*, Vol. 15, No. 3, pp. 213-24. On the growth of Brazilian Merchant Marine, see Farrell, S. (1984), *Brazilian Merchant Marine Policy 1958-80: A Study in Planning and Development*, PhD Thesis, The University of Liverpool.

9   The Gerschenkron model means his theory of industrialisation to be discussed in Chapter 2 of this book.

10   On its concept in the Gerschenkron model, see Gerschenkron, A. (1957), "Reflections on the Concept of 'Prerequisites' of Modern Industrialisation", L'Industria, No. 2, pp. 357-72. This was reprinted in his book (1962) *Economic Backwardness in Historical Perspective: A Book of Essays*, pp. 31-51, Harvard University Press, Cambridge, Massachusetts. This subject will be discussed in detail in Chapter 2 of this book.

11   Gerschenkron, A. (1952), 'Economic Backwardness in Historical Perspective', in Hoselitz, B. (ed.), *The Progress of Underdeveloped Counties*, pp. 3-29, Chicago University Press, Chicago. This was reprinted in his book (1962), op. cit., pp. 5-30. On his other works, see Chapter 2 of this book.

12   Gerschenkron, A. (1952), op. cit., p.8.

13   On the role of the Russian government in industrialisation, see Gerschenkron, A. (1970), *Europe in the Russian Mirror: Four Lectures in Economic History*, pp. 101-3, Cambridge University Press, London. On the role of the governments in Western countries, see Gerschenkron, A. (1952), op. cit., pp. 14-20.

14   Smith, T. C. (1955), *Political Change and Industrial Development in Japan: Government Enterprise, 1868-1880*, p. 63, Stanford University Press, Stanford.

15   The term is defined as the actual motivating power to move a person from inside to a set line of conduct. The bearers of a particular ethos at a given moment in history react or generally behave in accordance with that ethic which has become their own, and in this sense it may be reworded as 'Menschentum' ('modal personality') or 'Geisnnung' ('temper'). Weber, M. (1958), 'The Protestant Sects and the Spirit of Capitalism', in Gerth, H. H. and Mills, C. W. (ed.) *From Max Weber: Essays in Sociology*, p. 321, Oxford University Press, Oxford. On further discussion on this subject, see Chapter 5 of this book.

16   On List's nationalism, see Roll, E. (1973), *A History of Economic Thought*, pp. 227-31, Faber and Faber Limited, London.

17   On the Saint-Simonism, see Oser, J. (1963), *The Evolution of Economic Thought*, pp. 114-8, Harcourt, Brace & World, New York.

18   On his propositions, see Gerschenkron, A. (1962), op. cit., pp. 353-4. These will be discussed in Chapter 2 of this book.

2 The Gerschenkron model and its applicability to the shipping industry: The case of Korea

Introduction

The controversies between developed and developing countries over the establishment or expansion of merchant marines in developing countries were summarised in the previous chapter. It seems that the adversaries could come to no agreement about the controversies. This was partly because the developing countries viewed the establishment or expansion of shipping in the general perspective of overall economic development, and at the same time regarded shipping as an industry of strategic value, discarding realism or relevance in applying conventional economic theories, e.g. a comparative advantage and laissez-faire policy, to shipping in developing countries.

It was also partly because, from the historical economic point of view, economic conditions inherent in developing countries were not on the whole considered in the course of the controversies over the establishment of their merchant fleets. To understand this point, it is helpful to refer to the following: without materials derived from history and the economic intuition deriving from familiarity with them, theory feeds upon itself, models become artificial and involuted, hypotheses become unreal. If stripped of materials and 'craftsmanlike' methods of economic history, economics will become an ornamental, rather than a useful, art.[1]

An alternative approach is, therefore, required to overcome the limits and problems which the approaches taken in the course of the controversies did not clearly solve. For this, we introduce Gerschenkron's theory of industrialisation, which we will call the Gerschenkron model, to play such a role. The model starts from a criticism of the way of thinking which regards industrialisation as a uniform process of a universal character, unaffected by considerations of time and space and rests on the fact that every historical event which takes place changes the course of all subsequent events. Gerschenkron's attention is limited to the understanding of backward and advanced countries in the process of industrialisation. These relations consist mainly of exchanges of industrial technology, skilled labour and capital, not to mention relations of international competition.

The arguments put forward in this chapter are: that Korea, as a typical late-comer in the shipping sector, has taken the advantages of relative backwardness and substituted lack of prerequisites[2] for shipping development in the context of the Gerschenkron model; and that the model will be appropriate for analysing the growth of the Korean shipping industry from more historical and comprehensive points of view than those of pure economic theories.

What is the Gerschenkron Model?

Alexander Gerschenkron (1904-78), Harvard University economic historian, was born in Odessa, Russia. He received his doctor's degree at the University of Vienna, which was one of the major neo-classical economics centres in Europe, with the spirit of the Austrian School.

The Gerschenkron model was first set out in the essay entitled *Economic Backwardness in Historical Perspective* in 1952,[3] developed *in Social Attitudes, Entrepreneurship and Economic Development* in 1955[4] and *Reflections on the Concept of 'Prerequisites' of Modern Industrialisation* in 1957,[5] and summarised in *The Approach to European Industrialisation: A Postscript* in 1962.[6]

This section will be devoted to discussing the main features and contentions of the Gerschenkron model based on his own major works[7] and previous studies on the validity and tests of the model carried out by many researchers.[8]

Gerschenkron's propositions

An integral part of Gerschenkron's view of European industrialisation is the belief that changes in the speed of industrial growth in the early stages of industrialisation were intimately associated, on the one hand, with the relative backwardness of the countries concerned, and, on the other, with a number of specific features of the industrialisation process itself.[9] Industrialisation was characterised in a systematically varying fashion by sudden accelerations, that is to say, by identifiable discontinuities in the form of great spurts.[10] Such discontinuity is not accidental. It is ascribed to the result of the existence of complementarity and indivisibilities in economic processes.[11]

Gerschenkron, comparing the concepts of the take-off[12] and the great spurt, notes that they both stress discontinuity[13] in economic development, but that great spurts are confined to the area of manufacturing and mining, whereas take-offs refer to national output.[14] He specifies two quantitative characteristics of a great spurt of industrial growth: a sudden and substantial rise in the rate of growth, and a continuation of the spurt across a period of international depression without any conspicuous diminution in the rate of growth.[15] This situation is accompanied by both micro- and macro-economic effects; in the average size of plant and in an eruptive, that is, revolutionary, industrial development.

Gerschenkron describes a few basic elements in the industrialisation processes of European backward countries[16] from the nineteenth century and up until the beginning of the First World War. One of them is that in a backward country prior to industrialisation, there is a situation of tension between the actual low state of economic activity and the obstacles to industrial development, on the one hand, and the great promise inherent in development, on the other. He cites as examples the serfdom of peasantry[17] or the far-reaching absence of political unification as the obstacles in Russia.[18]

In general the whole process of industrialisation has to overcome many considerable obstacles from all parts of the social and historical structure. They came from groups whose previously unchallenged dominant position in society is threatened by the industrial entrepreneurs; artisans whose small shops are being ruined by the competition of the factory; intellectuals whose sense of both compassion and beauty is outraged by the conditions of factory labour, the misery and ugliness of the worker's suburbs; and all those whose preference for security, stability and aversion from change are offended by the uncertainties and hazards of the new dynamic economy.[19] Many examples can be found in all developing countries. Indeed, they provide much of the content of recent history.

No country in which industrialisation took place has been free of such obstacles. Thus, his view is that unless certain formidable institutional obstacles are removed, no industrialisation can take place. However, their intensity varies considerably with a direct relationship with the degree of relative backwardness of the country concerned on the eve and in the early stages of its industrialisation.

Borrowed technology is one of the primary factors assuring a high speed of development in a backward country.[20] Industrialisation seems the more promising, the greater the backlog of technological innovations which the backward country can borrow from the more advanced country. Gerschenkron, on a criterion of technology imports, notes conclusively the tendencies in backward countries to concentrate much of their effort on the introduction of the most modern and expensive technology, their emphasis on large-scale plant, and their interest in developing investment goods industries need not necessarily be regarded as flowering, mainly from a quest for prestige and economic megalomania.[21]

Assuming that sufficient industrial labour has been raised, to the extent that industrialisation takes place, it is largely by application of the most modern and efficient techniques that backward countries can achieve success, particularly in the case of competition from the advanced countries. Thus, the advantages inherent in the use of technologically superior equipment is strengthened by its labour-saving effect. This seems to explain the tendency on the part of backward countries to concentrate at a relatively early point of their industrialisation on the promotion of those branches of industrial activity in which recent technological progress has been particularly rapid. Furthermore, in the context of the Gerschenkron model, industrialisation in a backward country, with its heavy emphasis on large size and on the most modern and capital-intensive techniques, seems to result largely from its inability to form an industrial labour force quickly. Gerschenkron maintains that, for countries of this type, the notion that labour is cheap and capital is expensive must be reformulated. On this point, he notes that 'industrial labour, in the sense of a stable, reliable and disciplined group that has cut the umbilical cord connecting it with the land and has become suitable for utilisation in factories, is not abundant but extremely scarce in a backward country'.[22]

Under these circumstances, capital-intensive investment may become the most attractive and efficient form of progress. However, it is based on the more subtle argument that, while there may be an apparent superabundance of labour in the backward country and while relative factor costs seem to militate against capital-intensive techniques, skilled workers are in fact scarce and labour-saving devices more necessary even than in advanced economies.[23] Underdeveloped areas have a great deal of disguised underemployment, e.g. through extended families.

Moreover, a distinctive feature of the underdeveloped economy with a labour surplus is the predominance of an agricultural sector characterised by widespread disguised unemployment and high rates of population growth, side by side with a small but growing industrial sector and an acute shortage of capital. Indeed, it has become commonplace to argue that a means of developing these economies is to employ surplus labour in the construction of capital goods. In a two-sector setting, the main problem of economic development lies in the gradual shifting of the economy's centre of gravity from the agricultural to the industrial sector through labour reallocation.[24] In this process, it is doubtful whether labour-saving technology in underdeveloped countries is able to solve unemployment. It seems that this is the weakest proposition in the Gerschenkron model.

Gerschenkron contended that from the point of view of underdeveloped countries, advanced countries are sources of technical assistance, skilled labour and capital goods,[25] and maintained that because underdeveloped countries borrow these things (in particular the latest forms of technology) from advanced countries, they may succeed in the process of industrialisation. He observed that the more backward a country is, the greater the gap of the level of technology between it and advanced countries, and that patterns of industrialisation in backward countries change in accordance with the degree of their backwardness, and processes of rapid industrialisation started in several of those countries from very different levels of economic backwardness.[26] Noting that the course and character of industrialisation tended to vary in a number of important respects, he summarised those variations in the form of six propositions:

1. The more backward a country's economy, the more vigorous its industrialisation process; tending to start discontinuously as a sudden great spurt and proceeding at a relatively high rate of growth of manufacturing output.

2. The more backward a country's economy, the more pronounced in its industrialisation was the stress on size of both plant and enterprise.

3. The more backward a country's economy, the greater in its industrialisation was the stress upon producers' goods as against consumers' goods.

4. The more backward a country's economy, the heavier was the pressure in the course of its industrialisation upon the levels of consumption of its population.

5. The more backward a country's economy, the greater was the part played in its industrialisation by special institutional factors designed to increase the supply of capital to the nascent industries and, in addition, to provide them with less decentralised and better informed entrepreneurial guidance; the more backward the country, the more pronounced was the coerciveness and comprehensiveness of those factors.

6. The more backward a country, the less likely was its agriculture to play any active role in the process of industrialisation by offering to growing industries the advantages of an expanding industrial market based in turn on the rising productivity of agricultural labour.[27]

Institutional instruments and ideology

As mentioned above, the effect of basic factors, which historically were peculiar to economic situations in backward countries, and made for higher speed of growth and different productive structure of industries, was reinforced by the use in backward countries of certain institutional instruments (mainly banks and the State) and the acceptance of specific industrialisation ideologies.[28]

The institutional instruments for industrialisation suggested by Gerschenkron consist of the banks and the State. This sub-section is devoted to discussing how the institutional instruments and ideology played roles in different backward countries in the context of the Gerschenkron model and what specific factors they have.

Banks Although the banking system is by no means the only element in the Gerschenkron model of the distinctive patterns of industrialisation in various European countries, he considers that it plays a key role at certain stages of the industrialisation process. From the view of the banker's role, the fifth proposition, as enumerated above, is important:[29] the more backward a country's economy, the greater was the part in its industrialisation played by special institutional factors designed to increase the supply of capital to the nascent industries and, in addition, to provide them with less decentralised and better informed entre-preneurial guidance; the more backward the country, the more pronounced was the coerciveness and comprehensiveness of those factors.

Gerschenkron divides the European countries into three groups: advanced area, area of moderate backwardness and area of extreme backwardness, with respect to capital and entrepreneurship. He chose Britain, Germany and Russia as representatives of three groups of countries,[30] and considered that their development patterns take the form of a series of stage models. Thus, under the fifth proposition above he maintains that in the course of development, in moderately backward countries, the banks first undertake the leading role in industrialisation, and at the next stage industry advances to a position independent of the banks. To give one example, when Germany began to industrialise, she, as an area of moderate backwardness, had few potential entrepreneurs and less liquid capital. Under this situation the banking system became the prime source of both capital and entrepreneurship. On the role of the banks in Germany, he states:

> In Germany, the various incompetencies of individual entrepreneurs were offset by the device of splitting the entrepreneurial function: the German investment banks - a powerful invention, comparable in economic effect to that of the steam engine - were in their capital-supplying functions a substitute for the insufficiency of the previously created wealth willingly placed at the disposal of entrepreneurs. But they were also a substitute for entrepreneurial deficiencies. From their central vantage points of control, the banks participated actively in shaping the major - and sometimes even not so major - decisions of individual enterprises. It was they who very often mapped out a firm's paths of growth, conceived far-sighted plans, decided on major technological and locational innovations, and arranged for mergers and capital increases.[31]

Gerschenkron accepts, with several qualifications, the example where a German bank accompanied an industrial enterprise from establishment to liquidation over the period of its existence.[32] He has focused attention on what he sees as the vital role of investment banking in large parts of Europe. He argues that in a relatively backward economy, the bloc of investment required for industrialisation will be particularly great. However, a relatively backward country will have an undeveloped capital market and a scarcity of entrepreneurial talent, and it will need a larger than average-size of plant and concentration on branches with relatively high capital-output ratios. Reliance upon the banks in such a country will be much greater than in a country like Britain, where industrialisation was able to proceed more gradually, and where, consequently, capital accumulation, first from earnings in overseas plantations, e.g. sugar, trade and modernised agriculture and later from industry itself, was sufficient.[33]

Thus, Gerschenkron speaks of a truly momentous role of the investment banking of the period for the economic history of France and of large portions of the Continent.[34] Furthermore, he contends that 'the continental practices in the field of industrial banking must be conceived as specific instruments of industrialisation in a backward country'.[35]

The State   In the Gerschenkron model, it is the State which first undertakes the leading role in industrialisation in very backward countries, at the second stage the banks take over this function, and at the third stage industry attains independence from the banks.[36]   In other words, Gerschenkron holds that where neither private entrepreneurial activities nor banking activities are sufficient, the State must move in to provide the impetus for industrialisation.[37]   Thus, the State becomes one of the institutional instruments in the Gerschenkron model.

For example, in Russia, which was even more backward than Germany, not even the banking system was adequate for the task of providing capital and entrepreneurship for industrialisation.   There the imperial government played the major role in supplying capital for the needs of industrialisation through the compulsory machinery of the government, that is to say, its taxation and budgetary policies.[38]   Gerschenkron maintained that not only in their origins but also in their effects, the policies implemented by the Russian government in the 1890s were closely similar to those of banks in Central Europe.[39]   Thus, he argued from the example of Russia that the more backward the economy, the greater the reliance on the State rather than on the bank or private enterprise.[40]

In the world of the Gerschenkron model, the State also contributes to the removal of institutional obstacles to industrialisation through its powerful policies or ideology, organising resources efficiently and effectively.   Taking the case of Russia in the nineteenth century, Gerschenkron argues that the more backward the economy, the more important the role of government, and the more powerful a government the economy needs.

Of some studies on the validity and the quantitative test of the Gerschenkron model applied in Japan, H. Rosovsky maintained that the Japanese government played a role in rapid industrialisation, as did the Russian government in the 1890s, and that the government's encouragement was a necessary condition for future growth.[41]

Ideology   The role of ideology, like that of the State, tends to increase with the degree of backwardness; and indeed the two go hand in hand.   Here, there is a functional justification: some kind of psychological reassurance and inspiration is necessary to comfort the members of a society in their years of privation and stimulate them to labour for better times to come; and the more necessary, the more difficult the effort; the more ambitious the goal, the greater the sacrifices demanded.[42]

On the need and role of ideology for industrialisation, Gerschenkron notes that:

> To break through the barriers of stagnation in a backward country, to ignite the imaginations of men, and to place their energies in the service of economic development, a stronger medicine is needed than the promise of better allocation of resources or even of the lower price of bread.   Under such conditions even businessman, even the classical daring and innovating

entrepreneur, needs a more powerful stimulus than the prospect of high profits.[43]

The process of industrialisation needs to overcome resistance which comes from a social structure. It reflects the level of backwardness of the country concerned on the eve and in the early stages of its industrialisation. It can be said in the context of the Gerschenkron model that unless they are removed, no industrialisation takes place. Here, the creation of specific industrialisation ideologies to play a role in removing such resistances is needed. It is therefore, not surprising that in backward countries an attempt was made to justify the process of industrialisation and to make palatable the indubitable ills it implied, by associating it with values that could be expected to find approval in large segments of society and to overcome, or at least to mitigate, those resistances.[44]

Gerschenkron enumerates Saint-Simonism in France and nationalism in Germany which can be justly regarded as dominant industrialisation ideologies.[45] In each case, there is little doubt that to some not inconsiderable extent, those ideologies fulfilled their function not only in reducing external resistance to industrialisation, but also in calming the uneasy consciences of the industrialisers themselves and providing them with a strong spiritual incentive in addition to the more materialistic profit motive.[46] Thus, ideologies of this type were undoubtedly helpful in the creation of industrial economies, being confined to brief initial periods of rapid spurts.

Prerequisites for industrialisation

In the Gerschenkron model, certain major obstacles to industrialisation must be removed and certain things favourable to it must be created prior to industrialisation through some more or less discrete stages. This is common ground between both Rostow[47] and Gerschenkron.[48] But Gerschenkron criticises Rostow's conception of prerequisites or preconditions of industrial development on two grounds: some of the factors that had served as prerequisites in the advanced country either were not present at all, or at best, were present to a very small extent, in the more backward countries; the great spurt of industrial development occurred in those countries despite the lack of such prerequisites.[49] The Gerschenkron argument raises the following question: 'In what way and through what devices did backward countries substitute for the missing prerequisites?'[50]

Let us discuss this question in terms of the nature, validity and usefulness of the concept of prerequisites, selecting from the listing of various prerequisites the one of capital availability.

Assuming that a prerequisite of availability of capital takes the form of original accumulation of capital, Gerschenkron criticises Marx's concept of it in the sense that:

the concept lies in the fact that it presupposes a type of economic development which encompasses a big spurt of industrialisation. It is this assumption which makes the concept of the 'beginning' a meaningful one, and it is the large amounts of capital needed to launch and to sustain such a spurt that alone justify the concept of original, that is, prespurt, accumulation. Without the industrial spurt the concept is destitute of meaning.[51]

Gerschenkron maintains that, as a matter of history, this concept is properly applicable only to Britain and then on a much smaller scale than is usually supposed. Thus, from the point of view of theory, it cannot be regarded as a universal precondition for industrialisation. He concludes that original accumulation of capital was not a prerequisite for industrial development in major countries on the European continent.[52] In order to support such a conclusion he suggests examples of the substitution for lack of original accumulation of capital for industrialisation in backward countries. To give one example, the focal role in capital provision in Germany must be ascribed not to any original capital accumulation but to the role of credit-creation policies on the part of the banking system.[53] In other words, the previously discussed role of banks in Germany can be regarded as a specific substitute for the inadequate original accumulation of capital in that area of moderate backwardness. As another example, the budgetary policies of the Russian government under Count Witte may be seen both as a substitute for insufficient original accumulation and as a substitute for policies of credit creation by investment banks for which conditions in Russia were not yet ripe.[54]

Moreover, the existence of capital-abundant areas abroad has discoloured the problem of original accumulation. Thus, Gerschenkron says that 'to the extent that capital can be imported from abroad, the importance of previously created domestic wealth is *pro tanto* reduced'.[55]

Gerschenkron maintains that although backward countries do not have factors which in a more advanced country served as prerequisites for industrial development, they would be on the road of industrialisation if there exist substitutes for the lacking factors which occurred in the process of industrialisation in conditions of backwardness.[56] Accordingly, one of the ways of approaching the problem is to ask what substitutes and what patterns of substitution are required for the lacking prerequisites in the process of industrialisation.

Gerschenkron states that in backward countries with high illiteracy levels and low standards of education, the resulting difficulty in training skilled labour and efficient engineers, and the lack of a pool of technical knowledge can be overcome by immigration from more advanced countries, by using the training facilities of those countries and by importing technological knowledge from more advanced countries as sources of technical assistance, skilled labour and capital goods.[57] He suggests banks and activities of governments, as possible substitutes for the prerequisites, on the grounds of historical studies on Central Europe and Russia.[58] In Russia, the activities of the government effectively substituted for the missing prerequisites of minimum acceptable standards of commercial honesty, issuing specific injunctions against the involvement of banks in long term credit operations. Moreover, the government's policies of industrialisation had to function as a substitute for the missing prerequisite of craft-guild experience.[59] Conclusively, Gerschenkron notes that 'the lack of something that might be regarded as a general set of prerequisites of industrial development does not necessarily diminish the heuristic value of the concept of prerequisites. It is precisely by starting from the concept and by trying to understand how a given country managed to start its process of industrialisation despite the lack of certain prerequisites, that one can arrive at some differentiated and still co-ordinated view of industrialisation in conditions of graduated backwardness.[60]

However, Gerschenkron emphasises that the absence of certain prerequisites should not be regarded as advantages of backwardness. Furthermore, he adds that such advantages result from overcoming the lack of preconditions for economic progress, and the process as a rule is a costly one.[61] In other words, the various processes of substitutions for prerequisites are accompanied by difficulties, strains and costs.

The applicability of the Gerschenkron model to the Korean shipping industry

For a country to be included in tests of the Gerschenkron model, it must have experienced a great growth spurt, and as a practical consideration, there must be sufficient data available to make the necessary computations. Two problems must be solved before tests can be made. First, the beginning of the spurts must be dated. Second, the countries must be ranked according to relative backwardness just prior to their great spurts. The approach calls, first of all, for some measurement of the rate of growth of the shipping industry during the period under review. These necessitated, therefore, the construction of indices of the Korean shipping industry. With the Gerschenkron model in mind, they will be in turn handled.

Great spurts and relative backwardness in the Korean shipping industry

Great spurts

Gerschenkron regards the two quantitative characteristics of a great spurt as a sudden and substantial rise in the rate of growth, and as a continuation of the spurt across a period of international depression without any considerable decrease in the rate of growth.[62] In this study, the concept of a great spurt is applied to the shipping industry, using the same two quantitative characteristics as above.[63]

24

To measure a sudden and substantial rise in the rate of shipping growth in Korea, it is necessary to construct an index of shipping tonnage for the years 1958-81. It seems that the index sufficiently serves the purpose, which is to obtain a general view of the speed of the Korean shipping growth in various periods and sub-periods. The index indicating the growth of gross tonnage on the basis of 1975 = 100 in the period 1958-81 is presented in Table 2.1.

Table 2.1
Index of Korean shipping gross tonnage (1958-81)

Year	Index	Year	Index	Year	Index	Year	Index
1958	7	1964	8	1970	52	1976	111
1959	8	1965	8	1971	58	1977	154
1960	6	1966	12	1972	65	1978	183
1961	7	1967	19	1973	68	1979	243
1962	6	1968	29	1974	75	1980	267
1963	7	1969	47	1975	100	1981	317

(1975 = 100)

Sources: calculated from Table 1.1.

According to the Gerschenkron approach, the choice of sub-periods into which a fairly long stretch of growth should be divided is made arbitrarily.[64] For the purposes of a presentation that aims at isolating the great upsurge, an inspection of the data from Table 2.1 seems to yield the following divisions, for which the rates of growth implied in the index for these sub-periods are given in Table 2.2.

Table 2.2
Rates of growth of Korean shipping tonnage for sub-periods

Division	Period	Percentage change[+]
Stagnation	1958 - 62	-3.8
Moderate growth	1962 - 66	18.9
Very rapid growth	1966 - 70	34.3
	1976 - 81	23.3
Reduced rate of growth	1970 - 81	13.4
Whole period	1958 - 81	18.0

Note: + *Computed on the assumption of a geometric rate of growth between the first and last years of the specified periods.*

Source: derived from Table 2.1.

In terms of the index of tonnage, the Korean shipping industry experienced very rapid growth twice in the period 1958-81, i.e. in the sub-periods 1966-70 and 1976-81. The growth rates recorded 34.3 and 23.3 per cent in the same sub-periods, respectively. Even a sub-period with 'reduced rate of growth', i.e. the period 1970-76, recorded 13.4 per cent.

Table 2.3
Value added in the Korean shipping sector (1962-81) (at 1975 prices)

Year	Amount (in Won)[+] (A)[++]	(A) as percentage of total transport sectors %	Annual percentage change in the growth rate in:		
			(1)[+++]	(2)*	GNP
1962	5.7	7.6	-	-	-
1963	6.4	7.1	12.5	19.4	9.3
1964	7.3	7.1	14.1	13.6	8.9
1965	9.2	7.4	26.0	19.8	8.1
1966	10.7	7.4	16.8	18.0	11.9
1967	12.8	8.1	19.6	21.8	7.8
1968	18.8	9.5	46.9	24.0	12.6
1969	25.6	11.1	36.2	18.0	15.0
1970	33.6	13.0	31.3	11.8	7.9
1971	41.7	14.7	24.1	9.8	9.2
1972	46.1	14.8	10.6	9.4	7.0
1973	60.1	15.1	30.4	28.6	16.7
1974	62.3	15.1	3.7	3.4	8.7
1975	66.8	14.5	7.2	11.5	8.3
1976	93.7	17.6	40.3	16.4	14.3
1977	122.1	17.8	30.3	19.7	10.3
1978	146.1	17.6	19.7	17.8	11.6
1979	181.3	19.4	24.0	12.9	6.4
1980	203.0	21.4	12.0	1.7	-6.2
1981	235.9	23.1	16.2	7.6	7.1

Notes: [+] *Won is the Korean currency unit.*
[++] *(A) indicates the amounts of value added in shipping sector based on constant market prices in 1975.*
[+++] *(1) indicates shipping sector.*
* *(2) indicates all transportation sectors.*

Source: KMPA (1980), *Hankook Haeoon Hangman Sasipyeonsa*, [The Forty Years History of Korean Shipping and Ports], Chapter 2, KMPA, Seoul, Korea.

This implies that during a period of international depression for shipping caused by the oil shocks in the 1970s, Korean shipping showed sustained growth from the level of rate of tonnage growth, as indicated in Table 2.2. Table 2.3 presents the value added in the Korean shipping sector during the period 1962-81.

The value added in the Korean shipping sector amounted to 235.9 billion won in 1981 from 5.7 billion won in 1962, at 1975 prices. The average annual growth rate of real added value over the period 1962-81 is 21.6 per cent. The share of the value added in the shipping sector of total value added in all transportation sectors in Korea increased to 23.1 per cent in 1981 from 7.6 per cent in 1962. From the point of view of value added, it can be said from the figures in Table 2.3 that Korean shipping became an important transport industry in Korean economy. Table 2.4 presents the index showing the growth in the value added in the Korean shipping industry on the basis of 1975 = 100 in the period 1962-81.

Table 2.4
Index of value added in the Korean shipping sector (1962-81) (at 1975 prices)

Year	Index	Year	Index	Year	Index	Year	Index
1962	9	1967	19	1972	69	1977	183
1963	10	1968	28	1973	90	1978	219
1964	11	1969	38	1974	93	1979	271
1965	14	1970	50	1975	100	1980	304
1966	16	1971	62	1976	140	1981	353

(1975 = 100)

Source: calculated from Table 2.3.

After a glance at the data from Table 2.4, the sub-periods to indicate big upsurge in terms of value added can be presented as follows:

1962-66   Moderate growth
1966-71   Very rapid growth
1971-75   Reduced rate of growth
1975-81   Very rapid growth

Table 2.5 presents the rates of growth implied in terms of the index of value added in the Korean shipping sector, on the basis of 1975 = 100, during the period 1962-81.

Table 2.5

Rates of growth of value added in the Korean shipping sector for sub-periods (at 1975 prices)

Division	Period	% change per year
Moderate growth	1962 - 66	15.4
Very rapid growth	1966 - 71	31.1
	1975 - 81	23.4
Reduced rate of growth	1971 - 75	12.6
Whole period	1962 - 81	21.3

Note: *Computed on the assumption of a geometric rate of growth between the first and last years of the specified periods.*

Source: derived from Table 2.4.

The Korean shipping industry experienced the very rapid growth division twice in the period 1962-81 in terms of value added, i.e. in the periods 1966-71 and 1975-81. For these two very rapid growth divisions, their annual average rate of growth of value added was 31.1 and 23.4 per cent, respectively. The starting year, 1966, of the first very rapid growth division in value added in the shipping sector coincides with that of shipping tonnage in Korea. (See Table 2.2.) For the second very rapid growth division, the starting year in value added in shipping was 1976, while that in shipping tonnage was 1975. They both experienced nearly the same starting year.

On the other hand, it can be observed from Table 2.5 that even in a period of shipping depression, caused mainly by the two oil shocks, Korea recorded a continuous growth, i.e. 12.6 per cent in the period 1971-75, in terms of percentage change in value added in shipping.

Two points seem to emerge with sufficient clarity from the data contained in the preceding tabulations; firstly, the Korean shipping industry has satisfied the first condition - a sudden and considerable growth within a short period - to qualify as a great spurt. Secondly, despite the fact that the growth of the world shipping tonnage stagnated during the early 1970s owing to the oil shock in 1973, the industry has recorded slow but continuous growth in terms of gross tonnage and value added. This means that the industry fulfilled the second condition to qualify as a great spurt - a continuation of the spurt across a period of international depression, without any conspicuous diminution in the rates of growth in gross tonnage and value added in Korea. In other words, it was found that, on the whole, the presence of the two distinguishing features, i.e. two quantitative characteristics mentioned above, were sufficient for our purposes in recognising a great spurt of shipping growth in Korea.

In order to rank countries according to relative backwardness, of its several measures[65] Gerschenkron chose the lateness of the spurt because of unreliable data and the ambiguity of index numbers and disagreement as to the accuracy of per capita income as a measure of backwardness.

To calculate relative backwardness in shipping, the shipping conditions of a backward country on the eve of its spurt should be compared with those in advanced countries at that date. The first difficulty in this stems from selecting the indicators to represent relative backwardness in shipping. In this study, the absolute size of gross tonnage is chosen as its indicator because it is regarded as a source to earn and/or to save foreign exchange and at the same time a measure of transportation capacity in developing countries. To cover any weaknesses which the indicator may have, the relative backwardness on general economic conditions of European countries on the eve of their spurts is also suggested.

Table 2.6
Date of the spurt and the size of gross tonnage on the eve of the spurt

Country	Spurt date	Gross tonnage[+]
France	1829	663[++]
Germany	1850	569[++]
Sweden	1880	542[+++]
Italy	1896	564[*]
Japan	1900	488[*]
Korea	1967	306

Notes: [+]   *In thousand tons.*
   [++]   *Gross tonnage in 1843.*
   [+++] *Sailing and steam vessels.*
   [*]   *Excluding tonnage of sail and barges.*

Sources: On the beginning dates of the great spurts in five European countries, see Barsby, S. L. (1969), 'Economic Backwardness and the Characteristics of Development', *Journal of Economic History*, Vol. 29, No. 3, pp. 449-72. On the beginning dates of the great spurt in Japan, see Rosovsky, H. (1961), *Capital Formation in Japan, 1868-1940*, The Free Press of Glencoe, New York; Rostow, W. W. (1960), *The Stages of Economic Growth*, p. 38, Cambridge University Press, Cambridge. On shipping tonnage in European countries, see 'Tables Showing the Progress of Merchant Shipping', *Accounts and Papers*, Vol. 28, pp. 46-9, 1903. On Japanese shipping tonnage, see *Lloyd's Register of Shipping Statistical Tables 1987*. On the data of Korean shipping tonnage, see Table 1.1.

The second difficulty is raised in selecting particularly advanced countries and in weighting them to form a single standard for such comparisons. To avoid these problems, only one country will be used as the standard. Use of a single country is a second choice, but one made necessary by the lack of criteria for using a combination of countries.

On the standard country, as maintained by S.L. Barsby,[66] Britain appears to be the best choice because: (1) it was undoubtedly the most advanced country in Europe in almost every respect until around the end of the nineteenth century; (2) Britain was the first country to experience a great spurt, and as such it is the only single country to which all others can be compared; and (3) if one of the countries included in this study were used, there would be no way to determine its own relative backwardness.

The relative backwardness of European countries and Japan are simply shown in Table 2.6 according to the dates of their spurts based on general economic conditions and the size of gross tonnage, while the date of spurt in Korea, 1967, was based on the result of analysis carried out in the previous section.

It is fairly certain from Table 2.6 that, from comparing Korean shipping tonnage on the eve of its spurt with that of advanced countries at that date, the Korean shipping condition was under relative backwardness.

Hypotheses on the Korean shipping industry based on the Gerschenkron model

As discussed in the previous sub-sections, the Korean shipping industry had its relative backwardness and also experienced two great spurts. Based on a series of historical facts, prerequisites for shipping growth, for example capital accumulation for acquiring ships and know-how in shipping business, which had served as prerequisites in advanced maritime countries, either were not present at all, or at best were present to a very small extent in Korea. Despite this lack of prerequisites, great spurts occurred in the Korean shipping industry. Such a fact raises the question: 'In what way and through what devices did Korea substitute for the missing prerequisites?'.

This sub-section is devoted to making hypotheses about the Korean shipping industry on the basis of the Gerschenkron model, as the preparatory stage for testing them and answering the above question in the following chapters. With a series of historical questions or expectations in mind, the hypotheses derived from the Korean shipping industry are given below.

Hypothesis I In the relative backwardness of Korea, when the banks did not participate in the process of shipping development until a certain degree of shipping growth had been achieved, the Korean government played the main role in shipping growth through its economic policies, e.g. outward-looking strategy or export-oriented industrialisation and fiscal policies.

Hypothesis II In Korea, where national shipping finance could not be raised sufficiently at home and, also, the Korean shipping industry could not attract the required capital for its development from other economic sectors in Korea during the 1960s and 1970s, a special shipping financing system was designed and employed for the acquisition of ships.

Hypothesis III In conditions of extreme backwardness in the Korean shipping industry, a powerful ideology would have been needed in order to overcome the barriers of stagnation in the shipping industry, to ignite the imaginations of men in the shipping industry and to place their energies in the service of shipping development.

Hypothesis IV Prior to building merchant marines in Korea, a maritime educational institution established after the Liberation from Japan in 1945 served as a prerequisite for shipping growth, making it possible to combine low-wage Korean seamen with uneconomic Japanese ships through international division of labour in shipping and, as a result, substituting the prerequisite of original accumulation of capital for acquiring ships. Japan, as an advanced maritime country, was a source of technical assistance including ship operating skills, know-how in shipping business and also of capital for the purchase of ships in Korea.

Conclusions

Referring to European countries which began their rapid industrialisation during the nineteenth century, Gerschenkron stated that the greater a country's relative backwardness on the eve of its spurt (1) the more rapid was the subsequent rate of manufacturing growth, (2) greater was the stress on large size of plant and enterprise, (3) greater was the stress on producers' goods as opposed to consumers' goods, (4) the less rapid was the increase in the level of consumption, (5) greater was the role played by special institutional factors designed to speed industrialisation, and (6) the less the agricultural sector contributed to economic growth, as measured by the rate of increase in agricultural labour productivity.

This chapter has reviewed the Gerschenkron model so that it may be applicable to shipping, bearing the Korean case in mind. The applicability of the Gerschenkron model to the Korean shipping sector was found from the following points: (1) that when Korea started to develop shipping, it did so in a setting broadly reminiscent of what Gerschenkron described as relative backwardness compared with those in European countries and Japan; (2) that the Korean shipping industry satisfied the two quantitative characteristics to qualify a great spurt and experienced two great spurts, i.e. the first in 1967 and the second in 1975.

Hypotheses I, II, III and IV made in this chapter will be tested in turn in Chapters 3, 4 and 5, bearing in mind that one of the ways of approaching the problem of shipping growth in backward countries can be done by asking what substitutions and what patterns of substitutions for the lacking prerequisites occurred in the backward Korean shipping industry.

Notes and References

1   Parker, W. N. (1986), 'An Historical Introduction', in Parker, W. N. (ed.), *Economic History and the Modern Economist*, p. 9, Basil Blackwell, Oxford.

2   The concept will be further discussed in this chapter.

3   Gerschenkron, A. (1952), 'Economic Backwardness in Historical Perspective' in Hoselitz, B. F. (ed.), *The Progress of Underdeveloped Areas*, pp. 3-29, The University of Chicago Press, Chicago, reprinted in his book (1962) *Economic Backwardness in Historical Perspective: A Book of Essays*, pp. 5-30, Harvard University Press, Cambridge, Massachusetts.

4   Gerschenkron, A. (1987), 'Social Attitudes, Entrepeneurship and Economic Development', in Robinson, A. (ed.), *Economic Progress*, Proceedings of a conference held by the International Economic Association at Santa Margherita Ligure, Italy, pp. 256-74, Macmillan, London. This book was first edited by Dupriez, L. H. and published by Institut de Recherches Economiques et Sociales, Louvain in 1955. It was reprinted in Gerschenkron's book (1962), *Economic Backwardness in Historical Perspective: A Book of Essays*, op. cit., pp. 52-71.

5   Gerschenkron, A. (1957), "Reflections on the Concept of 'Prerequisites' of Modern Industrialisation", *L'Industria*, No. 2, pp. 357-72. This was reprinted in his book (1962), op. cit., pp. 31-51.

6   Ibid., pp. 353-66.

7   Besides, there are his works for further understanding of the Gerschenkron model:

Gerschenkron, A. (1951), 'Uses and Misuse of Russian Statistics', *Review of Economics and Statistics*, Vol. 33, No. 1, pp. 76-8.

Gerschenkron, A. (1955), 'Notes on the Rate of Industrial Growth in Italy, 1881-1913', *Journal of Economic History*, Vol. 15, No. 4, pp. 360-75.

Gerschenkron, A. (1965), 'Agrarian Policies and Industrialisation, Russia 1861-1917' in *The Industrial Revolutions and After: Incomes, Population and Technological Change (II)*, Vol. 6 of *The Cambridge Economic History of Europe*, Habakkuk, H. J. and Postan, M. (ed.), 6 volumes, pp. 706-800, Cambridge University Press, Cambridge.

Gerschenkron, A. (1963), 'The Early Phases of Industrialisation in Russia: Afterthoughts and Counterthoughts', in Rostow, W. W. (ed.), *The Economics of Take-off into Sustained Growth*, pp. 151-69, St Martin's Press, New York.

Gerschenkron, A. (1967), 'The Discipline and I', *Journal of Economic History*, Vol. 27, No. 4, pp. 443-59.

Gerschenkron, A. (1968), *Continuity in History and Other Essays*, Harvard University Press, Cambridge, Massachusetts.

Gerschenkron, A. (1969), 'History of Economic Doctrines and Economic History', *American Economic Review*, Papers and Proceedings, Vol. 59, No. 2, pp. 1-17.

Gerschenkron, A. (1970), *Europe in the Russian Mirror: Four Lectures in Economic History*, Cambridge University Press, London.

Gerschenkron, A. (1972), 'Ideology as a System Determinant' in Eckstein, A. (ed.), *Comparison of Economic Systems: Theoretical and Methodological Approaches*, pp. 269-89, Oxford University Press, Delhi, India. The first edition of the book was published in 1971 by University of California Press.

Gerschenkron, A. (1977), *An Economic Spurt That Failed: Four Lectures in Austrian History*, Princeton University Press, Princeton.

8   Rosovsky, H. (1961), *Capital Formation in Japan 1868-1940*, The Free Press of Glencoe, New York.

Rosovsky, H. (ed.) (1966), *Industrialisation in Two Systems: Essays in Honour of Alexander Gerschenkron by a Group of his Students*, John Wiley and Sons, New York.

Landes, D. S. (1965), 'Technological Change and Development in Western Europe, 1750-1914', in *The Industrial Revolutions and After: Incomes, Population and Technological Change (I)*, Vol. 6 of *The Cambridge*

Economic History of Europe, Habakkuk, H. J. and Postan, M. (ed.), 6 volumes, pp. 274-601, Cambridge University Press, Cambridge.

Barsby, S. L. (1969), 'Economic Backwardness and the Characteristics of Development', *Journal of Economic History*, Vol. 29, No. 3, pp. 449-72.

Cameron, R. (ed.) (1972), *Banking and Economic Development: Some Lessons of History*, Oxford University Press, New York.

Findlay, R. (1978), 'Relative Backwardness, Direct Foreign Investment and the Transfer of Technology: A Simple Dynamic Model', *Quarterly Journal of Economics*, Vol. 92, No. 1, pp. 1-16.

9   Gerschenkron, A. (1967), op. cit., p. 443.

10   Ibid., p. 444.

11   Gerschenkron, A. (1952), op. cit., p. 8.

12   Rostow defines take-off as the interval during which the rate of investment increases in such a way that real output per capita rises and this initial increase carries with it radical changes in production techniques and the disposition of income flows which perpetuate the new scale of investment and perpetuate thereby the rising trend in per capita output. Rostow, W. W. (1960), *The Process of Economic Growth*, p. 274, The Clarendon Press, Oxford. This book was first published in 1953.

13   Gerschenkron criticises continuity in history in the sense: (1) that it means that the historical roots of a given phenomenon reach very far back into the past; (2) it is used to indicate periodic recurrence of events on a broad historical scale; and (3) it is also made to imply a very gradual change, the degree of which is hardly perceptible. Gerschenkron, A. (1962), op. cit., p. 37.

14   Ibid., ft. 1 on pp. 353-4.

15   Gerschenkron, A. (1963), op. cit., p. 163.

16   In the nineteenth century, France, Germany and Russia were among the backward countries. Britain was excluded because Gerschenkron's hypothesis was concerned with follower countries which could make extensive use of borrowed technology from more advanced countries and have advantages of backwardness, Barsby, S. L., op. cit., p. 450.

17   Gerschenkron, A. (1965), op. cit., pp. 706-12.

18   Gerschenkron, A. (1952), op. cit., pp. 5-6.

19   Gerschenkron, A. (1972), op. cit., p. 279.

20   An idea usually associated with the names of Veblen, T. and Gerschenkron is that the greater the relative disparity in development levels between a country at the outset of a process of industrialisation and the already industrialised part of the world, the faster the rate at which the backward country can catch up. Veblen applied this hypothesis to Germany vis-à-vis Britain, and Gerschenkron used it in a broader framework embracing Britain at one extreme and Russia at the other, with France, Germany and Italy in between. Veblen, T. (1915), *Imperial Germany and the Industrial Revolution*, Macmillan, London; Findlay, R., op. cit., p. 2.

21   Gerschenkron, A. (1952), op. cit., p. 25.

22   Ibid., p. 7.

23   Landes, D. S. (1965), op. cit., pp. 588-9.

24   For further discussion of this position, see Galenson, W. and Leibenstein, H. (1955), 'Investment Criteria, Productivity and Economic Development', *Quarterly Journal of Economics*, Vol. 69, No. 3, pp. 343-70; Leibenstein, H. (1957), 'The Theory of Underemployment in Backward Economies', *Journal of Political Economy*, Vol. 65, No. 2, pp. 91-103; Oshima, H. T. (1958), 'Underemployment in Backward Economies: An Empirical Comment', *Journal of Political Economy*, Vol. 66, No. 3, pp. 259-64; Fei, J. C. H. (1963), Innovation, Capital Accumulation and Economic Development', *American Economic Review*, Vol. 53, No. 3, pp. 283-313.

25   Gerschenkron, A. (1952), op. cit., p. 47.

26   Gerschenkron, A. (1962), op. cit., p. 353.

27   Ibid., pp. 353-4; Gerschenkron, A. (1963), op. cit., pp. 152-3.

28   Gerschenkron, A. (1952), op. cit., p. 9.

29   Cameron, R., 'Introduction', in Cameron (ed.), op. cit., pp. 9-10.

30   Gerschenkron, A. (1962), op. cit., pp. 354-6.

31   Gerschenkron, A. (1968), op. cit., p. 137.

32   Gerschenkron, A. (1952), op. cit., p. 12.

33   Ibid..

34   Ibid., p. 10.

35   Ibid., p. 13.

36   Gerschenkron, A. (1962), op. cit., p. 355.

37   Rudolph, R. L., op. cit., p. 27.

38   Gerschenkron, A. (1957), op. cit., pp. 368-9.

39   Gerschenkron, A. (1952), op. cit., pp. 18-9; Cameron, R., op. cit..

40   Landes, D. S. (1965), 'Japan and Europe: Contrasts in Industrialisation', in Lockwood, W. W. (ed.), *The State and Economic Enterprise in Japan: Essays in the Political Economy of Growth*, p. 100, Princeton University Press, Princeton.

41   Rosovsky, H. (1961), op. cit., p. 100.   On the role of the Japanese government in industrialisation, Smith also remarks that the government was responsible for overcoming the initial difficulties of industrialisation: Smith, T. C. (1955), *Political Change and Industrial Development in Japan: Government Enterprise, 1968-1880*, p. 63, Stanford University Press, Stanford.   On the other hand, Orchard maintains that there are few modern industries in Japan today which do not owe their existence to government initiative and that Japanese industry of the present day owes its state of development primarily to the efforts of a highly paternalistic central government: Orchard, J. E. (1930), *Japan's Economic Position: The Progress of Industrialisation*, p. 90, New York.

42   Landes, D. S. (1965), op. cit., p. 597.

43   Gerschenkron, A. (1952), op. cit., p. 23.

44   Gerschenkron, A. (1972), op. cit., pp. 279-80.

45   On the role of the Saint-Simonism in industrialisation, see Gerschenkron, A. (1952), op. cit., pp. 22-4.

46   Gerschenkron, A. (1972), op. cit., p. 280.

47   See Rostow, W. W. (1960), *The Stages of Economic Growth*, Chapter 3, Cambridge University Press, Cambridge.

48   Gerschenkron, A. (1962), op. cit., p. 356; Gerschenkron, A. (1963), op. cit., pp. 151-69.

49   Gerschenkron, A. (1962), op. cit., pp. 357-8.

50   Ibid., p. 358.

51   Ibid., p. 99. On his detailed criticism on the concept, see Gerschenkron, A. (1957), op. cit., pp. 33-8; and Gerschenkron, A. (1968), op. cit., pp. 98-101.

52   Gerschenkron, A. (1957), op. cit., p. 368.

53   Ibid.; Gerschenkron, A. (1963), op. cit., p. 167.

54   Ibid., pp. 167-8; Gerschenkron, A. (1957), op. cit., pp. 368-70.

55   Ibid., p. 369.

56   Ibid., p. 368.

57   Ibid., p. 369.

58   Ibid., pp. 369-70.

59   Ibid., pp. 370-1.

60   Ibid., p. 372.

61   Ibid.

62   Gerschenkron, A. (1963), op. cit., p. 163.

63   Comparing the concepts of the take-off and the great spurt, Gerschenkron notes that great spurts are confined to the area of manufacturing and mining, whereas take-offs refer to national output. Gerschenkron, A. (1962), op. cit., pp. 353-4.

64   Gerschenkron, A. (1955), op. cit., p. 363.

65   Gerschenkron suggested the following for its measurement: the levels of output, the degree of technological progress achieved, the skill of the population, the degree of its literacy and the standard of honesty and time horizon of entrepreneurs. To supplement the levels of output, i.e. per capita income as a measure of backwardness, he considered two additional independent measures, that is to say, the percent of the labour force employed in the agricultural sector and lateness of the spurt. Gerschenkron, A. (1957), op. cit., p. 44; Barsby, S. L., op. cit., pp. 451-2.

66   Ibid., pp. 453-4.

3 The role of the Korean government in shipping growth

Introduction

To a greater or lesser extent, every government is concerned with the mobilisation and allocation of resources, the stabilisation of the national economy and the promotion of technological innovation. Furthermore, a government may play many roles in economic development: as a major investor and at the same time as a consumer; as a source of selective development planning and financing; as a powerful agent of social change, e.g. through education; and as a motivating force behind investment decisions by private business.[1] Gerschenkron relates the increasing role of the government to the degree of backwardness found in the society in which the growth process is being initiated. In a very backward country, where neither private entrepreneurial activities nor the banking system are adequate for the task of providing capital and entrepreneurship for industrialisation, he maintains that the government may play the major role in supplying capital for the needs of industrialisation through the compulsory machinery of the government (e.g. taxation) or in making favourable investment environments to attract capital through fiscal and monetary reforms. Government can also play a role in the transfer of established technology and forms of organisational structure. This was true in the later development of at least some Western European countries and it has particular relevance to developing countries.[2]

In this chapter, I shall attempt to place the growth of Korean shipping in the period 1962-81 into the context of Gerschenkron's model, which was discussed in the previous chapter, and to review the role of the government in the process of that growth.

Although Korea did not have any systematic shipping policy until the First Five Year Economic Development Plan launched in 1962, the government has employed various policy initiatives to develop the shipping industry since the Liberation from Japan in 1945. The major measures taken by the government were:

39

- establishment of the Korean Shipping Corporation in 1950;
- enforcement of the waiver system in 1965;
- establishment of the Shipping Information Centre in 1962 financed jointly by the government and shipping companies;
- various tax allowances;
- implementation of the government-financed shipbuilding programme, i.e. 'Keihek Zoseon' in Korea in 1975;
- favourable money policy; and
- establishment of the Korea Maritime and Port Administration (KMPA) in 1976.

To review the role of the government in shipping growth it will be helpful to categorise the above measures as (1) direct subsidies and special funds; (2) taxation; (3) the 'Keihek Zoseon' scheme; (4) investment in maritime transportation infrastructure; and (5) cargo reservation, i.e. the waiver system.

Direct subsidies and special funds

Shipping is generally considered to be a capital-intensive industry and financial assistance from government can take the form of subsidies, direct and indirect. These may be used permanently or only when times of financial difficulty are faced by the shipping industry.

It was the Shipping Bureau of the Ministry of Transportation which was responsible for implementing financial assistance in Korea until 1976 when the KMPA was established. Before launching the First Five Year Economic Development Plan (1962-66), the Korean government did not provide sufficient operating subsidies because it had difficulties in raising public funds for the expansion of the national fleet and investment priority was given to road transportation and infrastructure for the Korean economy.

As the First Five Year Plan was successfully implemented, the economy grew, export and import industries expanded, and the demand for seaborne trade increased rapidly. Transporting raw materials and supplies into Korea and shipping Korean products out presented special problems. With the exception of transportation to and from Japan, all goods have to travel long distances by sea to keep Korean trade moving. Few steamers made scheduled and regular trips. Ships under the Korean flag were limited in size and number, and could not cope with the growing export requirements. For a good deal of its shipping, Korea had to rely on tramp steamers with lengthy delivery times and frequent and irregular stops en route. This made it difficult to attract customers, as firm delivery dates could not be given. As an inheritance from the Korean War, stevedore charges were higher at the Korean ports than at the nearby ports in Japan.

To cope with this, the Korean government organised a programme to finance the expansion of the national fleet and the development of shipbuilding. Before

1967, the government gave financial assistance to shipping in the form of subsidies to mutual aid passenger ship projects (1962 and after); and government financial aid for ship improvement projects (1964-66). The amount of loans and subsidies provided in the period of the First Five Year Plan totalled 813.3 million won[3] and 655.6 million won, respectively, and with these, ships totalling 28,814 gross registered tonnage were built. The tonnage accounted for 32.3 per cent of the net increase of shipping tonnage during the same period.

The legal basis for operating subsidies to shipping companies is contained in the Shipping Promotion Law, 1967.[4] Since 1967, financial assistance to the shipping industry has been implemented on the basis of this law.

During the period 1969-73, a total of 836.8 million won was granted under the law to shipping operators, against a total of 3,101.3 million won requested in the same period (an annual average ratio of grant implementation was only 27 per cent). The reason for this was a lack of government funds.

In 1970 a programme of grants to the operators of full container vessels was implemented in order to encourage the development of container services and to relieve financial difficulties during the initial stage of operation. Between 1970 and 1973 six liner companies were compensated by the government for operating losses incurred, with a total of 460.6 million won. However, in 1973 the subsidy programme came to a halt because of a lack of government funds.

During the Fourth Five Year Economic Development Plan (1977-81), the Korean government provided Korean shipping with short term and special funds companies in two main areas. First, a soft loan to finance short term working capital was given to shipping companies for 90 days at a 10 per cent interest rate. Compared with the interest rates of 15 per cent to the 19 per cent on commercial lending from domestic banks in the late 1970s in Korea, these terms were very favourable. The total amount of such funding to a company was limited to 10 per cent of the company's annual revenue in the previous year, based on US dollar freight earning overseas. Total financing of this type amounted to 12.8 billion won in 1977 at 1980 prices. Since then the total amount has increased dramatically and reached 119.1 billion won in 1981 at 1980 prices. Second, special loans to shipowners with a view to assisting in the payment of principal and interest on payments on ship mortgage began in 1977.

These loans were offered on the following terms: period of three years with a moratorium of one year on repayments; an interest rate of 16 per cent; loans not available for mortgages on conventional liner vessels in Korea/Japan and Korea/ Southeast Asia trades, as well as oil tankers; and a maximum loan of 50 per cent of the total principal and interest payment in a given year.[5] However, the total of this type of financing to shipping companies in 1979 amounted to 2.4 billion won at 1980 prices, having decreased considerably from 5.9 billion won in 1978. These loans were stopped in 1980 and 1981.

Taxation in shipping

A tax allowance for a shipping company is an indirect form of assistance by a government. It enables the shipping company to pay no taxes or lower taxes than it would otherwise have to pay. Often, the government, by means of tax subsidies, stimulates new investment by reducing or eliminating taxes on the ships acquired. Developing countries often opt for this form of shipping subsidy which is easier to justify than other forms of shipping protectionism, e.g. cargo preferences and cargo reservation. Moreover, unlike other direct subsidies, a tax allowance does not require the developing countries to raise additional public funds.

As mentioned in the previous section, in the early 1960s the Korean government did not supply sufficient financial assistance to shipping companies according to the shipping promotion measures because of an insufficient budget and shortage in foreign exchange. Thus, financial assistance for shipping development was limited only to the following tax privileges:[6]

- exemption from business tax and corporate tax for ocean-going shipping companies in 1958;
- exemption from tax on imports of ships stores in 1964;
- exemptions from the insurance gains related to ships in 1969;
- exemption from the acquisition tax on ships in 1970; and
- exemption from tax on imports of ships in 1973.[7]

The government promoted competitive fleet acquisition by not imposing duties on imported ships and exempting them from acquisition taxes. These reduced the capital costs of foreign vessel acquisition. Thus, these exemptions not only stimulated shipowners to import second-hand ships but the exemption of tax on ship's stores also contributed to the reduction in operating costs of ships and to the increase in international competitiveness in operating such ships.

In particular, the exemptions from business and corporate taxes, which ranged from 30 per cent to 40 per cent of taxable income, were used to accumulate the income from ocean-going operations. It may be concluded that the above tax incentives contributed to the development of shipping in Korea in the 1960s and 1970s.

Government-financed shipbuilding programme: Keihek Zoseon

As a result of the development of heavy and chemical industries during the Third Five Year Economic Development Plan (1972-76), the Korean shipbuilding industry expanded its capacity rapidly and became a strategic export industry.

The 1973 Arab oil embargo and the subsequent doubling of oil prices greatly reduced world demand for tankers and the market crashed as numerous orders for tankers were cancelled in Japan and Europe. In these circumstances, the Korean shipbuilding industry also experienced a decrease in overseas demand for shipbuilding. According to the policy of encouraging and fostering the heavy and chemical industries, the Korean government established the 'Keihek Zoseon' scheme. The primary purpose of the scheme was to develop the shipbuilding industry, to link the industry to the shipping industry and to develop both industries together.

Since the introduction of the scheme in 1975 shipbuilding activity in Korea has grown remarkably during the Fourth Five Year Plan, resulting in continuous growth and contributing to the expansion of the Korean merchant fleet.

In the period 1975-81 a total of 94 new ocean-going ships amounting to 1.3 million grt. were ordered under the scheme. New ocean-going vessels amounted to 91.4 per cent of the total tonnage ordered through the scheme, the rest being coastal and fishing vessels. The tonnage of bulk carriers amounted to about 1 million grt., i.e. 78.5 per cent of total tonnage. The 0.2 million grt. of containerships built through the scheme amounted to 17.9 per cent of the total tonnage during the same period. However, oil tankers amounted to only 45,600 grt., i.e. 3.6 per cent of the total tonnage. The dead-weight tonnage completed during the same period accounted for nearly 11 per cent of the Korean merchant fleet at the end of 1981.

Financing sources and terms for the Keihek Zoseon scheme

This section examines the financing terms of the 'Keihek Zoseon' scheme and compares them with those in Japan and the other OECD countries to identify the sources of financing for the scheme and their significance from the point of view of shipping growth in Korea.

The rule set for the financing of the scheme is that 10 per cent is to be self-financed by the owner (8 per cent for full containerships), 50 per cent of domestic fund loan at an interest rate of 13 to 14 per cent at the initial stage of the Keihek Zoseon scheme for a total period of 10.5 years including a two and a half year grace period, and the rest with a foreign currency re-loan[8] for a total of seven years including a two-year grace period.

Between 1975 and 1981, about 70 per cent of the funds needed came from the National Investment Fund raised by the Korean government and 30 per cent from the Industrial Facility Fund supplied by the Korea Development Bank (KDB).[9] The former fund is raised by taking a certain portion of the new savings deposited with commercial banks each year, whereas the latter is raised by selling long term government bonds through the KDB. The purpose of raising both funds is to channel the funds to the strategic industries, e.g. shipbuilding, machinery and electronic industries.

Table 3.1
Sources of financing for the Keihek Zoseon scheme in Korea (1975-81)
(at 1980 prices)

	Self-financing (in million won)+		Domestic funds (in million won)		Foreign currency loan (in thousand US $)		Total by year (in million won)
	Amounts	%	Amounts	%	Amounts	%	
1975	1,428	8.4	15,613	91.6	-	-	17,041
1976	4,330	14.4	14,506	48.1	[9,100]	37.5	30,163
1977	7,421	8.0	40,046	43.0	[42,333]	49.0	93,026
1978	8,428	8.6	54,810	56.1	[39,092]	35.3	97,747
1979	7,471	7.8	48,682	50.7	[52,992]	41.5	96,057
1980	3,998	4.4	53,718	59.0	[48,554]	36.6	90,983
1981++	1,211	2.6	31,044	66.5	[22,568]	30.9	46,706
Total by source	34,289	7.3	258,419	54.8	[214,639]	37.9	471,723

Notes: + *US $ is equivalent to 485 won until 12 January 1980 and 681 won for 1981.*
++ *The data were based on the Keihek Zoseon scheme in 1981.*

Source: Yoon, S. S. (1982), 'Haewoon-gwa Zoseon' [Shipping and Ship-building], *Journal of the Society of Naval Architects of Korea*, Vol. 19, No. 3, p. 104.

Of the amounts invested in the period 1975-81 for the 'Keihek Zoseon' scheme, i.e. about 47.2 billion won at 1980 prices, the shares of self-financing and foreign currency loans were 7.3 per cent and 37.9 per cent respectively. They were below the regulated percentages of financing for the scheme, i.e. 10 per cent for self-financing and 40 per cent for foreign currency. That is to say, they indicated a shortage of 2.7 per cent and 2.1 per cent respectively. One reason for this is that the owner's ability to finance equity was limited partly by low profitability and partly by the small size of Korean shipping companies. Another reason is that the Korean economy experienced a lack of foreign currency. For the domestic fund, its share was 54.8 per cent, i.e. 4.8 per cent higher than the 50 per cent regulated. Table 3.1 shows the sources of financing for the 'Keihek Zoseon' scheme and their percentage of the total.

The interest rates available under Keihek Zoseon financing for ocean-going vessels have been a source of some controversy, particularly when they are compared with the rates available to export ships. The interest rates under the scheme ranged from 9 per cent to 17 per cent in the period 1975-81. The scheme provided the Korean shipowners with an opportunity to obtain financial support at lower interest rates than those from domestic commercial banks, which varied between 15.5 per cent and 20 per cent. However, interest rates under the scheme were unfavourable compared with those under shipyard credits for an export ship in Korea. The latter terms are similar to the interest rates of shipyard credits in the OECD. Thus, unlike the Korean owners, foreign owners ordering ships at Korean shipyards obtained export credit at standard OECD financing terms. In fact, this meant that internal conflicts between the shipping and shipbuilding industries arose with regard to financing terms. Most Korean shipowners who had ships built under the scheme claimed that they paid more for the ships than they would have cost if they had been contracted in a neighbouring country, Japan.

Effects of the Keihek Zoseon scheme on the Korean shipping industry

Maritime transportation is an extremely capital intensive industry. It had long been recognised that the question of ship financing - i.e. the possibility for developing countries to obtain favourable conditions for financing - was a major stumbling block which had frustrated many of the efforts or intentions of those countries to establish or expand their national merchant fleets.

Since the introduction of the Keihek Zoseon scheme in 1975 in Korea, it has contributed to expanding the Korean merchant fleet, resulting in a 13.8 per cent increase in fleet capacity in the period 1975-81. It has also played an important role in rescuing and developing the shipbuilding industry in Korea.

The government played an important role in supplying additional shipping finance for the scheme through the Industrial Facility Fund from the KDB and the National Investment Fund. In other words, from the point of view of supplying shipping finance for new shipbuilding, the government contributed to the development of the Korean merchant marine.

On the other hand, some conflicts between the shipowner and the shipyard in Korea arose in the course of the Keihek Zoseon scheme. The primary emphasis of the scheme was placed on securing the shipbuilding industry. From the shipowner's viewpoint, the terms of financing under the scheme were more unfavourable than those under the Japanese government financed shipbuilding programme, the OECD and even an export ship in Korea in the light of interest rates and the loan period, including a grace period. However, although the scheme has some drawbacks in terms of financing, its beneficial effects on increasing new tonnage were undeniable.

Favourable money policy

The Korean government mobilised both internal and external resources by making use of the market mechanism in implementing an export-led industrialisation strategy. The strategy in the mid-1960s contributed to the maintenance of an exchange rate near the free market level. In addition, the growth-oriented Korean government encouraged the influx of foreign capital. Exchange rate policy in Korea facilitated the inflow of foreign loans. An application for the inducement of foreign capital for the acquisition of ships was approved by the government in order to review the basic requirements for the expansion and development programme of the Korean shipping industry. Since corporate borrowing from abroad could only be undertaken with the government's authorisation and guarantee, this constituted a substantial augmentation of the government influence. These private long term loans were covered by The Foreign Capital Inducement Law, which was enacted in 1960 and amended in 1962 and 1966 to make it more attractive to investors and lenders. Under this Law, Korean shipowners were able to obtain the Korea Exchange Bank's or Commercial Banks' guarantees on repayment (both amortisation and interest payments). The Law facilitated the import of foreign loans since foreign lenders were guaranteed repayment regardless of the domestic shipowner's credit standing by the domestic lending banks for the Korean shipping companies.

The government also committed itself to a variety of economic incentives for shipping growth because of the lack of both budget and foreign exchange in the 1960s. There were, for example, various tax exemptions on the imports of second-hand ships, ship's stores and income in ocean-going shipping companies, and preferential loans for the government financed shipbuilding programme, i.e. in Korea, the Keihek Zoseon scheme, as discussed in the previous section. They all contributed to the expansion of the national fleet.

Investment in maritime transport infrastructures

When the Government launched the First Five Year Plan, Korea had only two major ports for international trade. The Port of Incheon on the west coast is close to the major manufacturing centre of Seoul, but has a 30 foot tidal range and, therefore, ships could not load or unload outside the docks. The Port of Pusan on the south-east coast of Korea has no such problem, but its docking facilities were unable to accommodate ships over 10,000 grt.. The limitations of port facilities and capacity were the major factors contributing not only to congestion and in turn to increased transportation cost, but also to preventing modern and large ships from calling there.

The Korean government recognised: that seaports can play a major role in promoting international trade by generating commercial and industrial activities which directly assist the economic progress of the country; and that, without an efficient port, the cost of physical distribution becomes higher, industrial development more difficult, and exports of goods less competitive.

Korean seaports are classified as First Class Ports and Second Class Ports, according to their relative size and economic importance. The former are used for international traffic, while the latter for the coastal and ferry services and harbours of refuge. The paramount need of port developments in Korea has been further emphasised by the adoption of an export-oriented industrialisation policy in the 1960s and by the fact that the Korean economy is heavily dependent on imports of raw materials because of a lack of natural resources. Thus, since 1962 the government has included investment in the maritime infrastructure in the overall social overhead investment sector. Table 3.2 presents the amount invested for port developments.

Table 3.2
Port investments by the government in the period 1962-81
(million won at 1980 prices)[+]

Year	Real amount	Rate of real increase (%)	Year	Real amount	Rate of real increase (%)
1962	23,871	-	1972	38,048	-19.1
1963	10,731	-55.0	1973	39,211	3.1
1964	7,760	-27.7	1974	48,414	23.5
1965	13,290	71.3	1975	82,780	71.0
1966	22,322	-68.0	1976	105,927	28.0
Sub-total	77,994	Average 14.2	Sub-total	314,380	Average 1.3
1967	25,088	-12.4	1977	108,967	2.9
1968	43,871	74.9	1978	112,393	3.1
1969	67,410	53.7	1979	95,716	-14.8
1970	46,342	-31.3	1980	113,458	18.5
1971	47,039	1.5	1981	101,795	-10.3
Sub-total	229,750	Average 17.3	Sub-total	532,329	Average 0.1

Grand total: real amount: 1,154,443 million won
Average: 13.2%

Note: [+] *Investments are mainly concerned with the construction of quay walls, lighter's wharf, breakwater, groin, seawall, pier and dredging.*

Source: KMPA (1980), *Hankook Haewoon Hangmansa*, [History of Korean Shipping and Ports], pp. 841-876, KMPA, Seoul, Korea. The Bank of Korea, *Economic Statistics Yearbook*, various issues. KMPA (1986), *Haewoon Hangmancheong Sibnyeonsa*, [10 Years History of Korean Shipping and Ports], p. 288, KMPA, Seoul, Korea.

During the Third Five Year Plan, the government developed industrial ports to meet the needs of increasing seaborne trade, e.g. iron, steel, crude oil, petrochemical plants and ship-yards, according to the Heavy and Chemical Industry Development Plan set up in 1973.[10] For example, the Port of Ulsan was constructed mainly to serve the oil industry and nearby petrochemical complexes, power plants and manufacturing plants; the Pohang New Port for the Pohang Iron and Steel Company, which imports bulk cargoes such as oil, coal, iron and other ores and export steel products.

Over the two Five Year plans (1967-76), in the Port of Incheon, which has one of the largest tidal ranges, a lock system was constructed to connect the outer and inner harbours. As a result, the handling capacity of the port increased from 1.4 million tonnes in 1971 to 8.7 million tonnes in 1976 and its number of berths from seven in 1971 to 27 in 1976.

In 1970, the government launched a project for the construction of piers for a container terminal and for the repair and expansion of other existing piers in the Port of Pusan in order to handle the rapidly increasing seaborne trade. Based on the report on the feasibility of port development and with the loans of US $115 million from IBRD and Saudi Arabia,[11] the first stage of the project was mainly concerned with the construction of piers: Pier Number 5 for the container terminal, Pier Number 7 for coal, iron and ore and Pier Number 8 for special cargo. The government launched the second stage of the project in 1979. This involved the construction of Pier Number 6, a container terminal, and repair and expansion of other existing piers in the Port of Pusan. Thanks to such considerable investments by the government, the handling and berth capacities of the Port of Pusan significantly increased for the former, from 5.7 million in 1971 to 19.6 million tonnes in 1981 and, for the latter, from 33 ships in 1971 to 56 ships in 1981. Table 3.3 shows that both capacities increased because of the government's port investments.

Table 3.3
Berth and handling capacities of Korean major ports

Year	Incheon (H)[+]	(B)[++]	Pusan (H)	(B)	Pohang (H)	(B)	Ulsan (H)	(B)	Others (H)	(B)	Total (H)	(B)
1961	1.4	7	4.0	32	0.4	-	-	-	3.3	24	9.1	63
1966	1.4	7	5.0	32	0.4	-	0.5	1	7.4	27	14.7	67
1971	1.4	7	5.7	33	0.4	6	1.3	8	9.9	37	18.7	91
1976	8.7	27	7.0	33	5.0	12	1.5	9	11.8	48	34.0	129
1981	9.7	na	15.0	56	24.2	na	2.7	na	35.8	na	87.4	199

Notes: [+]   *(H) cargo handling capacity in port (in million tonnes).*
　　　　[++]   *(B) berth capacity in port (number of ships).*

Source: KMPA (1980), *Hankook Haewoon Hangmansa*, [History of Korean Shipping and Ports], p. 894, KMPA, Seoul, Korea.

Cargo reservation: The waiver system

Cargo reservation is an administrative way of reducing the competition from foreign ships in the transport of domestic cargoes. This affects different parts of the country's seaborne trade; in some cases, a country may even reserve 100 per cent of its cargo for its own fleet which thus enjoys a full monopoly of transport.

Korea adopted a typical form of cargo reservation, the waiver system, in 1959. However, the system was further developed when the enforcement of 'The Outline of the Procedure for Issuing Waivers' was published by the Ministry of Transportation in 1965. In the same year, the government adopted a resolution to require that over 50 per cent of inbound cargo procured with aid, loans or other government funds should be transported aboard Korean flagged ships. This strengthened the waiver system. In 1967, the most comprehensive attempt at cargo reservation was embodied in the Shipping Promotion Law. This declared the intention of the government to reserve major cargoes of imports and exports for the national fleet in order to improve the balance of payments and, at the same time, to promote the development of an ocean-going shipping industry in Korea. The major contents of the waiver system contained in the law were:[12]

- Imports of iron ore, coal, raw chemical products, grain, fertilisers, crude oil, and government purchases as well as exports of plywood, cement, and steel are reserved for Korean-flag vessels unless a waiver is granted to a foreign vessel by the Korean Shipowners' Association.
- There are two cases in which the waiver is issued: when the cargo is transported on routes where no Korean flag ship is serving, and when no Korean flag ship is available on the date on which cargo must be loaded, although the cargo can be shipped on routes where Korean flag ships are serving.
- If a foreign carrier is nominated on the Letter of Credit, no waiver is necessary.

It is worth discussing how the system influenced the expansion of Korean shipping in detail, along with the increase of seaborne trade thanks to Korean economic policies, i.e. export-oriented industrialisation in the 1960s and import-substitution in the 1970s. As a preparatory stage to this, the following section briefly reviews the remarkable growth of the Korean economy in the past few decades.

General overview of economic policies (1962-81)

In Korea, a protectionist strategy of import substitution for light non-durable consumer goods, processed food, beverages and tobacco and finished textiles characterised industrial growth in the period 1953-62.[13] In 1962 when the nation launched the First Five Year Plan, Korea had in principle two alternative approaches to economic development. One was an inward-looking development strategy[14] based on import substitution. The other was an outward-looking development strategy emphasising trade.[15] For Korea, with a long inward-looking tradition, the 1963 change to the outward-looking strategy was indeed remarkable. It is to the credit of the political leadership at that time that such a strategy was adopted. However, there were powerful economic reasons for the policy, including poor natural resource endowment, small domestic markets and the existence of an abundant and well trained and educated labour force with relatively low wages.[16]

The essence of the outward-looking strategy adopted in the early 1960s was to promote labour-intensive manufacturing exports in which it was considered that Korea had a comparative advantage. In order to implement this strategy, the Korean government mobilised both internal and external resources by making use of the market mechanism. The most important elements of the policy were fiscal and monetary reforms, which were aimed at increasing public and private saving, and the establishment of a uniform exchange rate, which was the last step in the gradual adoption of a complete set of export incentives. For example, to mobilise domestic savings, the government raised interest rates on deposits to commercial banks from 5.8 per cent to 20.2 per cent in real terms. As a result, savings deposits in Korean banks nearly doubled each year. In addition, in order to promote exports, the government readjusted the exchange rate in 1964, and kept it near the free market level.[17] Furthermore, the Korean won was devalued by nearly 100 per cent, thus eliminating a bias against the export sector.[18]

The Korean government incentive policies were not directed toward perfectly free trade during this rapid growth period. There were, for example, government measures such as tax incentives and preferential loans that led to the expansion of several inefficient domestic as well as export industries, and import restrictions along with high tariffs that stimulated import substitution, not only in consumer durables, but also in various intermediate goods, including chemicals, electrical machinery and transportation equipment. The government continued to give its full support to the export-oriented growth strategy. This basic strategy of export-oriented industrialisation was carried out under the subsequent Second, Third and Fourth Five Year Economic Development Plans.

In the decade after 1965, the growth of manufactured exports and the rise in domestic demand fuelled a much faster rate of industrialisation. An average annual rate of growth in the index of manufacturing output of 11 per cent between 1955 and 1965 rose to 24 per cent between 1965 and 1975. Underlying the acceleration of growth in manufacturing output, the share of exports in gross manufacturing output rose from roughly 6 per cent in 1965 to almost 25 per cent in 1975. In the decade 1965-75, the share of GNP originating in the manufacturing sector was more than doubled. Manufactured exports became increasingly diversified, so that by 1975 Korea was a major exporter of footwear, transport equipment, electrical machinery and appliances, and various manufactures of metal and non-metallic minerals - in addition to textiles, clothing and plywood, which had generated the initial growth of exports.[19]

In the early 1970s the government began to modify its outward looking development strategy by emphasising import substitution,[20] particularly in the heavy and chemical industries and in agriculture. This change in economic strategy resulted from a number of disturbing external developments. For one thing, in 1971 the Nixon administration reduced the US troop levels in Korea by one third. This led the government to develop its own defence industry. Korea's resolve in this direction was reinforced by Democratic Presidential Candidate Jimmy Carter's 1976 campaign promise to carry out total US troop withdrawal. In addition, in 1971 the Bretton Woods system began to fall apart.[21] It was widely believed that the system itself encouraged protectionism because it discouraged balance of payments adjustments via exchange rate modification. However, the advent of the flexible exchange rate system failed to reverse this trend. On the contrary, the protectionist trend accelerated. Thus, Korea was forced to diversify its trading partners and to produce and export higher value-added industrial goods.

Although emphasis has been placed on export-oriented industrialisation, since the early 1970s import substitution in selected major industries was also promoted by means of tax concessions and the allocation of preferential credits. The import-substituting industries promoted, included shipbuilding, iron and steel, machinery and petro-chemicals,[22] although some of these, in particular shipbuilding, have recently become new export industries. Consequently, the machinery industry is now promoted not only for import substitution but also for export expansion. In addition to assisting these major industries, the government has provided both tax and credit incentives for coal mining and the livestock industry, while still controlling the prices of their products to consumers.[23]

By introducing the import-substitution strategy, the Korean economy achieved a high average annual growth rate of real GNP of 9.5 per cent at 1980 prices between 1972 and 1978 and the upgrade of its export structure. The share of heavy and chemical industrial products in total exports rose from 21.3 per cent in 1972 to 34.7 per cent in 1978.

Employment of shipping is dependent upon the volume and pattern of seaborne trade. The size of shipping tonnage is, therefore, ultimately governed by the volume of seaborne trade, the distances over which it is to be transported and the efficiency of seaports. The nature of each of the commodities and the quantity in which it is transported determine the type of shipping required to carry it. While general cargo, which moves in small parcels or consignments, is transported by liner ships, bulk cargo, which consists of homogenous commodities individually moving in large quantity, usually in shiploads, is carried by tramps and bulk carriers. The scope for employment and growth of tramp shipping is dependent upon the volume of bulk cargoes in import and export trades of a country as well as the international cross trades in which it can participate.[24]

To analyse how the waiver system, along with the economic policies which led to the growth of foreign trade, contributed to the Korean shipping expansion, it is helpful to raise and answer the following questions. What changes occurred in the types and volume of commodities imported and exported as the Korean seaborne trade expanded in the period 1962-81 and the Korean fleet changed its composition and gross tonnage? Where did this seaborne trade come from and go to? What shares of imports and exports have been carried by the Korean fleet? These questions will be answered below.

Seaborne cargoes in import trade (1962-81)

Table 3.4 shows a breakdown of seaborne imports by item in the period 1962-81. There are no consistent data available of primary commodities in the whole period, stemming from a disparity in the criteria for data collection.

Table 3.4
Seaborne import trade volume by item (1962-81)

	1962	1966	1967	1971	1976	1981
Grains	452	558	1,061	2,928	3,131	7,300
Fertiliser	993	831				
Cement	198	189				
Oil			3,580	12,651	18,546	25,421
Coal			95	58	1,689	12,463
Logs	484	1,012	1,334	3,082	5,552	5,107
Iron ore			3	19	2,635	11,804
Anthracite	23	20				
Minerals	3	40				
Phosphate			112	700	893	1,130
Machinery			103	98	516	717
Iron material			645	1,221	2,416	3,923
Others	1,548	4,123	2,804	3,498	6,068	11,158
Total	3,701	6,773	9,737	24,255	41,446	79,023

(unit: thousand tonnes)

Source: The Ministry of Transportation, *Statistics Yearbook of Transportation*, various issues.

The volume of Korea's seaborne import trade grew by 21.35 times in the period, i.e. from about 3.7 million tonnes in 1962 to about 79.0 million tonnes in 1981, when the volume constituted approximately 75 per cent of the total seaborne foreign trade volume.

The oil and coal industries chiefly produce fuels (used by the mining, agriculture, forestry, fishery, service and transport industries, and by households) and raw materials (for the petrochemical industry). With the expansion of production, Korean imports of crude oil increased at annual rates of 26.7 per cent in order to meet demand. Crude oil constituted the most important commodity in terms of quantity in Korea's import trade. In 1971, crude oil imports amounted to 12.6 million tonnes, more than half of the total import trade. Crude oil was imported mainly from the Middle East, e.g. from Iran, Kuwait and Saudi Arabia.

The First and Second Five Year Plans called for construction of housing, factories, roads, harbours and bridges. The resulting construction boom led to expanded demand, not only for iron and steel products, but also for plywood. In order to meet the demand for plywood, logs, out of which plywood is made, were imported from Malaysia, the Philippines and Indonesia. Imports of logs amounted to 5.1 million tonnes in 1981. Increased demand for ferrous metal products brought increased imports of scrap iron, including imports of steel plates. Scrap iron is imported chiefly from the USA in terms of value. In 1981 imports of iron material constituted 3.9 million tonnes and grew by seven times during 1967-81.

During the Third and Fourth Five Year plans, was the largest import commodity in terms of quantity crude oil, and this continuously grew to 25.4 million tonnes in 1981, from 12.6 million tonnes in 1971. However, its share of the total import trade in terms of volume fell by 32 per cent in 1981 from 51 per cent in 1972.

As a result of emphasising import substitution in the chemical and heavy industries, the first stage of the Pohang Iron and Steel Company (POSCO) was completed and production of pig iron and hot steel coil began in 1973. POSCO therefore needed imports of iron ore, as one of the raw materials for iron and steel products. Imports of iron ore began to increase sharply from 1974 and grew by approximately 12 times until 1981 when they amounted to 11.8 million tonnes compared with 1 million tonnes in 1974. The oil crisis and the establishment of POSCO have played a role in sharply increasing imports of coal as an alternative fuel.

Imports of coal amounted to 12.5 million tonnes in 1981, i.e. 16 per cent of total sea-borne import trade. The principal bulk cargoes consist of grains, crude oil, coal, logs and iron ore imports as set out in Table 3.4 and amounted to 62.1 million tonnes in 1981, i.e. approximately 59 per cent of total seaborne foreign trade.

The above figures show the importance of bulk cargoes in quantum terms in Korea's total seaborne foreign trade. Although in terms of value bulk cargoes were far less important than the quantity figures indicate, it is the quantity of cargo carried and not the value of cargo carried which gives employment to a large fleet.

Seaborne cargoes in export trade, 1962-81

Table 3.5 presents the seaborne export trade volume by main item in Korea in the period 1962-81. During the Second Five Year Plan, in terms of quantity the bulk cargoes in Korea's export trade were mainly cement, ores and oil. In 1971, they amounted to 2.1 million tonnes, i.e. about 50 per cent of the total export trade in Korea. Cement was the most important commodity in quantity terms in Korea's export trade. Cement production grew under the stimulus of domestic demand generated by the First and Second Five Year Plans and was used extensively in building roads, ports, dams and other forms of initial investment in social overhead capital, in addition to factories, housing and multi-storey buildings.

Table 3.5
Seaborne export trade volume by item (1962-81)

	1962	1966	1967	1971	1976	1981
Grains	64	57				
Oil			-	340	1,216	371
Fertiliser	-	6	10	80	157	809
Cement	-	18	27	910	3,094	5,546
Lumber	7	36	62	248	1,623	902
Anthracite	294	152				
Minerals	253	842				
Iron ore			608	478	14	30
Other ore			254	327	629	587
Machinery			0	3	186	595
Iron material			4	112	1,476	5,218
Others	185	551	821	1,695	5,913	12,238
Total	803	1662	1,786	4,193	14,308	26,296

(unit: thousand tonnes)

Source: The Ministry of Transportation, *Statistics Yearbook of Transportation*, various issues; KMI, *Haewoon Tonggye Yoram 1986,* [Maritime Statistical Yearbook 1986].

In Korea, the export of cement in 1967 and 1971 amounted to 27,000 and 910,000 tonnes respectively. In 1971, it amounted to 21.7 per cent of the total export trade and constituted more than half of the total bulk dry cargo of Korea's export trade. Approximately 10 per cent of total domestic production of cement was exported, mostly to Vietnam.

In the 1960s, plywood was also an important Korean export. Its quantum data are not available, but, considering that in 1968 the contribution of plywood to total exports had reached 14.4 per cent,[25] it can be estimated that plywood represented a significant export volume. Throughout the 1960s, 80-90 per cent of plywood exports in terms of real value went to the USA, while during the latter half of the decade, plywood exports to Canada and Japan started to increase, as shown in Table 3.6.

More than 90 per cent of Korea's exports of electronic components in terms of value went to the USA, followed by much smaller proportions going to Japan, FR Germany, Hong Kong and Canada. Exports of wigs followed a similar pattern with most of Korea's wigs being exported and very few sold domestically.

Table 3.6
Export of plywood in Korea (1964-70) (at 1970 prices)

Year	USA	Canada	Japan
1964	13,820	7	77
1966	30,850	3,934	16
1968	65,773	3,027	554
1970	73,635	4,890	11,637

(unit: thousand US $)

Source: *Statistical Yearbook of Foreign Trade*, Seoul, Korea, various issues.

With regard to raw silk, 80-90 per cent of exports went to the USA during the first half of the 1960s, while during the latter half of the decade 70-90 per cent went to Japan instead. This was also the case with cotton fabric: while during the earlier part of the 1960s cotton fabric was exported exclusively to the USA, it then began to be exported first to Hong Kong, then to Japan, and then to the UK, Italy and Nigeria.[26] The data of these commodities in terms of quantity were included in the category of 'others' and their separate data were not available.

The chief characteristic to be observed so far is that Korea conducted most of its export trade with only two partners - the USA and Japan. Throughout the 1960s, these two countries received 60 per cent to 70 per cent of Korea's exports. Moreover, the proportion of exports bound for the USA and Japan showed a tendency to increase, from 60 per cent in the early 1960s to 70 per cent in the late 1960s.[27]

Thanks to the construction boom in the Middle East, cement continued to keep its principal position in terms of quantity in Korea's export trade during the 1970s. The export of cement in 1981 amounted to 5.5 million tonnes, which constituted 20 per cent of the total export trade. POSCO, which began operating in 1973, immediately secured an internationally competitive position and has contributed to both import substitution and export expansion. Exports of iron material have sharply increased since 1975 and amounted to 5.2 million tonnes in 1981, which consisted of 20 per cent of Korea's total export trade. POSCO contributed, of course, to exports of manufactured goods, such as steel plates.

As a result of shifting the emphasis of policy to import substitution and thanks to a substantial change in the industrial structure during the Third and Fourth Five Year Plan periods, one of the distinctive features of the Korean export trade is that the composition of export commodities has changed from simple labour-intensive manufactured goods (such as textiles and footwear) to high value-added industrial goods (such as iron and steel manufactures, non-ferrous metal goods, shipbuilding, machinery, electronics and petrochemicals). It can be observed from Table 3.5 that exports of machinery were only 11 million tonnes in 1972 but since 1975 sharply increased to 176 million tonnes. Although the share of machinery in the total export trade was still only 2 per cent in 1981, its growth trend is remarkable.

The growth of the merchant marine fleet

In 1962, the Korean fleet totalled 40 steam and motor vessels of 103,870 grt. (an average size of 2,600 grt.). Since the implementation of the Five Year Economic Development Plan, the fleet has expanded, with the rate of growth accelerating over the years. By 1981, the number of vessels had risen from 40 to 1,634 (an average 21.6 per cent growth rate per annum) and gross tonnage from 103,870 grt. to 5.1 million grt. (average 22.8 per cent growth rate per annum), as shown in Table 3.7.

Table 3.7
Gross tonnage and seaborne foreign trade volume in Korea (1962-81)

Year	Number	Steam and motor gross tonnage[+] (in thousand tonnes)	Foreign trade volume (in million tonnes)
1962	40	104	4.5
1967	196	306	11.5
1972	446	1,057	30.7
1977	1,042	2,495	68.3
1981	1,634	5,142	105.3

Note: [+] *Including all fishing type ships, passenger, ferries and others.*

Source: *Lloyd's Register of Shipping Statistical Tables*, 1987; KMPA (1980), *Hankook Haewoon Hangmansa*, [History of Korean Shipping and Ports], pp. 400, 458 and 493, KMPA, Seoul, Korea.

Thanks to the export-oriented industrial strategy from the early 1960s and shifting emphasis to import substitution in the early 1970s, total foreign trade increased remarkably with volumes growing from 4.5 million tonnes in 1962 to 105.3

56

million tonnes in 1981, i.e. a 2,340 per cent increase. The annual average growth rate over the period 1962-81 was 10 per cent.

The principal bulk cargoes in import and export trades aggregated 20.3 million tonnes out of a total import and export trade of 28.4 million tonnes in the period 1962-71. The trade in bulk cargo, therefore, constituted over 71 per cent of Korea's total foreign trade. Most bulk cargoes were reserved for Korean flag ships by the waiver system, with some exceptions, for example agricultural commodities imported from the USA under the terms of Public Law Number 480 and cargo carried by bilateral agreements.

Table 3.8 presents Korean shipping tonnage by ship type during the period 1962-81. In 1971 Korean ships carried about 21 per cent of the country's total foreign trade. It can, therefore, be observed that prima facie there was great scope for expansion of the country's tramp shipping for carriage of bulk cargoes.

Table 3.8
Gross tonnage by ship type (1962-81)

	1962	1966	1967	1972	1976	1981
Oil tankers	8	15	152	401	652	1,296
Dry cargo ships	103	219	278			
Liquefied gas					1	12
Passenger ships	3	5	6			
Ore and bulk				155	263	2,098
General cargo+				406	548	936
Chemical carriage				8	3	18
Container ships				3	36	312
All fishing types						
Car carriers						24
Others						
Total	113	239	436	973	1,511	4,696

(unit: thousand grt.)

Note: + *Including passenger ships.*

Source: KMI, *Haewoon Tonggye Yoram, 1986*, [Maritime Statistical Yearbook, 1986]; *Lloyd's Register of Shipping Statistical Tables*, 1971-72.

As shown in Figure 3.1, the growth of the Korean merchant marine fleet was in line with that of total seaborne foreign trade, although in 1967 the gap between the two curves began to grow. However, from 1970 the growth rate of seaborne foreign trade was relatively higher than that of the gross tonnage.

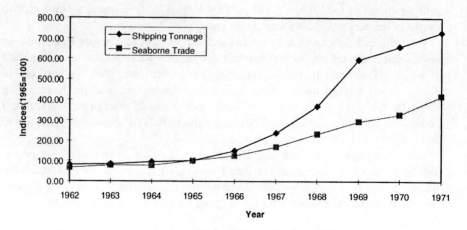

Figure 3.1   Growth trends in shipping tonnage and seaborne trade volume in Korea (1962-71)

The Korean oil tanker fleet experienced a remarkable 46-fold expansion of its tonnage during 1962-71, rising to 373,000 grt. in 1971 from 8,000 grt. in 1962. This expansion can be ascribed partly to the waiver system and also to a relative increase in oil imports.

There has been considerable growth of bulk shipping in Korea in the period covered by the First and Second Five Year Plans. Thus, the growth in the shipping industry was more in tramp shipping and tanker shipping than in liner shipping, unlike shipping in India and other developing countries. In other words, unlike most developing countries, the development pattern of the Korean merchant marine fleet was in the second stage of development out of the four distinct stages development of merchant marines that have been identified.[28]

Ore and bulk tonnage amounted to 0.16 million grt. in 1972, which was 16 per cent of the total Korean merchant fleet. By 1981, this had increased to 2.1 million grt., i.e. 44 per cent of the fleet. Its annual average growth rate was about 30 per cent. For oil tankers, tonnage grew to about 1.3 million grt. in 1981 from 0.4 million grt. in 1972, i.e. a three-fold increase during the period 1972-81, although their share of the total Korean merchant fleet fell to 28 per cent in 1981 from 41 per cent in 1972.

On the other hand, total seaborne trade volume increased to 105.3 million tonnes in 1981 from 30.7 million tonnes in 1972. The annual average growth rate was 13.1 per cent during the period 1972-81.

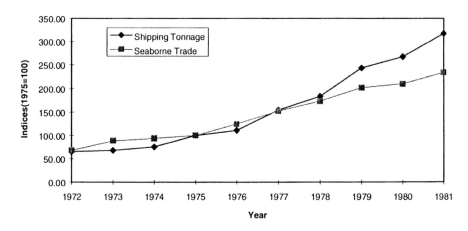

Figure 3.2   Growth trends in shipping tonnage and seaborne trade volume in Korea (1972-81)

From Figure 3.2, it can be seen that the growth trend of the Korean merchant marine fleet was roughly equivalent to the expansion of total seaborne volume with a similar pattern to the period of 1962-71 (see Figure 3.1). This means that Korean shipping growth was accompanied by an increase of seaborne trade volume which in turn can be ascribed to the Korean government's economic policies, i.e. a successful outward looking economic policy in the 1960s and an import-substitution policy in the 1970s. The growth pattern of the shipping industry becomes more obvious when Figures 3.1 and 3.2 are combined into one figure (see Figure 3.3). Figure 3.3 relates to the growth trends of the total gross tonnage and seaborne trade volume in Korea over the whole period 1962-81. In this figure, the two curves run in a parallel pattern over the whole period.

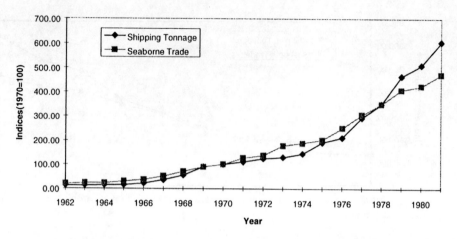

Figure 3.3   Growth trends in shipping tonnage and seaborne trade volume in Korea (1962-81)

Conclusion

The purpose of this chapter was to discuss the role of the Korean government in shipping growth in the period 1962-81. The role of the government was reviewed in terms of financial assistance, taxation, the government-financed shipbuilding programme ('Keihek Zoseon'), port investment and the waiver system.

An export-oriented industrialisation policy brought about rapid export growth, which in turn increased the imports of raw materials in Korea since the early 1960s. As a result, the extensive expansion of foreign trade has been achieved and caused the government to accelerate the expansion of the merchant fleet.

In addition, the waiver system has reserved considerable cargoes - for example, crude oil, grain, iron ore, cement and plywood - for Korean flag ships and provided the opportunity for substantial increases in Korean shipping tonnage. Various tax exemptions for the importation of ships and ship's stores enabled Korean shipowners to save on operating and capital costs and thus to operate their ships competitively. On the other hand, one thing that must never be disregarded is that the government has attempted to provide some visible infrastructure such as port construction and related facilities for shipping development in every Five Year Economic Development Plan since 1962. The 'Keihek Zoseon' scheme contributed to the increase of new shipping tonnage since 1975. In the light of the above, it can be said that the Korean government played important direct and indirect roles in Korean shipping growth.

In investigating the relationship between foreign trade and shipping tonnage in this chapter it is clear that there existed a positive interrelationship between volumes of foreign trade and shipping tonnage. However, it must be mentioned that the expansion of shipping tonnage does not depend solely on the capacity of foreign trade; for Korea, the waiver system reserved considerable cargo, in particular bulk cargoes, for the Korean national fleet. In addition, thanks to the export-led economic industrialisation, rapid export growth in the whole period 1962-81 was a relevant factor which helped to determine shipping growth. In other words, the point to be emphasised is that in the case of demand for a great deal of final shipping services, foreign trade has played the decisive role. The expansion of shipping in Korea was a response to the export-oriented industrialisation policy. The diversification of export commodities and export markets has led to an increase in shipping tonnage and a change in the composition of the fleet in Korea. It must also be noted that there was a gradual acquisition and upgrading programme by the Korean government and Korean shipowners, most of whom employ their ships in Korean trading routes as well as in cross trades.

Notes and references

1   On the role of government in economic development, Gamba, C. (1953), The Role of the State in Underdeveloped Areas, Economic Record, Vol. 29, pp. 245-56; Aitken, H. G. J. (ed.) (1959), *The State and Economic Growth*, Social Science Research Council, New York; Whang, I. J. (1987), *The Role of Government in Economic Development: The Korean Experience*, Asian Development Review, Vol. 5, No. 2, pp. 70-88.

2   On the Gerschenkron model, see Chapter 2.

3   Korean currency unit.

4   Sohn, T-H. (1982), *Hankook Haewoonsa*, [History of Korean Shipping], p. 455, A-Seong Publishing Company, Pusan, Korea. H. Kokuryo translated main contents of this Law included in the above book into English. See Kokuryo, H. (1985), *Korean Shipping and Shipping Policy - Shipping Industry Rationalisation Plan*, JAMRI Report No. 8, Japan Maritime Research Institute, Tokyo.

5   Temple, Barker and Sloane, Inc. and Korea Maritime Institute (1985), *An Overview of Prospects and Strategy for the Development of the Korean Shipping Industry*, a project prepared for the World Bank and Port Administration, p. I-9, Korea Maritime Institute, Seoul, Korea.

6   KMPA (1980), *Hankook Haewoon Hangmansa*, [History of Korean Shipping and Ports], pp. 541-7, KMPA, Seoul, Korea.

7   The complete exemption from the tax applied only to a cargo ship of more than 3,000 grt. with less than 10 years old. For the other ship, the tax rates of 5 to 30 per cent were applied. Ibid., p. 543.

8   A foreign currency re-loan means that the Korea Development Bank, the Long Term Credit Bank and Korean commercial banks borrow foreign currencies from foreign commercial banks and Euro-money markets and lend them to domestic strategic industries, e.g. the shipbuilding, chemical, electric and motor industries.

9   The Korea Development Bank (1985), *Hankookeui Haewoon Zoseonup Hyeonhang*, [Current Issues of the Korean Shipping and Shipbuilding Industries], unpublished report, p. 59, KDB, Seoul, Korea.

10   On the development of industrial ports in Korea, see Kim, H. N. (1986), 'Industrial Port: Policy and Planning Issues in the ROK.', MSc Thesis, The University of Wales Institute of Science and Technology, Cardiff.

11   KMPA (1986), *Haewoon Hangmancheong Sibnyeonsa*, [10 Years History of Korean Shipping and Ports], (in Korean version), pp. 291-2, KMPA, Seoul, Korea.

12   Temple, Barker and Sloane, Inc. and Korea Maritime Institute, op. cit., p. I-7.

13   Suh, S. T. (1975), *Import Substitution and Economic Development in Korea*, Working Paper No. 7519, p. 261, The Korea Development Institute, Seoul, Korea.

14   On the subject of inward- and outward-looking strategy, see Balassa, B. (1970), 'Growth Strategies in Semi-Industrial Countries', *Quarterly Journal of Economics*, Vol. 84, No. 1, pp. 24-47.

15   On the outward-looking development policies, see Keesing, D. B. (1967), 'Outward-looking Policies and Economic Development', *Economic Journal*, Vol. 77, No. 306, pp. 303-20. On various reasons why developing countries changed their industrialisation strategies from import substitution to export promotion, see Little, I. M. D. et al. (1970), *Industry and Trade in Some Developing Countries: A Comparative Study*, Oxford University Press, London; Ballance, R. H, Ansari, J. A. and Singer, H. (1982), *The International Economy and Industrial Development*, Chapter 2, Wheatsheaf Books Limited, Sussex.

16   On further discussion on the reasons for adopting an outward-looking strategy, see Balassa, B. (1971), 'Industrial Policies in Taiwan and Korea', *Weltwirtschaftliches Archiv*, Vol. 105, No. 1, pp. 60-1; Krueger, A. O. (1979), *The Development Role of the Foreign Sector and Aid*, p. 82, Harvard University Press, Cambridge, Massachusetts; Dornbusch, R. (1987), *Korean Growth Policy*, Brookings Papers on Economic Activity, No. 2, pp. 439-41.

17   Suh, S. T., op. cit., p. 261.

18   For further details of financial policies in Korea, see Kanesa-Thasan, S. (1969), *Stabilising an Economy - A Study of the Republic of Korea*, International Monetary Fund Staff Papers, Vol. 16, pp. 1-26.

19   Westphal, L. E., Rhee, Y. W. and Pursell, G. (1981), *Korean Industrial Competence: Where It Came From*, The World Bank Staff Working Paper No. 469, p. 13, The World Bank, Washington, D.C.

20   Import substituting industrialisation remains a controversial issue in the literature of development economics. The issue has become more controversial so because economic development of developing countries has become an ever-more pressing problem and efforts to accomplish rapid economic development through import substitution have often been frustrated. For an analytical relationship between import substitution and economic development, see Chenery, H. B. (1960), 'Patterns of Industrial Growth', *American Economic Review*, Vol. 50, pp. 625-54. For a comprehensive review of the theoretical and empirical concept and problems of import substitution and an analysis on the issue for the Korean economy, see Suh, S. T., op. cit.

21   Kim, K. W. (1984), *The Korean Economy: Past Performance, Current Reforms and Future Prospects*, pp. 9-10, Korea Development Institute, Seoul, Korea.

22   On the level of import substitution in them, see Watanabe, T. (1978), 'Heavy and Chemical Industrialisation and Economic Development in the Republic of Korea', *Developing Economies*, Vol. 16, No. 4, pp. 385-407.

23   Mason, E. S, et al. (1980), *The Economic and Social Modernisation of the Republic of Korea*, pp. 131-2, Harvard University Press, Cambridge, Massachusetts.

24   Sanklecha, S. N. (1966), *Tramp Shipping in India*, p. 88, The University of Bombay, Bombay.

25   Balassa, B. (1971), op. cit., p. 61.

26   Institute of Developing Economies (1975), *Development of Manufacturing in Korea in the 1960s - A Statistical Analysis*, I.D.E. Statistical Data Series No. 17, p. 20, Institute of Developing Economies, Tokyo.

27   Ibid., p. 19.

28   First, a liner fleet is established and expanded. Second, operations with tanker and bulk carrier fleets begin, leading to the third stage, which is participation in horizontal integration of shipping with other transport as well as non-transport activities. Apart from the oil-exporting countries that began directly with tanker and bulk operations, most less-advanced countries are in the first stage. Abrahamsson, B. J. (1980), *International Ocean Shipping: Current Concepts and Principles*, p. 15, Westview Press, Boulder, Colorado; Norwegian Shipping News, 19 September and 10 October 1975.

4 Shipping finance and shipping growth in Korea

Introduction

Having decided to purchase a vessel, a shipowner may consider several different sources of shipping finance. The main sources are:

- self-financing, including joint ventures, e.g. by retained profits or equity issues;
- special national shipping finance funds;
- shipyard credits, e.g. ship export credits;
- leasing arrangements;
- bilateral or government-to-government assistance;
- international or regional development banks;
- mezzanine finance;
- securitisation finance;
- international commercial banks;
- bare boat charter finance;
- time charter finance;
- the Shikumisen financial arrangements.[1]

The above major sources of shipping finance can be roughly summarised into two, that is, self-financing and external financing methods. The advantages and disadvantages of the various sources depend upon a number of factors: the down-payment, which in turn determines the amount of capital to be financed; the effective rate of interest; the repayment period; the security that the borrower is asked to provide; the currency specified; and special conditions which may be tied to the finance. Taxation may also be relevant, as may capital and operating subsidies.

In the context of the Gerschenkron model, the banking system plays an important role at a certain stage of the industrialisation process in relatively backward countries, having a poorly developed capital market and a scarcity of entrepreneurial talent. That is, the banks undertake the leading role in industrialisation, providing the prime source of capital and entrepreneurship in moderately backward areas.

This chapter aims to test hypothesis II established in Chapter 2: in Korea, where there was no original capital accumulation in the shipping sector, a special shipping finance system was designed and thus contributed to acquiring ships and to expanding the Korean merchant marine. For this, the following questions will be raised and answered: what methods of shipping finance were mainly employed in this growth of the fleet in Korea? What served as a substitute of the original for capital accumulation in the shipping sector?

Methods of acquisition of the Korean merchant fleet

The methods of ship acquisition by which Korean shipowners have developed their significant national fleet in the period 1962-81 can be classified largely into:

- general domestic shipbuilding;
- government financed shipbuilding programmes, i.e. "Keihek Zoseon", as discussed in Chapter 2;
- the importing ships;
- the bareboat charter with purchase option (BBCPO).

As shown in Table 4.1, the expansion of the Korean merchant fleet was largely attributable to the methods of imports and bareboat charter with purchase option. Apart from 1976, these two methods contributed to the expansion of more than 60 per cent of the total annual tonnage increased during the period 1975-81. Since its introduction in 1975, the method of Keihek Zoseon has also played a role in adding new tonnage to the Korean fleet as discussed in Chapter 3, unlike the other two methods, while increased tonnage by the method of general domestic shipbuilding amounted to 55 per cent of the total increased tonnage in 1976 and since then, it has decreased sharply.

For testing hypothesis II, the following sections discuss the sources and mechanism of shipping finance by the method of ship acquisition and how each of these methods contributed to expanding the merchant marine in Korea, along with some attention given to the growth trends of the Korean shipping tonnage by the method of ship acquisition.

Table 4.1 shows annual tonnage increases by each method in Korea during the period 1975-81.

66

Table 4.1
Annual increasing tonnage by method of acquisition of ships in Korea
(1975-81)

Year	General domestic shipbuilding	Planned shipbuilding	Imports	BBCPO[+]	Total by year
1975	11	-	135	156	302
	(4)[++]	-	(45)	(51)	(100)
1976	454	-	143	230	827
	(55)	-	(17)	(28)	(100)
1977	147[3][+++]	74[10]	187[21]	207[17]	615[51]
	(24)	(12)	(30)	(34)	(100)
1978	84[4]	136[13]	530[44]	277[13]	1,027[74]
	(8)	(13)	(52)	(27)	(100)
1979	21[1]	202[19]	461[22]	82[8]	766[50]
	(3)	(26)	(60)	(11)	(100)
1980	2[1]	178[21]	337[21]	345[14]	862[57]
	(0)	(21)	(39)	(40)	(100)
1981	11[1]	193[12]	706[34]	384[16]	1,294[63]
	(1)	(15)	(54)	(30)	(100)
Total by method	730	783	2,499	1,681	5,693
	(12.8)	(13.8)	(43.9)	(29.5)	(100)

Notes: [+]   BBCPO indicates the bareboat charter with purchase option.
   [++]   Figures in ( ) indicate the percentage of total tonnage increased per annum.
   [+++]   Figures in [ ] indicate number of ships. Data on number of ships for 1975 and 1976 were not available.

Sources: Korea Shipping Information Centre, *Hankook Haewoon Tonggye Yoram*, [Korea Maritime Statistical Yearbook], 1981 and 1982; Sohn, T-H. (1982), *Hankook Haewoonsa*, [History of Korean Shipping], p.448, A-Seong Publishing Company, Pusan, Korea.

The ship importation method

It can be estimated from Table 4.1 that among the methods of ship acquisition in Korea, the importation of ships played a dominant role in expanding the Korean merchant fleet in the 1970s. The tonnage acquired by this method amounted to approximately 2.5 million grt., i.e. 43.9 per cent of the total tonnage increased in the period 1975-81.

The availability of data on tonnage and the financing terms of imported second-hand ships over the period 1962-81 was extremely limited because of the secretive nature of shipping companies and the lack of a centralised organisation to deal with them. Thus, it is difficult to make a precise assessment of the impact of the importation method: it is impossible, firstly, to acquire a complete set of statistics of financing terms and amounts raised for the method; and secondly, much information is simply not available at all as it has never been collected. Moreover, nothing further is available in the way of unpublished data, either processed or in a crude state, and facilities do not exist to enable an outside research worker to collect such data.

In the 1960s and 1970s, financing sources employed for importing ships into Korea were:

• National Investment Fund Loans in local currency;
• Industrial Facility Fund by the Korea Development Bank (KDB) in local currency;
• foreign currency tied-loan by the KDB and the Long Term Credit Bank (LTCB);
• foreign commercial bank loan;
• foreign currency re-loan by the KDB, the LTCB and Korean commercial banks.

For a shipowner who wished to import a second-hand ship, 10 per cent of the ship's price was required to be self-financed. A number of interviews carried out in 1981 indicated that most shipowners depended on local commercial banks for financing even this 10 per cent of the ship's price.[2]

Table 4.2 shows the principal repayment balance of imported ships at the end of 1983. This data was not comprehensively collected until the Shipping Industry Rationalisation Plan was launched in 1983.[3]

The term principal repayment balance means the remainder of borrowed money to repay by the financing source in a certain year after the importing of the ship. In the Korean shipping industry, the total principal repayment amounted to US $764.3 million in foreign currency and 17,185 million won in Korean currency at the end of 1983, respectively.

It can be estimated from Table 4.2 that among the above-mentioned five financing sources, the main sources used for importing ships into Korea were foreign commercial bank loans and foreign currency re-loans by the KDB, the LTCB and Korean commercial banks. The interest rates on foreign currencies were based mainly on LIBOR. Therefore, despite the fact that there existed differences in interest rates between Korean shipping companies depending on their creditworthiness and the lender's financing sources, it is not difficult to regard LIBOR as a representative interest rate of foreign currencies employed for importing second-hand ships into Korea, giving some allowances.

Table 4.2
Principal repayment balance of imported ships

Financing sources	1983	1984	1985	1986
NIFL[+]	1,286	643	643	0
IFF[++]	1,739	1,514	1,252	1,098
Other	14,460	11,781	11,080	3,449
Sub-total[+++]	17,485	13,938	12,975	4,547
Foreign currency tied-loan	94,596	80,519	66,246	53,054
Foreign commercial bank loan	294,682	252,481	197,515	138,479
Foreign currency re-loan	375,034	281,683	212,688	150,873
Sub-total[*]	764,312	614,683	476,449	342,406
Grand total[**]	628,635	505,685	393,492	278,472

Notes: [+] *NIFL indicates the National Investment Fund Loans by KDB in local currency, i.e. million won.*

[++] *IFF indicates the Industrial Facility Fund by KDB in local currency, i.e. million won.*

[+++] *In Korean currency, i.e. million won.*

[*] *In foreign currency, i.e. US $ million.*

[**] *In million won.*

Source: based on various internal documents of the Korea Shipowners' Association.

General information about LIBOR is open to the public for inspection. Consequently, this section is forced to be confined to the analysis of financing terms for importing second-hand ships from the aspect of interest rates for the purpose of testing the Gerschenkron model. It is possible to make one or two observations on shipping financing terms used for importing ship into Korea if both LIBOR as a representative interest rate of foreign currency and domestic bank lending rate as a representative interest rate of local currency loans could be chosen, though too much reliance should not be placed on them.

Table 4.3 presents the annual average cost of capital in Korea in the period 1966-80. During most years of the 1960s and 1970s, the real interest rate Korean borrowers paid on foreign loans was negative, as shown in the table. In the period 1966-70, LIBOR adjusted for an exchange rate change which was lower than the rate paid on domestic borrowing by as much as 15 percentage points, depending on how expected exchange rate changes are estimated. Even in the period 1971-79, the foreign borrowing rate was consistently lower than the domestic rate, though the differential narrowed considerably. Much of the differential could be explained by the artificially low level of domestic interest rates and the overvaluation of the exchange rate while inflation was accelerating.

Table 4.3

Table 4.3
Annual average cost of foreign capital in Korea

	1966-70	1971-75	1976-80	1981-83
a) Domestic bank lending rate[+] (Curb market interest rate)	24.4	17.0	18.0	12.5
b) LIBOR[++]	6.4	7.9	11.5	11.1
c) Foreign inflation rate (GNP deflator)[+++]	4.9	8.4	5.9	4.1
d) Exchange rate depreciations[*]	5.1	7.8	5.5	10.1
e) GDP deflator (rate of change): Korea[**]	14.6	19.8	20.7	9.8
f) Real foreign interest rate: (b - c)	1.5	-0.5	5.6	7.0
g) Interest rate differential between home and foreign markets: (a - b - d)	12.9	1.3	1.0	-8.7
h) Real private cost of borrowing abroad: (b + d - e)	-3.1	-4.1	-3.7	11.4

(unit: %)

Notes: [+]   *Discounts on bills of deposit money banks (three-year moving averages).*
    [++] *LIBOR (90 days).*
    [+++] *Average of Japan and the USA.*
    [*] *The Bank of Korea standard concentration rate (three-year moving averages).*
    [**] *Three-year moving averages.*

Sources: Park, Y. C. (1986), 'Foreign Debt, Balance of Payments, and Growth Prospects: The Case of the Republic of Korea, 1965-88', *World Development*, Vol. 14, No. 8, p.1025.

It is not difficult to conclude that during the latter part of the 1960s, the enormous influx of foreign capital was certainly induced by the interest rate differential, partly caused by the Korean government's fiscal policy and that as a consequence, this interest rate differential was one of the most powerful incentives to Korean shipping companies to borrow from abroad and to import ships. In other words, Korean shipowners turned to foreign borrowing as an alternative source of credit in shipping financing. Thus, low interest rates combined with the Korean government's guarantee given to the shipowners and the sharp increase of foreign trade, as discussed in Chapter 3, resulted in a strong demand for foreign loans which in turn contributed to expanding Korean shipping tonnage from the latter part of the 1960s until the end of the 1970s.

Table 4.4
Tonnage by ship type acquired by BBCPO method in Korea (1976-81)

Year	Gen. cargo carrier	Log carrier	Bulk carrier	Container ship	Oil tanker	Other	Total
1976	26.9	-	117.7	-	85.4	0.5	230.5
	[3]		[5]		[4]	[1]	[13]
1977	12.0	25.5	35.5	-	129.0	5.1	207.1
	[2]	[7]	[3]		[2]	[2]	[17]
1978	16.4	-	126.6	19.1	112.5	2.3	276.9
	[3]		[6]	[1]	[2]	[1]	[13]
1979	21.9	4.0	53.4	-	2.2	-	81.5
	[2]	[1]	[3]		[2]		[8]
1980	-	-	232.1	13.3	99.0	0.6	345.0
			[11]	[1]	[1]	[1]	[14]
1981	20.4	4.3	311.0	48.6	-	-	384.3
	[2]	[1]	[10]	[3]			[16]
Total by	97.6	33.8	876.3	81.0	428.1	8.5	1,525.3
type	(6.4)	(2.2)	(57.5)	(5.3)	(28.1)	(0.5)	(100)

Notes: *Figures in [ ] indicate the number of ships. Figures in ( ) indicate the percentages of tonnage by ship type of the total tonnage acquired in the period 1976-81.*

Source: Korea Shipping Information Centre, *Hankook Haewoon Tonggye Yoram*, [Korea Maritime Statistical Yearbook], 1980 and 1982.

The bareboat charter with purchase option (BBCPO) method

The growth trends of tonnage by the BBCPO method is shown in Table 4.1; the tonnage acquired by BBCPO method in Korea amounted to approximately 1.7 million grt. in the period 1975-81, i.e. 29.5 per cent of the total increas in tonnage during the same period.

71

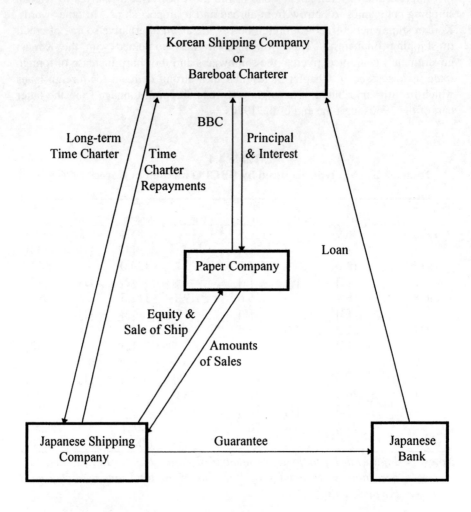

Source: depicted by the author.

Figure 4.1 The mechanism of a BBCPO arrangement

Table 4.4 presents a breakdown by ship type of the tonnage acquired by BBCPO method in the period 1976-81. Prior to 1975, the data of the tonnage by ship type was not available. Of a total of 1.5 million grt. acquired by BBCPO method throughout the period 1976-81, as presented in Table 4.4, bulk carriers amounted to approximately 0.8 million grt., i.e. 57.5 per cent of the total tonnage increased by the method during the same period. Oil tankers and general cargo carriers made up 28.1 and 6.4 per cent of the total tonnage respectively. It should be noted from Table 4.4 that the BBCPO method contributed in particular to the growth of the bulk carrier sector in the Korean shipping industry.

The mechanism of the BBCPO method For most developing countries where shipping finance cannot be sufficiently raised at home, capital is scarce and potential investors are not maritime-motivated and prefer less risky sectors, the investment barrier is one of the most serious obstacles to the development of maritime transport. Moreover, finance for purchase of second-hand ships is even more difficult to obtain. In Korea there was no original accumulation of capital in the shipping sector and she also faced the above problems during the 1960s and the 1970s. However, a peculiar shipping finance source, i.e. BBCPO arrangement, was generated between Korea and Japan in 1965. Figure 4.1 represents a typical mechanism of a BBCPO arrangement. It presents the parties as they stand in legal and financial relationship to each other in the BBCPO arrangement. Its events may be described as:

(1)   The sale, in which a Japanese shipping company gives a title to its affiliate, i.e. paper company, abroad in exchange for the sale's proceeds. The paper company was established in open registry countries.

(2)   The bareboat charter, in which the paper company charters the ship to a Korean shipping company under the condition of the BBCPO, with a pre-contracted long term time charter with the previous Japanese shipping company, i.e. the mother company of the paper company. In such circumstances, a ship manned by a Korean crew is delivered to a Japanese company in the form of a time charter. Between the above three parties, i.e. paper company, Japanese shipping company and Korean shipping company, the so-called bareboat charter and time charter (BBCTC) is generated.

(3)   The execution of mortgage and notes by the paper company, which promises to repay the principal sum and interest.

(4)   The execution of the long term charter party by the Japanese shipping company as the charterer and the affiliate in the above (3) as shipowner, whereby the charterer promises to make periodic time charter payments.

(5)   The disbursement by the mortgagee - the Korean shipping company or bareboat charterer - of proceeds of the loan to the paper company, which uses the money to purchase the ship.

Table 4.5
Time charter hire and hire base of MV Sangjin:
A case of the bareboat charter with purchase option method

Details of the ship		Annual costs and hire base on February 1974 (US $)	
Name of vessel:	Sangjin	Crew:	175,228.75
Year built:	1968	Maintenance & repair:	19,000
Classification society:	NK[+]	Survey:	1,820
Type:	bulk/log carrier	Ship stores, spares, etc:	58,630
Dead-weight ton (dwt.):	17,072	Marine insurance:	79,917.18
Purchase price:	US $ 3,996,000	Communication charges:	700
Current market price (at February 1974):	US $ 6,000,000	Other expenses:	2,750
Terms of repayment:		Repayment of ship: (2 × $364,000)	728,000
i) period:	Jul '74 - Jun '80		
ii) bi-annual payment:	US $ 364,000	General administration:	65,510
Purchase condition:	BBCPO	Non-operating expenses:	13,500
Time charterer:	Hinode Shipping	TOTAL:	1,145,055.93
Revenue on time charter hire per month per dwt. (m/dwt.):	US $ 5.975	Hire base per day:	3,137.14
		Hire base per month per dwt.:	5.513

Note: [+] *NK means the Japanese classification of society, i.e. Nippon Kaiji Kyokai.*

Source: based on various internal documents at the A-jin Shipping Company.

The BBCPO has a characteristic of the sale and charter-back or sale and lease-back[4] to the extent that the Japanese shipping company sells the ship to an affiliate company abroad; the ship is registered under a flag of convenience country and is chartered back to the original company through the Korean bareboat charterer. The company obtains the sales price in cash and retains the full economic use of the vessel for the term of the charter party. In this process, general trading companies in Japan introduced sources of finance for the BBCPO to the Korean shipping company. This bareboat charter was first introduced by Seoul Shipping Corporation, which acquired the ship Seoul of 3,997 grt. in 1965.[5]

There were a number of economic factors behind the creation of the BBCPO arrangements from the mid-1960s. The first of these lay in low Korean crew costs and high operating costs under a Japanese flag caused by sharply rising Japanese crew costs. For example, in 1974 a ship, Sangjin, was acquired by the BBCPO from both a Japanese shipping company, i.e. Hinode Shipping Company Limited and a Korean shipping company, i.e. A-jin Shipping Company Limited. The ship was a six years old, 17,000 dwt. bulk and log carrier. The A-jin Company contracted a long term charter of the ship from July 1974 to July 1980 with the Hinode Company. Table 4.5 presents the time charter hire and hire base of the ship Sangjin as February 1974.

Hire base is defined as a certain total annual cost per month per dwt. required to operate a ship, which is calculated by the following equation:

$$\text{Hire base per month per dwt.} = \frac{\text{annual direct costs} + \text{annual indirect costs}}{\text{dwt.} \times \text{total operating days during one year}} \times 30 \text{ days}$$

As shown in Table 4.5, the difference between time charter hire and hire base per month per dwt. is US $0.462 ($5.975 - $5.513 = $0.462). This difference enabled the Korean bareboat charterer not only to repay the principal and interest on the ship under BBCPO arrangements but also to raise the net revenue per month of US $7,887.264 ($0.462 × 17,072 dwt. = $7,887.264). In other words, from the Korean charterer's viewpoint, he is able to make a profit through BBCPO only when time charter hire is higher than hire base.

After the completion of all repayments of principal and interest on the ship Sangjin, the Korean bareboat charterer, i.e. the A-jin shipping company came to own the ship and began to be a shipowning company. This explains why a number of Korean shipping companies emerged in the early 1970s. This will be discussed in the following section, which deals with the effects of BBCPO arrangements on the Korean shipping industry.

In 1972, Japanese costs per ship with a crew of 32 was US $326,700 per year, excluding various allowances and social security instead of US $175,228.75 for the Korean ship. The resulting difference of crew costs makes a saving of US $151,471.25 in the hire base cost, i.e. 13.2 per cent.

The second factor behind the creation of BBCPO arrangements is that Japanese shipowners needed to dispose of old ships and at the same time improve their merchant fleet, replacing them with new ships. These needs coincided with the Korean bareboat charterers' desire to become shipowners. At that time they could not raise funds, domestically or internationally, to purchase second-hand ships. BBCPO arrangements thus played an important role in enabling the Korean bareboat charterers to own their ships. A long term charter party from a Japanese shipping company with a high reputation was enough of a guarantee to raise funds for BBCPO dealings from a financier in Japan, despite the lack of a developed capital market in Korea.

The third factor which enabled the Korean shipowners to acquire their ships without accumulating a great deal of capital was the high demand for shipping caused by rapid industrial expansion in Japan. Japanese shipping companies thus met the need for more ship tonnage to some extent through BBCPO arrangements.

The fourth economic factor behind BBCPO arrangements was that because ships under the arrangements were registered in open registry countries, the Japanese shipowners enjoyed a cheap labour supply from Korea and in turn could reduce total crew costs. The ships under BBCPO arrangements included mainly bulk carriers and oil tankers which were long term chartered to Japanese shipping enterprises. The types may be grouped together as tramps because of the economic aspects of their operations.

Let us now turn our attention to the discussion of the implications for crew costs in the context of second-hand tramps within BBCPO arrangements. Sturmey classified shipping costs into national and international costs.[6] He regarded crew costs, maintenance, capital charges and agency and office expenses as national costs by the fact that they are variable between nations. He defined international costs, for example, depreciation, insurance, cargo handling, stores, port charges and repairs, as invariant with respect to the nationality of shipowners. The national and international costs were again classified into organisation overhead costs, voyage overhead costs and variable costs, depending on liners, tramps or tankers. Crew costs belong to voyage overhead costs in liners and to variable costs in tramps and tankers.

Given equivalent ships, an owner in a low-wage country, i.e. the Korean shipowner, will continue to operate his vessels at freight rates at which the high-wage operator, i.e. the Japanese shipowner, has to lay up.

The conclusion reached is that tramp shipping under BBCPO arrangements is something in which a low Korean crew wage excels. However, the cost advantage of lower wage rates in Korea may be offset by higher repair costs and slower speeds of vessels so that higher-quality tramps and bulk carriers operated by developed countries might be able to compete.[7]

Financing for BBCPO arrangements The terms of financing during the early years of the acquisition of ships through the BBCPO method in Korea, are presented in Table 4.6. Most ships acquired were 3,000 to 4,000 grt., approximately 15 years old and cost US $0.4 to US $0.5 million in the early stages of the BBCPO arrangements. Financial sources for them were approximately US $0.1 million of self-financing, i.e. about 25 per cent of the ship's price, loans from general trading companies in Japan at the interest rate of 5.75 per cent, and surcharge rate for the rest of the ship's price. While the interest rate was based on the prime rate at that time, the surcharge rate amounted to 1.5 per cent more or less in which commission and management charges and guarantee fees were included.

During the period 1977-81, the financing terms for BBCPO arrangements were 10 per cent of self-financing of the ship's price and the other 90 per cent consisting of loan from LIBOR, mainly of six months deposit from banks.[8] This was drawn from unpublished data available in a crude state in the KMPA, by which shipping companies were required to submit the project report for the permission for BBCPO arrangements prior to the implementation of the arrangements. The report contained details of the vessel to be acquired, its financing terms and its profitability. In interviews with a number of financial managers in shipping companies in Korea,[9] it was found that even this 10 per cent of self-financing was raised from domestic commercial banks.

Table 4.6
Major ships acquired by BBCPO arrangement in Korea

Purchaser: Korean party	GT (Year built)	Ship's price	Self-financing	Loan	
				Amounts	Interest[+] rates (%)
Cho Yang Shipping Co., Ltd.	3,914 (1947)	337,778	100,000	333,000	5.75
Young Poong Shipping Co., Ltd.	4,185 (1950)	402,778	98,000	392,000	5.75
Samick Lines Co., Ltd.	3,715 (1949)	455,000	97,600	390,400	5.75
Daedong Shipping Co., Ltd.	3,710 (1949)	391,666	97,000	380,000	5.75
Cho Yang Shipping Co., Ltd.	3,373 (1957)	606,606	100,000	506,600	5.75
Shinhan Shipping Co., Ltd.	2,732 (1947)	312,000	62,000	249,600	5.75
Korea Shipping Co., Ltd.	4,746 (1947)	577,842	100,000	477,842	5.75

(unit : US $)

Note: [+] *Based on the prime rate in the United States of America.*

Source: Sohn, T.-H., op. cit., pp. 410-1.

Effects of the BBCPO arrangements on the Korean shipping industry: Their peculiarities In Korea where the shipping industry could not attract the required capital for its development from other economic sectors over the 1960s and 1970s, the method of the BBCPO has played an important role in expanding the merchant marine. This method enabled Korean shipowners to acquire ships without having a great deal of capital. It was particularly important for the

Korean shipowners, whose names and reputations were not yet firmly established, to overcome low creditworthiness and thus to secure bank guarantees.

The BBCPO arrangements have influenced the shipping industry in Korea in a number of ways. Its first impact on the industry was that they played a major role in increasing employment and inducing the establishment of training facilities for Korean seamen. Thus, the extensive employment of Korean seamen in this way provided a reservoir of trained labour on which the Korean shipping industry could subsequently draw. The arrangements contributed to the training of officers, crew members and other personnel vital to the Korean shipping industry.

The second impact, as a consequence of the first, is that the increase of seamen employed abroad contributed to improving the balance of payments through the remittances of crew income in foreign currency. Its significance can be drawn from Table 4.7, which shows a comparison of freight earnings with the wage income of crew employed abroad, and the share of the latter of the total credit of other goods, service and income in Korea.

Table 4.7
Korea's total freight earnings and wage income of
Korean crew employed abroad (1965-81) (at 1980 prices)

Year	Freight earnings (A)	Wage income of crew (B)	B/A (%)	Credit of other goods service & income (C)	B/C (%)
1965	35.7	4.2	11.8	320.2	1.3
1967	75.5	8.9	11.8	810.5	1.1
1969	143.6	14.5	10.1	1,191.3	1.2
1971	185.2	23.3	12.5	1,052.3	2.2
1973	317.0	54.0	17.0	1,661.5	3.2
1975	487.0	74.3	15.3	1,351.8	5.5
1977	822.6	115.4	14.0	3,956.9	2.9
1979	1,413.7	153.6	10.9	5,397.1	2.8
1981	2,182.7	231.8	10.6	6,003.6	3.9

Sources: Korea Shipping Information Centre (1981), *Hankook Haewoon Tonggye Yoram*, [Korea Maritime Statistical Yearbook], Seoul, Korea; KMI (1987), *Hankook Haewoon Tonggye Yoram*, [Korea Maritime Statistical Yearbook], Seoul; KMPA (1984), *Maritime and Port Statistics*, Seoul; The Association of Management for Korean Seamen's Power (1984), *Hankook Seonwon Seonbak Tonggye Yeonbo*, [Statistical Yearbook for Korean Crew and Ships], Pusan, Korea; IMF (1987), *International Financial Statistics Yearbook*.

In 1965, shipping freight earnings amounted to US $35.7 million and increased to US $2,182.7 in 1981 at 1980 prices. In the period 1965-81 its average growth rate was 29.3 per cent per annum in real terms. On the other hand, the wage income of the Korean crew employed in foreign merchant ocean-going vessels increased to US $231.8 million in 1981 at 1980 prices. Its real annual average rate of growth was 28.5 per cent during the same period in Korea.

Table 4.8
Number of Korean shipping companies and their new entries (1962-78)

Year	Member company of KSA+ of which		No. of new entry
	Total grt (in thousands)++	Total number	company+++
1962	100.4 [41]	11	2
1963	108.8 [48]	14	1
1964	122.6 [50]	12	0
1965	171.7 [60]	15	5
1966	223.5 [72]	18	3
1967	389.7 [87]	22	6
1968	469.7 [87]	21	3
1969	727.2 [97]	22	2
1970	758.2 [95]	21	7
1971	820.7 [113]	19	4
1972	810.0 [129]	21	5
1973	850.4 [142]	30	9
1974	1,190.2 [164]	45	5
1975	1,354.0 [195]	49	5
1976	1,928.9 [219]	55	2
1977	2,263.6 [311]	68	3
1978	3,191.8 [546]	62	1
1979	3,677.8 [415]	67	0
1980	3,949.0 [448]	66	0
1981	4,857.8 [468]	68	1

Notes: + *The number of shipping companies indicate members of the Korea Shipowners' Association (KSA).*

++ *Figures in [ ] indicate number of ships which belonged to the total shipping companies under KSA.*

+++ *Indicates total number of shipping companies newly established in the Korean shipping industry every year.*

Sources: KMPA (1981), *Hankook Haewoon Hangmansa*, [History of Korean Shipping and Ports], pp. 643-77, KMPA, Seoul, Korea; KMPA (1984), *Hankook Haewoon Hangmansa*, [History of Korean Shipping and Ports], pp. 730, 734 and 738, KMPA, Seoul, Korea.

During the period 1965-81 the ratio of wage income of crew to shipping freight ranged from 10.1 to 17.0 per cent. Its share of total credit of other goods, service and income reached 5.5 per cent in 1975, which contributed to improving the net deficit of US $679 million in the sector of other goods, service and income. This significant ratio is attributable to the increase of crew employment on foreign ships. The increase of foreign ships available to employ the Korean crew was initiated under BBCPO arrangements.

The third impact on the Korean shipping industry is that thanks to the economic factors behind the generation of BBCPO arrangements, the arrangements easily provided an opportunity for the creation of shipping companies in Korea. As can be seen from Table 4.8, which shows how many shipping companies were established in Korea between 1962 and 1978, the number of members of the Korean Shipowners' Association increased from 11 in 1962 to 62 in 1978, i.e. more than five times, largely for this reason.

Of the nine newly established companies in 1973, five had participated in operating ships under BBCPO arrangements. Thanks to the peculiarity of the arrangements in terms of financing, they became shipping companies which owned Korean flagged ships, despite the lack of original accumulation of capital for the acquisition of ships within the companies.

Conclusions

In the Gerschenkron model, the banking system, along with the state and ideologies, plays a key role in industrialisation in backward countries, supplying the prime source of capital and entrepreneurship.

In this chapter, hypothesis II, established on the basis of the Gerschenkron model, was tested and found to be acceptable. Firstly, prior to its test, the sources of shipping finance available to developing countries were discussed; and secondly, the ingenious methods of shipping finance employed for the expansion of the Korean shipping growth were analysed.

During the late 1960s and the 1970s, when there was no original capital accumulation in the shipping sector and insufficient capital, domestic and foreign, or acquisition of ships, BBCPO arrangements, as a special shipping financial system, played an important role in expanding the national fleet in Korea. The arrangements were particularly important for Korean shipowners whose names and reputations were not firmly established, to overcome low creditworthiness and thus to secure bank guarantees.

Foreign borrowing, encouraged by much interest rate differential between home and international financial markets, as shown in Table 4.3, and exchange rate policy which facilitated the inflow of foreign capital, along with various tax exemptions in the shipping industry, as discussed in Chapter 3, was employed to acquire second-hand ships. During the 1960s and 1970s, as a result, the high degree of reliance on imports of second-hand ships also made an important contribution to the expansion of Korean shipping growth.

Notes and references

1   "Shikumisen" means the ship that was built in the Japanese shipyard by the order of a foreign shipowner, who had already acquired the long term contract of affreightment with the Japanese importer of raw materials, and had raised ship finance for building the ship from the Export-Import Bank of Japan. The ship was employed on major Japanese trade routes and began to take a partial share of the shipping market which Japanese shipowners had formerly held. The "Shikumisen" finance was initiated by Japan and was a major type of shipping finance for over two decades in Japan and Hong Kong. For further discussion on this subject, see Lee, T-W. (1989), *The Growth of Korean Shipping 1962-1981*, PhD Thesis, University of Wales, Cardiff; Sohmen, H. (1983), *Shipping in Crisis: 1974-1983*, Fairview Printing Production, Hong Kong; Sohmen, H. (1986), *Shipping in Transition: 1983-1986*, Fairview Printing Production, Hong Kong; The Long Term Credit Bank of Japan Limited (1978), *Transactions of International Shipping Finance*, The Long Term Credit Bank of Japan Limited, Tokyo.

2   Lee, T-W (1981), *A Study on the Profitability of Imported Ships into Korea*, p. 45, MBA Dissertation, The Yonsei University, Seoul, Korea.

3   On the background and contents of the plan, see Kokuryo, H. (1985), *Korean Shipping and Shipping Policy: Shipping Industry Rationalisation Plan*, JAMRI Report No. 8, Japan Maritime Research Institute, Tokyo; Kim, S. K. (1987), *The Reorganisation of Korean Shipping Industry*, MSc Thesis, The University of Wales Institute of Science and Technology, Cardiff.

4   The term "charter back" is used for second-hand Japanese vessels sold overseas and simultaneously chartered back to their previous owner, usually with lower operating costs through non-Japanese crew.

5   KMPA (1981), *Hankook Haewoon Hangmansa*, [History of Korean Shipping and Ports], p. 645, KMPA, Seoul, Korea.

6   Sturmey, S. G. (1962), *British Shipping and World Competition*, pp. 266-8, Athlon Press, London.

7   Ibid., p.275.

8   Lee, T-W.(1981), op. cit., p.45.

9   Ibid., pp. 46-7.

5   Ideology and shipping growth in Korea

Introduction

An ideology is a set of ideas and values guiding individuals and organisations in interpreting their environment, choosing goals in regard to maintaining or changing the environment, and selecting the means to achieve these goals.[1] An economic ideology is a set of ideas related to economic action. Ideology may affect the economic system in various ways. It influences both the ends and the means of the system; what its goals are, including the priorities among them; the institutions[2] and instruments[3] of the system and the patterns of their use; and attitudes to changes in goals, institutions and instruments.

As discussed in Chapter 2, an ideology is the only autonomous non-economic factor in the Gerschenkron model, besides being closely connected as a cause of industrialisation. There is little doubt that such an ideology as Saint-Simonism, e.g. in its relation to industrialisation in the nineteenth century, carried out its function not only in reducing external resistance to industrialisation but also in calming the uneasy consciences of the industrialisers themselves and providing them with a strong spiritual incentive. Thus, it seems reasonable to say that ideology helped to clear the road for industrialisation. But it is not reasonable at all to say that Saint-Simonism was the primary determinant of what was called French capitalism. It remains to be added that the role of such ideology was confined to the brief initial period of rapid spurt.[4]

In this chapter, our primary concern is with testing hypotheses III and IV made in Chapter 2 based on the Gerschenkron model. After explaining the ideology which emerged in the Korean shipping sector, i.e. a set of ideas and values guiding individuals participating in the sector in its initial period, the chapter is concerned with finding out whether ideology played a role in its rapid growth in the context of the Gerschenkron model and, if so, discussing the embodying patterns of ideology and its effects on the shipping industry in Korea.

Ideology in the Korean shipping industry

The twentieth century has been a period of travail in Chosun, 'the land of the morning calm', another descriptive phrase applied to Korea, which was derived from the name of an old ruling dynasty, Koryo. Korea remained a closed pre-modern society until 1876. Subsequently, many world powers struggled for political and economic dominance over Korea. The first two protagonists were Japan and China. After the defeat of China in the Sino-Japanese War in 1894 and that of Russia in the Russo-Japanese War in 1904, Korea was annexed to Japan in 1910 and remained a colony until the end of the Second World War.

During the period 1910-45, the Korean economy was controlled by the totalitarian Japanese Colonial Government established in Korea.[5] At the beginning of the Japanese occupation of Korea, Japan allowed Koreans to operate shipping companies through equity participation, but gradually removed them, subsequently, Japanese arrived in large numbers and controlled the companies.[6]

Table 5.1
Major vested shipping enterprises and ships (April 1946)

Name of shipping enterprises[+]	Number of ships	Gross tonnage	Average gross tons per ship
Chosun Wooseon Choosik Haesa	5	8,693	1,740
Kyeong-In Sangseon Choosik Haesa	4	985	250
Kanghwa Hangwoon Chohap	6	350	60
Samkook Seoktan Choosik Haesa	23	683	30
Chosun Haeryook Woonsoo Choosik Haesa	25	1,368	55
Pusan Haehang Woonsoo Choosik Haesa	8	401	50
Chosun Michang Choosik Haesa	10	192	20
Bokdo Cho	9	310	35
Cheonnam Kiseon Choosik Haesa	6	253	40
Seo-Ilbon Kiseon Choosik Haesa	10	1,163	116
Chosun Seonbak Tongje Choosik Haesa	35	3,457	100
Chosun Keunhae Woosoo Choosik Haesa	11	370	35
Chosun Haesang Kooweon Choosik Haesa	7	276	40
Choil Cho	4	150	40
TOTAL	163	18,651	115

Note: + In transliterated Korean.

Sources: The Division of Shipping, the Ministry of Transport (1956), *Haewoon Sipnyeon Yaksa*, [A Brief 10 Years History of Shipping], pp. 119-20, Seoul, Korea; Recited from Shon, T-H. (1982), *Hankook Haewoonsa* [History of Korean Shipping], p. 369, A-Seong Publishing Compay, Pusan, Korea.

The Japanese left behind physical facilities on their defeat and withdrawal in 1945. Korea inherited over 2,500 operating industrial and business enterprises, as well as infrastructure, inventories, real estate, and 15 per cent of the nation's land; the official count was 166,301 items of such so-called 'vested property'.[7] As a result, in the Korean shipping sector, physical capital, ships and shipping enterprises from Japan were available from 1945. Table 5.1 shows the major vested shipping enterprises and their ships in Korea.

As shown in Table 5.1, 14 major shipping enterprises and tonnage totalling 18,751 grt. were left in Korea in April 1946. The total number of ships was 163 and the average tonnage per ship was merely 115 grt. It was only 'Chosun Wooseon Choosik Haesa' which owned any ships over 1,000 grt.

Subsequently, ships supplied through the USA aid were added to the Korean shipping sector. Table 5.2 presents ships imported by an aid programme, the Government and Relief in Occupied Area (GARIOA), from the USA.

Table 5.2
Ships imported by the USA aid programme

Date	Number of ships	Total grt.	Grt. per ship
1947	23	38,560	1,677
1948	17	n.a.[+]	n.a.
Total	40		

Note: [+] n.a. = not available.

Source: Sohn, T-H. (1982), *Hankook Haewoonsa*, [History of Korean Shipping], p. 371, A-Seong Publishing Company, Pusan, Korea.

As can be seen from Table 5.2, the total tonnage of ships imported by the GARIOA aid programme was about 40,000 grt. and the number of ships was about 40. It can be said that from the point of view of tonnage, the aid ships contributed to the expansion of the Korean national fleet in the burgeoning period, but only with very small vessels.

In these circumstances, the presence of large stocks of liberated property, including ships, encouraged people to have two attitudes. The first attitude was the so-called parasitic characteristics. This involved acquisitive minds, irrespective not only of the means and ends for seeking gains from the liberated property, but also of the nature of the ethic of time. In Weber's words it appeared broadly around the process of expansion and institutionalisation of the spirit of capitalism in the case of modern, rational and industrial capitalism; it also appeared as the essence of acquisitive activities in the case of pre-modern capitalism, especially of merchants and financiers. In other words, it represented pre-modern capitalism, serving as negative elements at the occasion of the birth of a uniquely modern rational industrial capitalism.[8] Those who have such an attitude perceived themselves as legitimate heirs to at least a portion of it. As a consequence, they

employed all sorts of pressure from high-ranking military officers, representatives of national agencies, their civil affairs colleagues, and Korean friends
against the property custodians in order to acquire vested property and
concessions related to American aid for themselves.[9]

Those who had the second attitude, which Weber terms 'ethos',[10] devoted their
eagerness and passion to re-building their country, liberated from Japan after a
36-year occupation, with disinterested minds and stood beyond their personal
profit-seeking need.

Maritime officers who participated in the Korean shipping sector after the
Liberation from Japan generally showed the second attitude.[11] They were
educated in mercantile marine colleges in Japan and experienced ocean-going
navigation in the colonial period. They not only played the role of a leading elite
in shipping growth[12] but also were a class formed in social or economic mobility
in the shipping sector in Korea, as was the case in the rise of the bourgeoisie in
Western Europe. They possessed great enthusiasm for building a viable national
merchant fleet[13], perceiving in this a way in which it could contribute to the
economic development of Korea.

It can be said that in the Korean shipping sector a tension resulted from
conflicts concerning vested property between the first attitude of men who had
'pariah-Kapitalismus' characteristics and the second attitude of men who had a
strong passion for building their country, standing beyond that of individual
profit-seeking. The former can be regarded as an obstacle to shipping
development.

Other tensions were caused by social and economic disorder. The Liberation
and unexpected partition between North and South Korea created acute
disorganisation in every aspect of Korean society. There was also a sudden
evacuation of all Japanese entrepreneurs, managers and technicians and the
unanticipated separation of the Korean economy from the dismantled Japanese
economic bloc. Simultaneously, the partition severed economic links between
North and South Korea.[14]

In applying the Gerschenkron model to the Korean shipping sector, it can be
said that unless tensions existing in the sector shortly after Liberation are
removed, no shipping development takes place. Here, a functional role of
ideology is required. In the model, an ideology, therefore, contributes to breaking
such a situation of tension and obstacles to shipping growth and to guiding people
to organise resources in an efficient and effective manner. The importance of
ideology tends to increase with the degree of backwardness.[15]

The ideology which contributed to breaking the tensions and obstacles in the
Korean shipping sector resulted from three factors: firstly, it was based on anti-
Japanese nationalism and maritime officers' recognition of the role of shipping in
economic development in Japan, through their experiences in the Second World
War under the Japanese military regime. During the Japanese occupation, Korean
people were excluded from shipping businesses, but were permitted to enter
mercantile marine colleges in Japan in very limited numbers. Korean maritime

officers who were educated in Japan realised that sea transportation played an important role for the Japanese economy before and during the Second World War. They perceived that the establishment of merchant marines played an important role in building a country newly born from 36 years of occupation, opening a path towards complete economic independence from Japan.

Such an ethos resulted partly from an understanding of the capital intensity of merchant marines. Thus, they believed that the shipping industry cannot be a business for private profit acquisition and that the establishment and development of a merchant fleet is absolutely necessary to build their newly born country. In other words, they stressed that a shipping development must be one whose benefits do not accrue to a small, self-enriching minority but benefit the population in general.

The second factor of the ideology came from Confucianism and the respect it induces for education.

In the colonial period education was primarily at lower levels. However, after 1945 the situation was different in both quality and quantity. In the 20 years after Liberation, the number of college students rose 18-fold; middle and high school students 14-fold. This phenomenon reflected the high value that Korean society has traditionally placed on education as a cultural and social asset. In due course it also became an economic asset.

By the late 1950s and using formal education as a measure, Korea achieved the highest level of human resource development for its per capita GNP. Thus, Korea's human resource development was comparable to that of countries with per capita GNP equal to three times the Korean level. Since that time Korea's educational effort has increased still further in relation to the country's level of real output.[16] It can be said that such rapid growth and eagerness for education is consistent with the characteristics of Confucianism.[17] It can be found in a note on the significance of education in Confucian society as:

> ... education in Eastasia was the major path to individual success. The class structure, divided into the four classes of scholar, agriculturist, handi-craftsman, and peddler, reflected this emphasis on book learning. In pre-modern China and Korea even a lowly peddler's family could aspire, through education, to achieve the rank of scholar. Unlike the traditional castes of India, these categories were not fixed at birth but could be changed with effort. Educational systems took deep root in Eastasia, offering extensive private education in small academies with individual instruction. ... Eastasia learned early that education is too important an asset to leave to the aristocracy.[18]

Literary education was the yardstick of social prestige and a basic qualification for office in Korea. Scholars were not a hereditary social group like the Brahmans of India, for their position rested in principle upon their knowledge of writing and literature, not their birth. They had the same high prestige regardless of their social origin, though obtaining the requisite education often depended upon the wealth of the family. It is, therefore, evident that as far as education is concerned, this characteristic of Confucianism, which Weber characterised as the status ethic of the literati, played a leading role in the rapid expansion of education in Korea where an atmosphere of Confucianism is pervasive. As a consequence, Korea, in extreme backward conditions, could, to a great extent, reduce illiteracy and overcome the resulting difficulty in training skilled seamen. Finally, the ideology was partly based on anti-Communism.

In 1950 when the North Koreans moved down the peninsula, they added the destruction of war to the burdens of South Korea. The main movements of the Korean War took less than a year, after which ground action was largely confined to the centre of the country near the 38th parallel. However, in that one year, destruction was enormous. Nearly one million South Korean civilians plus 320,000 recruited South Korean soldiers were killed. Property damage was estimated at US $2 billion. Agricultural production fell 27 per cent from 1949 to 1952 and GNP fell 14 per cent. Approximately five and a half million people, or 25 per cent of the population, became refugees during the War.[19]

The Korean war ended in stalemate and armistice because the presence of United Nations forces ruled out the possibility of victory for North Korea in its aim of reuniting the Korean peninsula by force. The perception of military fear of the north is far from being merely an excuse for military involvement in domestic politics on the classic Latin American pattern. In the course of the last three decades until his death, Kim Il-sung, the North Korean leader, never abandoned the unification of the peninsula under his rule as an end, nor military force as a means to it.[20] This political situation led the military regime of Mr Park Chung-hee since 1961 to select anti-Communism as a major national policy. This was reflected in political, economic and social sectors in various forms. Its implication is the aim of preventing communism from being rooted in Korea and of reuniting the peninsula by peaceful means.

The ideology of anti-Communism forced Korean shipping to be regarded as a life line for transporting both imports and exports in peacetime and military goods in wartime. This was strengthened by the 'island' nature of the country caused by the divisions between North and South Korea and the complete absence of trade between them. Thus, growth of the means of shipping transportation was viewed as an insurance against a sudden military attack from North Korea. The use of capital for investment in shipping was considered to be of premium importance. The greater the scarcity of capital in Korea in the 1960s, the higher the premium was deemed to be.

The above three factors were channelled into a burgeoning period of the Korean shipping sector and formed an ideology. Let us now turn our attention to discuss how this ideology played a role in the Korean shipping sector.

The embodiment of ideology in the Korean shipping industry

The ideology or ethos of the second attitude of men was embodied in the following two patterns in the Korean shipping sector shortly after the Liberation from Japan: one was the establishment of an educational institution for producing maritime officers in 1945; and the other was the take over and management of the biggest vested shipping company, 'Chosun Wooseon Choosik Haesa'. (See Table 5.1.) They are in turn discussed below.

The establishment of a seamen's educational institution: Supply of maritime officers and entrepreneurs

When ships are purchased they have to be manned and managed. The point is often correctly raised that developing countries are, as a whole, unable to meet the manning requirements of their maritime industries, especially in the more skilled grades. Japan faced such problems in the nineteenth century and even until the early twentieth century. Although the Japanese government set up schools of navigation and marine engineering in 1875, foreign captains and officers formed a high portion of officers employed by the mercantile marine until 1900, and their numbers remained significant until 1914. In 1895 about two-fifths of the masters, navigating officers and engineers employed by Nippon Yusen Kaisha were foreigners. Even in 1910 more than a quarter of masters were foreigners.[21]

In 1945, shortly after Liberation, when Korea still had hardly any ocean-going ships, a mercantile marine college with the aim of educating and training high-grade maritime officers was established by maritime officers. It was named 'Jinhae Merchant Marine College'. The College, with a four year course, took over both 'Tonyeong Merchant Marine College' in 1946 and 'Incheon Merchant Marine College' in 1947. The name was changed to 'Korea Merchant Marine College' in 1957.[22] The establishment and success of this college epitomised the second attitude described above.

For many observers, it can be said that there is a relationship between education and economic growth. In analysing possible relationships, two outstanding perspectives may be employed. The first is the human capital theory, the other the status-conflict theory.[23] The former argument in the Korean shipping sector would go on asserting that the accumulation of educated manpower helped to lay a foundation for the rapid shipping growth which occurred after 1962. The export-oriented pattern of economic growth[24] increased the demand for shipping and it consequently required skilled seamen. Table 5.3 shows that educational expansion made maritime officers available to the Korean shipping industry in the period 1962-81.

Accelerated shipping growth effectively absorbed both accumulated educated human resources in the shipping sector as of 1962 and post-1962 increments. Effective utilisation of seafarer resources was reflected in the sharp increase of the employment rate from an average 14 per cent in the period 1948-64 to an average of approximately 100 per cent during the period 1965-81.[25]   Therefore, Korea could overcome the problems caused by lack of seamen which most developing countries commonly faced in establishing their merchant marines.

Table 5.3
Supply of maritime officers graduated from the
Korea Merchant Marine College[+]

Year of college graduation	Deck dept.	Engineer dept.	Total number	Total per cent employed in shipping
1948 - 1954	272	237	509	46%
1955 - 1961	390	393	791	less than 5%
1962 - 1964	152	159	311	approx. 51%
Total 1948 - 1964	841	789	1,603	14%
Sub-total 1965 - 1981[++]	1,351	1,398	2,749	100%
Grand total 1948 - 1981	2,165	2,187	4,352	

Notes: [+] *The name was changed to the Korea Maritime University in 1980.*
 [++] *In 1968, the enrolment size of each department increased to 100 persons and in 1975 and 1976 to 150 and 175 persons, respectively. In 1977, it increased to 200 persons.*

Sources: KMPA (1980), *Hankook Haewoon Hangmansa*, [History of Korean Shipping and Ports], pp. 1056-7, Seoul, Korea; The Korea Maritime University (1987), Unpublished internal documents, Pusan, Korea.

From the above discussion, we may note a peculiarity in the Korean shipping industry in that the education of merchant marine officers preceded the establishment of a merchant marine, unlike Japan and developing countries. In 1965 when BBCPO arrangements were introduced in Korea, well educated and low cost crew already existed in sufficient numbers to man ships under the arrangements. Thus, the availability of efficient seamen played an important role in establishing and expanding the merchant marines. In other words, the factor of Korean seamen plus bareboat chartering made it possible to substitute the prerequisite of original capital accumulation in the context of the Gerschenkron model for acquiring ships through internationally horizontal division of labour with Japan.

The Korea Merchant Marine College also played a major role in providing shipping entrepreneurs in the Korean shipping industry. A recent study[26] indicated that 70 to 80 per cent of the top management in ocean-going shipping companies graduated from the College. That is to say, almost all the board of directors in Korean ocean-going shipping companies were ex-seagoing officers, originally trained there. It can thus be said, that the high availability of skilled managers and directors has been a result of the establishment of the College. This is consistent with the fact that many shipping companies emerged and were founded in the 1960s and 1970s in Korea. Thus, Professor Sohn defined this phenomenon as a type of shipping growth led by maritime officers in Korea.[27]

The successful management of a vested shipping company

Shortly after the Liberation, two organisations, which mainly consisted of maritime officers, were founded in order to establish and develop the merchant marine in Korea.[28] The American Control Authority nominated representatives of both organisations and a few investors as members to take over and manage one of the biggest vested shipping companies, whose name is 'Chosun Wooseon Choosik Haesa' in Korean.

Unlike the other vested shipping companies as shown Table 5.1, 'Chosun Wooseon Choosik Haesa' was the biggest and at the same time owned and operated most of the ocean-going vessels in Korea until 1949. Brief details of ships operated by the company until 1949 are presented in Table 5.4.

Table 5.4
Ships owned by 'Chosun Wooseon Choosik Haesa' until 1949

Ship's name	Grt.	Dwt.	Machinery	Sea speed
Pusan	1,631	n.a.	compound steam engine	n.a.[+]
Kumcheon	3,081	4,800	compound steam engine	8
Chunkang	2,222	4,037	compound steam engine	6
Rudo	1,281	n.a.	compound steam engine	n.a.[+]
Pyeongan	1,578	2,091	compound steam engine	9
Hanyang	2,219	4,037	compound steam engine	6
Iljin	780	1,117	diesel engine	9
Anseong	883	1,604	diesel engine	6
Lihyangbo	875	1,623	diesel engine	6

Note: [+] *n.a. = not available.*

Source: Sohn, T-H., op. cit., p. 370.

'Chosun Wooseon Choosik Haesa' owned nine ships of 14,550 grt. until 1949, including the 'Pusan' and the 'Rudo' interned by North Korea and thus not available. The fleet consisted of typical merchant carriers, i.e. four 'three-island' type ships. Although most ships were small in terms of tonnage and had low speed compound steam engines using coal as fuel, it can be said that at that time tonnage owned by the company formed a significant proportion of the total Korean fleet.

The majority of the managers of the company were maritime officers. They operated the company successfully and made significant net profits every accounting period except for the first couple of years. (See Table 5.5.)

Table 5.5
Business performance of 'Chosun Wooseon Choosik Haesa',
1 October 1945 - 31 March 1949

Accounting period	Profit and loss amount	
1 October 1945 - 31 March 1947	Loss	1,622
1 April 1947 - 30 September 1947	Profit	8,868
1 October 1947 - 31 March 1948	Profit	1,049
1 April 1948 - 30 September 1948	Profit	1,200
1 October 1948 - 31 March 1949	Profit	2,093

(unit: thousands won)

Source: Ibid., p. 373.

Unlike the manufacturing sector, in the shipping sector the departure of Japanese technicians and entrepreneurs does not seem to have been a critical factor. The reason for this is that the effect of their exposure to modern technology and organisation in the Japanese shipping industry, and years of 'learning by watching and doing' on Japanese ships enabled maritime officers to step up to supervisory and technical positions required for the Korean shipping sector without any technical difficulties in operating the ships and managing the company.

In 1950 the 'Chosun Wooseon Choosik Haesa' was taken over by the Korea Shipping Corporation, a government-owned corporation,[29] where ex-seagoing officers, as shore staff, played a key role in successfully managing the corporation. This provided a field where they were able to accumulate know-how in the shipping business in the 1950s and 1960s. In 1968, when it was privatised,[30] a number of managers, who were mainly ex-seagoing officers, retired from the corporation and dispersed in the Korean shipping industry, thus a number of promising entrepreneurs existed in the industry at that time. This explains the process discussed in Chapter 4, involving many shipping companies being established by experienced ships' officers in the 1960s and 1970s, using the bareboat charter with purchase option financial arrangements, which was first introduced in 1965.

Conclusion

This chapter has described how the ideology based on anti-Japanese nationalism, Confucianism and anti-Communism emerged in conditions of extreme backwardness in Korea after the Liberation from Japan in 1945. For Korea, such ideol-

92

ogies were helpful in breaking tensions or obstacles to shipping development and stimulating energies and imaginations of maritime officers in shipping development during the initial period of rapid spurt. Therefore, it can be said that hypothesis III is acceptable.

The above ideology was embodied into two patterns in the Korean shipping sector: the establishment of a seafarer's education and the successful management of the biggest vested shipping company. The former produced and provided maritime officers required in the great spurt period in the Korean shipping industry and the latter produced entrepreneurs. The existence of Korean seamen enabled Korea to generate BBCPO arrangements, which in turn played a major role in expanding Korean merchant marines, substituting a missing prerequisite for shipping growth, i.e. original accumulation of capital. In other words, it can be said that it was Korean seamen, through the international horizontal division of labour, that served as a substitute for original capital accumulation in the shipping industry in Korea. Korea imported the capital for acquiring ships through BBCPO arrangements in association with general trading companies in Japan. Thus, it can be said that hypothesis IV is accepted.

Notes and references

1 There are at least three major components of any ideology: a set of value commitments, a set of historical generalisations and prophecies and a set of institutional preferences. On the definition of ideology and its subject, see Krishna, R. (1988), 'Ideology and Economic Policy', *India Economic Review*, Vol. 23, No. 1, pp. 1-26; Spengler, J. J. (1961), 'Theory, Ideology, Non-Economic Values and Politico-Economic Development', in Braibanti, R. and Spengler, J. J. (ed.), *Tradition, Values and Socio-Economic Development*, Duke University Press, Durham.

2 Institutions may be defined as relatively fundamental organisational arrangements for conducting production and distribution. They are often prescribed by law and not altered as easily as instruments. Examples of institutions include firms, households, markets in which firms exchange with other firms and with households, banks, trade unions, and government economic agencies. Each of these institutions in turn has various types and sub-types. An important aspect of any institution is the motivation of its participation, but they may have different motivations, with their relative strength and interaction determining the motivation of the institution as such. Bornstein, M. (1972), 'An Integration', in Eckstein, A. (ed.), *Comparison of Economic Systems: Theoretical and Methodological Approaches*, p. 345, Oxford University Press, Delhi, India.

3   Instruments refer to the tools used by the state when it intervenes to (attempt to) achieve social goals in the economic sphere. In comparison with institutions, instruments are more often subject to quantitative expression, are more easily and more frequently altered, and are used by only one kind of institution (government agencies). At least five types of instruments may be distinguished: (1) fiscal instruments include taxes, subsidies, transfer payments and government purchases; (2) monetary instruments involve changes in interest rates, reserve ratios and credit rationing; government lending and borrowing; management of existing debt; and control of consumer credit; (3) altering exchange rates is another instrument; (4) among direct controls are production assignments, allocation orders, fixing of prices and wages, and allocation of foreign exchange; and (5) changes in the institutional framework - e.g. in property rights or rules for the operation of markets - may be considered another types of instrument. Ibid., pp. 345-6.

4   Gerschenkron, A. (1972), 'Ideology as a System Determinant', in Eckstein, A. (ed.), op. cit., p. 280, Oxford University Press, Delhi.

5   Kim, K. S. and Roemer, M. (1979), *Growth and Structural Transformation*, Council on East Asian Studies, p. 2, Harvard University Press, Cambridge, Massachusetts.

6   On the history of Korean shipping in the period of Japanese occupation, see Sohn, T-H. (1982), *Hankook Haewoonsa*, [History of Korean Shipping], Chapter 5, A-Seong Publishing Company Limited, Pusan, Korea.

7   'Vested property' means an existing and disposable property in Korean territory left by the Japanese in 1945. The Korean government has a present, existing and disposable right to the immediate or future possession and enjoyment of the property. Jones, L. P. and Sakong, I. (1980), *Government, Business and Entrepreneurship in Economic Development: The Korean Case*, Council on East Asian Studies, p. 30, Harvard University Press, Cambridge, Massachusetts.

8   Weber, M. (1984), *The Protestant Ethic and the Spirit of Capitalism*, translated by Parsons, T., pp. 270-1 and note 58, George Allen & Unwin, London. For further concrete explanation of the concept, see Otsuka, H. (1976), *Max Weber on the Spirit of Capitalism*, IDE Occasional Papers Series No. 13, Chapter 2, Institute of Developing Economies, Tokyo.

9   Jones, L. P. and Sakong, I, op. cit., p. 32.

10   Weber used the word 'ethos' which includes in itself the practice of virtues as an inherent structural momentum, in order to emphasise that each man's participation in his society involves a personal commitment both to the behaviour patterns and to the material and ideal interests of a particular status group. Such styles of life frequently spread beyond the groups in which they originate. For example, many aspects of society were influenced by the domineering and patriarchal manner of the Junkers in Germany. Similarly, certain beliefs of early Protestantism, such as the idea of duty in one's calling, gained widespread influence far beyond the particular religious groups that developed them. An example is the Quakers. Thus, Weber attempted in each case to trace a style of life to the particular social group or groups from which a characteristic pattern of conduct and ideas had spread. In the light of this context, the maritime officers in the burgeoning period of Korean shipping can be regarded as a particular group which has a specific ethos. This will be further discussed in the text: Bendix, R. (1966), *Max Weber: An Intellectual Portrait*, pp. 260-1, Methuen & Co., London.

11   Sohn, T-H., op. cit., pp. 364-8; Kokuryo, H. (1985), *Korean Shipping and Shipping Policy - Shipping Industry Rationalisation Plan*, JAMRI Report No. 8, p. 7, Japan Maritime Research Institute, Tokyo; Kokuryo, H. and Tau, Y. M. (1983), 'Seamen's Situation in Korea', *Study of Maritime Traffic*, (in the Japanese version), No. 22, p.56.

12   On the role of an elite in economic growth, see Rostow, W. W. (1960), *The Stages of Economic Growth*, pp. 50-2, Cambridge University Press, Cambridge. On its historical example in Japan, see Lockwood, W. W. (1954), *The Economic Development of Japan,* Princeton.

13   Sohn, T-H., op. cit., p. 365.

14   Kim, K. S. and Roemer, M., op. cit., p. 25.

15   Taking the case of Russia in the nineteenth century, Gerschenkron argues that the more backward the economy, the more important the role of government and the more powerful a government the economy needs.

16   On further discussion of the subject, see Harbison, F and Myers, C. A. (1964), *Education, Manpower and Economic Growth*, pp. 31-48, McGraw-Hill, New York.

17   In Confucian society, the literati, as a status group, were privileged, even those who had only passed examinations but were not employed. The most important of status privileges for the literati were; freedom from the corvee

or compulsory labour; freedom from corporal punishment; stipends. They were also regarded as gentlemen. Considering a long history of such cultural background existing in East Asia, it is natural to say that an emphasis may be placed on education. Weber, M. (1964), *The Religion of China: Confucianism and Taoism*, p. 129, translated and edited by Gerth, H. H., The Free Press, New York; Hofheinz, R. Jr. and Calder, K. E. (1982), *The Eastasia Edge*, p. 45, Basic Books Inc., New York.

18   Ibid., p. 44.

19   Cole, D. C. and Lyman, P. N, (1971), *Korean Development: The Interplay of Politics and Economics*, p. 22, Harvard University Press, Cambridge.

20   Roberts, G. (1985), *South Korea to 1990: Liberalisation for Growth*, p. 36, The Economist Intelligence Unit, London.

21   Allen, G. C. (1962), *A Short Economic History of Modern Japan*, p. 90, George Allen & Unwin Limited, London.

22   Sohn, T-H., op. cit., pp. 367-8.

23   See McGinn, N. F., et al. (1980), *Education and Development in Korea*, Council on East Asian Studies, Chapter 3, Harvard University Press, Cambridge.

24   See Chapter 3 in this book.

25   Ibid., p. 111.

26   Kokuryo, H. and Tau, Y. M., op. cit., p. 56.

27   Sohn, T-H., op. cit., pp. 379-80.

28   Ibid., p. 366.

29   On 1 January 1950, 'The Korea Shipping Corporation' was established in accordance with the 'Korea Shipping Corporation Act'.

30   The 'Korea Shipping Corporation Act' was abolished in December 1957, turning the corporation into a stock company under the Commercial Law. However, its shares were held both by the Korean government and private investors. In 1968, the government sold all its shares to private investors, and the company became a completely private company.

6   Conclusion: Lessons from the case of Korea

The aims of the first part of this book were: to introduce the Gerschenkron model and show that it can be used for analysing the rapid growth of Korean shipping in the period 1962-81. This was achieved by specifying and testing certain hypotheses derived from the model and concluded that the Korean shipping industry had the advantage of relative backwardness and substituted some missing prerequisites for shipping development. It may thus be suggested that the model would be a useful tool to judge the validity of establishing merchant marines in various developing countries from more comprehensive and historical points of view than either the Prebisch model or the arguments of traditional maritime countries.

Summaries and conclusions have been provided at the end of each chapter; these will not, therefore, be repeated in detail. In this concluding chapter, emphasis will be given to the main findings that have been noted as the results of the hypotheses tested. This is intended to form an integrated assessment of Korean shipping growth and to suggest historical lessons in order to review the validity of the controversies regarding the establishment or expansion of merchant marines in developing countries since the early 1960s.

The results of the hypotheses tests and some peculiarities

For the Korean shipping industry to be included in the tests in the Gerschenkron model, three necessary conditions are required; firstly, the industry must have experienced a 'great spurt', which has two quantitative characteristics: a sudden and substantial rise in the rate of growth and a continuation of the spurt across a period of international depression without any considerable decrease in the rate of growth; secondly, the beginning of the spurt must be identified; thirdly, the industry must be ranked according to relative backwardness just prior to its great spurt. To measure a sudden and substantial rise in the rate of shipping growth during the period 1962-81, the indices showing the growth of gross tonnage and value added in the Korean shipping industry were used following the Gerschenkron approach.

In this study, it was found: that the Korean shipping industry satisfied the two quantitative conditions to qualify a great spurt; the industry experienced two great spurts in 1967 and 1975 respectively; and that the industry was subject to relative backwardness in terms of gross tonnage on the dates of their great spurts in European countries and Japan.

Four hypotheses were established on the basis of the Gerschenkron model, with a series of historical facts in Korea. They were related to the roles of the state and banking system, the existence and the role of ideology and the seafarer's role in the Korean shipping industry. In the course of testing them, a question was raised: in what way and through what devices did a backward country, i.e. Korea, substitute for the missing prerequisites in the process of shipping growth? The results of the hypotheses tested in this study may be summarised as follows.

Hypothesis I was concerned with the role of the Korean government in shipping growth in the context of the Gerschenkron model.

The government implemented the four Five Year Economic Development Plans successfully from 1962 to 1981. The essence of the outward-looking strategy adopted in the early 1960s was to promote labour-intensive manufacturing exports in which Korea had a comparative advantage. Moreover, the expansion of Korea's exports necessitated a corresponding increase of imports for the export production. As a consequence, Korea's seaborne foreign trade volume grew 18 per cent a year between 1962 and 1981. It was found that the growth trends of the Korean national fleet were in parallel with the expansion of Korea's total seaborne foreign trade volume in the same period, as depicted in Figure 3.3. The former was particularly supported by the Korean government's waiver system, which regulates to reserve major cargoes of imports and exports. Thus, it established a route towards the expansion of shipping tonnage in Korea. The Korean merchant fleet has expanded at an annual rate of as much as 22.8 per cent during the period 1962-81 to reach a total of about 5.1 million grt. at the end of 1981.

In other words, the point to emphasise here is that the road to expanding seaborne foreign trade was opened in response to a successful outward-looking economic policy in the 1960s and an import-substitution policy in the 1970s with the export growth policy, which in turn have played a decisive role in deriving shipping demand. In addition, the diversification of export commodities and export markets has led to increased shipping tonnage and changes to the composition of the fleet in Korea.

The Korean government mobilised both internal and external resources by making use of the market mechanism in implementing an export-led industrialisation strategy. The strategy in the mid-1960s contributed to the maintenance of an exchange rate near the free market level. In addition, the growth-oriented Korean government encouraged the influx of foreign capital. Exchange rate policy in Korea facilitated the inflow of foreign loans. An application for the inducement of foreign capital for the acquisition of ships was approved by the government in order to review basic requirements for the expansion and development programme of Korean shipping industry. Since corporate borrowing from abroad could only be undertaken with the government's authorisation and guarantee, this constituted a substantial augmentation of the government's influence. These private long term loans were covered by the 'Foreign Capital Inducement Law', which was enacted in 1960 and amended in 1962 and 1966 to make it more attractive for investors and lenders.[1] Under this law, Korean shipowners were able to obtain the Korea Exchange Bank's or commercial banks' guarantees on repayment (both amortisation and interest payments). The law facilitated the importing of foreign loans, since foreign lenders were guaranteed repayment regardless of the domestic shipowner's credit standing by the lending domestic banks for the Korean shipping companies.

The government also committed itself to a variety of economic incentives for shipping growth because of the lack of budget and foreign exchange in the 1960s. There were, for example, various tax exemptions on the imports of second-hand ships, ship's stores and income in ocean-going shipping companies, and preferential loans for 'Keihek Zoseon', i.e. the government financed shipbuilding programme. They contributed to the expansion of the national fleet.

Since the First Five Year Economic Development Plan in 1962, the government played an important role in port developments through the provision of considerable public funds: the expansion of major ports, e.g. Incheon and Pusan, the construction of industrial ports, container terminals and bulk terminals. It can be said that the investment in maritime infrastructure stimulated in indirect ways the growth of Korean shipping.

During the period 1966-79, the real interest rate Korean shipowners paid on foreign loans was mostly negative, as shown in Table 4.3 in Chapter 4. The foreign rate of interest, for example LIBOR adjusted for exchange rate change, was lower than the rate paid on domestic borrowing by as much as 15 percentage points. The interest rate differential was also, no doubt, a powerful incentive to Korean shipping companies to borrow abroad. As a result, very heavy foreign borrowing, excessively encouraged by distortions in interest rates, was employed to acquire second-hand ships. This explains the fact that during the 1960s and 1970s, the high degree of reliance on the importation of second-hand ships made important contributions to the expansion of Korean shipping growth.

Hypothesis II was related to a shipping financing system for shipping growth in Korea, substituting the prerequisite of original accumulation for acquiring ships through the system.

For most developing countries, where shipping finance cannot be sufficiently raised at home, capital is scarce, and potential investors are not maritime-motivated and prefer less risky sectors, the investment barrier was one of the most serious obstacles to the development of maritime transport. Moreover, finance for the purchase of second-hand ships was even more difficult to obtain. In Korea there was no original capital accumulation in the shipping sector and she also faced the above problems during the 1960s and the 1970s. However, a special shipping finance source, i.e. BBCPO arrangements, were generated between Korea and Japan in 1965. In Chapter 4, it was concluded that BBCPO arrangements have a similarity with the 'Shikumisen' financial arrangements. While the latter were used for increasing the number of new ships, the former contributed to expanding the second-hand fleet.

Of the total tonnage of about 9.9 million dwt. in 1981, the ships acquired by BBCPO arrangements amounted to 3.0 million dwt., i.e. 30.3 per cent of the total tonnage. As depicted in Figure 4.1 in Chapter 4, the basic mechanism of the arrangements is summarised as follows: a Japanese shipping company gives a title to its affiliate, i.e. a paper company, abroad, in exchange for the sales proceeds; the paper company charters the ship to a Korean shipping company or bareboat charterer with the conditions of the purchase option of the ship; and the Korean shipping company fully manned the ship with Korean crew and chartered her back to the previous Japanese shipping company.

In BBCPO arrangements, the combinations of economic factors; the Japanese shipowners' needs to dispose of inefficient and uncompetitive old ships caused by high operating costs under the Japanese flag, resulting from sharply rising Japanese crew costs; low cost and abundant Korean crew; and high demand for shipping caused by rapid Japanese economic expansion - produced a peculiar type of shipping finance and at the same time enabled Korean and Japanese shipowners to have benefits from a type of international division of labour in the shipping sector.

The ship under BBCPO dealings was to be let on a long term time charter to well-known companies in Japan. Therefore, the existence of a contracted charter party was enough to raise the creditworthiness of Korean shipping companies and served as a secure basis on which a bank guaranteed the loan for the acquisition of ships by BBCPO method. In other words, by means of the bareboat charter and time charter discussed in Chapter 4, the Korean shipping companies could draw finance from general trading companies in Japan, along with a guarantee from a time charterer or a Japanese shipping company. As a consequence, BBCPO arrangements played an important role in putting as collateral the time charter or mortgages the earnings on time charter hire and in turn in expanding merchant marines in Korea in the 1960s and 1970s. The BBCPO arrangements enabled the Korean shipping industry to a great extent to overcome its lack of capital.

The BBCPO arrangements have concurrently influenced the Korean shipping industry as follows.

•   Under BBCPO arrangements, a bareboat chartered ship was fully manned with Korean crew and delivered to a Japanese shipping company as a condition of the long term time charter. As a result, the so-called bareboat chartered ship with time charter (BBCTC) not only played an important role in increasing employment but also contributed to training officers, crew members and other personnel needed in the shipping industry in

100

Korea. The extensive employment of Korean seamen on BBCTC provided a reservoir of trained labour for the Korean shipping industry without any associated capital investment in ships by Koreans.

- The increase of seamen employed on BBCTC contributed to the improvement of the balance of payments through the remittances of crew income in foreign currency. The wage income earned by the Korean crew in foreign merchant ocean-going vessels increased to US $231.8 million in 1981 from US $4.2 million in 1965 at 1980 prices. In the period 1965-1981, the ratio of wage income of crew to shipping freight ranged from 10.1 to 17.0 per cent.

- Thanks to the above mentioned economic factors behind the generation of BBCPO arrangements, they easily provided Korean shipowners with an opportunity for the creation of shipping companies in Korea. While in 1962 the number of member companies which belonged to the Korea Shipowners' Association was only eleven, the number increased to 62 in 1978, i.e. a more than five-fold increase in the period 1962-78. This is because bareboat charterers could become shipowners after the completion of repayments on the ships acquired by BBCPO arrangements, despite the absence of capital accumulation for the acquisition of ships.

Besides BBCPO arrangements, the expansion of the Korean fleet was achieved through the 'Keihek Zoseon' scheme and importation of second-hand ships. The imports of vessels and BBCPO have played a far greater role in the expansion of the fleet than the 'Keihek Zoseon' scheme. This was partly because priority was given in shipbuilding to the construction of export ships as a means of earning foreign exchange and partly because the scheme was designed to support the shipbuilding industry. Moreover, there was a limit to the capacity and funds to build ships for national shipowners under the scheme.

Hypothesis III tested the existence of ideology and its role in the conditions of extreme backwardness in the Korean shipping industry.

The Liberation from Japan in 1945 and the Korean War in 1950 created some tensions and disorganisation in every aspect of Korean society. The presence of vested properties, e.g. ships and shipping companies, brought forth tensions in the Korean shipping sector. There were tensions between those who had parasitic characteristics and acquisitive minds for seeking gains from the liberated property and those who had an eagerness and passion beyond personal profit-seeking to build their country anew. In the context of the Gerschenkron model, the former can be regarded as an obstacle to shipping development. However, there existed a group to break the tensions. They were Korean maritime officers who were educated in Japan during the colonial period. They possessed great enthusiasm for establishing a viable national merchant fleet. The ideology that placed their

101

energies in a direction towards shipping development resulted from three factors as follows: anti-Japanese nationalism, Confucianism and anti-Communism.

Through their experiences under the Japanese military regime during the Second World War, the Korean maritime officers realised that shipping transportation had played an important role in carrying the goods required for the Japanese economy. In addition, they were also convinced that the development of a merchant fleet could not only help in building a newly born country but could also contribute to the achievement of a completely independent power from Japan.

By Confucianism, which places a high value on education as a cultural and social asset in Korea, the maritime officers trained and educated seamen and thus prepared one of the prerequisites for shipping development. As a result, Korea starting from extreme by backward conditions was able to improve the low standard of education and to overcome the resulting difficulty in training skilled seafaring labour without employing foreign seamen at the initial stage of establishment of merchant marine fleet.

Finally, anti-Communism, which originated from President S. M. Rhee and extended to the military regime of Mr C. H. Park after 1961, forced the national fleet to be regarded as a life line for transporting import and export goods for the Korean economy during peacetime and military goods during wartime. This implies that the question of security of service has been one major consideration in the development expansion of the Korean merchant marine, given the country's geographical position.[2]

For Korea, there is little doubt that to a considerable extent, the ideology fulfilled its function for shipping growth and that it was helpful in overcoming the constraints on shipping development through driving the energies and imaginations of maritime officers in that direction.

In the process of shipping growth in Korea, the above ideology produced two further outcomes, which will be further concluded in the following hypothesis IV: the establishment of a mercantile college for maritime officers and successful management of one of the biggest vested shipping companies.

Hypothesis IV was that prior to building merchant marines in Korea, a maritime educational institution served as a prerequisite for shipping growth by making it possible to combine low-wage Korean seamen with uneconomic Japanese ships through BBCPO arrangements; and that Japan was a source of skill and capital for Korean shipping growth.

At a time when Korea still had hardly any ocean-going ships, a mercantile marine college with the aim of educating and training high-grade maritime officers was established by the maritime officers in November 1945, i.e. shortly after the Liberation in August 1945. One of the peculiarities of the Korean shipping industry is therefore, that in Korea the education of merchant marine officers preceded the establishment of a merchant marine, unlike Japan and other developing countries.

In 1965 when BBCPO arrangements were introduced in Korea, abundant quantities of sufficiently well-educated, low cost and Korean crews already existed to man the ships under the arrangements, discussed in Chapter 4. In the process of shipping growth, Korea was, therefore, able to overcome a lack of seafaring labour which most developing countries commonly faced in establishing or expanding their merchant marines. Moreover, the existence of such Korean seamen made it possible to generate BBCPO arrangements with Japan through an internationally horizontal division of labour with Japan and, as a consequence, shipping finance was available to the Korean shipping industry. In other words, the availability of labour played an important role in establishing and expanding the merchant marines in Korea where capital was scarce. Subsequently, when there was no capital accumulation in the 1960s and 1970s, this in turn contributed to the substitution of a prerequisite of the original accumulation of capital in the context of the Gerschenkron model for acquiring ships, through combining uneconomic Japanese second-hand ships and abundant, well-trained and low wage Korean crews.

Moreover, the seamen's educational college also played an important, if indirect role in providing shipping entrepreneurs for the Korean shipping industry. It was found that about 75 per cent of top management in ocean-going shipping companies graduated from college. That is to say, almost all the board directors in Korean ocean-going shipping companies were ex-seagoing officers.

In 1950 a vested shipping company was taken over by the 'Korea Shipping Corporation', which operated in the form of a public corporation. The above ex-seagoing officers, as shore staff, successfully managed the corporation. At that time it was the only field in Korea where they were able to accumulate know-how in the shipping business in the 1950s and 1960s. In 1968 when it was privatised, the corporation produced a number of shipping entrepreneurs, mainly ex-seagoing officers, for new companies in the Korean shipping industry. Their know-how in the shipping business, along with a peculiar shipping financing system, i.e. BBCPO financial arrangements, enabled them to easily establish shipping companies. This explains why many shipping companies were set up in the 1960s and 1970s.

It was also found that some peculiarities of the two spurts in Korean shipping were the appearance of what Gerschenkron termed 'substitutions' for the 'missing pre-requisites' in the period 1962-81. The use of BBCPO arrangements, the Korean government economic and fiscal policies, the waiver system and the existence of Korean seamen were viewed as examples of such substitutions. It can therefore be said that the spurts of shipping development in Korea were engineered by factors quite unusual in the shipping history of developing countries. In other words, the effect of the above factors, historically peculiar to the Korean shipping industry, was reinforced by the use of certain institutional instruments, i.e. the state and banking system, and by the existence of an ideology and its role, taking advantage of relative backwardness from the viewpoint of the Gerschenkron model.

It was shown in the course of testing the above hypotheses that Korea had some peculiarities in the course of establishing or expanding her merchant marines over the period 1962-81, unlike other developing countries. Another peculiarity to be added is drawn from the pattern of shipping development in Korea. In most developing countries, a liner fleet was established and expanded from the initial development stage of their merchant marines. By contrast, Korea started from tramp shipping in the bulk sector and her fleet was expanded, taking a comparative advantage in shipping operating based on low cost and abundant Korean crew. The Korean shipping industry has also made a remarkable advance into cross trade. Since 1967, the cross trade cargo carried by the Korean fleet has risen rapidly, as discussed in Chapter 3.

Still another peculiarity in the process of shipping growth is that there existed a positive correlation between volumes of foreign trade and shipping growth in Korea. It is well known that Korea's rapid shipping growth rate, aided by the process of export-oriented industrialisation, has achieved a high level since the early 1960s. Its annual average growth rate marked 28.9 per cent during the same period, and has recorded a high level unmatched by other developing countries. The rapid growth rate reflects the expansion of seaborne trade volume caused by the successful performance of economic policies, i.e. export-oriented strategy in the 1960s. In addition to this, from the point of view of the shipping tonnage growth index based on 1962=100, the speed at which Korea has experienced the expansion of her merchant marine is ten times faster than that achieved by some newly industrialising countries and Japan in the period 1962-81, taking the 'compressed process' for its growth.[3]

Since shipping satisfied a demand derived from trade, and the volume of trade in many commodities depends increasingly on transportation efficiency and cost, efficient shipping is critical to development. The growth of volume of seaborne foreign trade can be one of the factors strong enough to provide a cornerstone for shipping growth in developing countries. However, it must be noted by developing countries that the growth of seaborne foreign trade is not a necessary or sufficient prerequisite for shipping growth. Within the bulk trades, the increase in freight rates resulting from reduced competition, i.e. the waiver system, in Korea, may be detrimental to the final consumer of sea transport. Under these circumstances, the growth of Korean shipping may not be desirable from the point of view of welfare, and it may be difficult to say that the Korean shipping industry has achieved genuine high rates of growth in the period 1962-81. In other words, the question is whether Korean-owned ships assure efficient, i.e. low-cost and competitive, transportation for her trades. It seems that this was not considered in the process of Korean shipping growth.

The results of this study have exposed areas for further research. First, it is suggested that based on the results of the hypotheses tested, developing countries should consider the criteria - what we would call 'criteria of the Gerschenkronian type' for shipping growth - to establish or expand merchant marines as follows: to identify what tensions exist between the shipping establishment and its potential optimisation; to grasp whether or not a government has a powerful and systematic enough organisation to be able to play a key role in breaking down the obstacles or tensions to shipping growth and in substituting missing prerequisites for shipping growth; to create a banking system to overcome the original accumulation of capital and supply entrepreneurship in the shipping sector; to check whether there exists an ideology to ignite men; and to break down the tensions inherent in backward countries or to develop such an ideology. For this, prior to establishing or expanding their merchant marines, developing countries should recognise certain pre-requisites for shipping growth and whether they exist; if some of them are missing, it is necessary to raise the following question: in what way and through what devices are backward countries able to substitute for the missing prerequisites?

Second, it is suggested that, to the developing countries which have been in the course of expanding their merchant fleets, all our approach can do is to enable their governments to discover and apply the most promising and appropriate pattern of substitutions for shipping growth.

Third, it is suggested that causal relations between trade and shipping growth in NICs, using econometric models[4], should be investigated, referring to the case of Korea in this study and to the following:

> The foreign trade of many newly industrial and advanced developing countries, such as South Korea, Singapore, Malaysia, and Taiwan, has grown more rapidly than that of the developed countries. This growth is often credited as a major contributing factor to their rapid development. It is interesting to note that most newly industrialised countries put a high priority on shipping development as an essential element towards their trade and economic growth.[5]

In applying the Gerschenkron model, we should, however, note that in trying to describe and interpret a model, a responsible scholar must be conscious of, and search for, the limits of its applicability. Thus, even though findings may be unique to Korea with a high rate of shipping growth, they may provide other developing countries with significant insights into the consideratioin of their future shipping development.

Notes and references

1   Mason, E. S., et al. (1980), *The Economic and Social Modernisation of the Republic of Korea*, Council on East Asian Studies, pp. 200, 268, Harvard University Press, Cambridge.

2   Hansen, H. (1981), *The Developing Countries and International Shipping*, The World Bank Staff Paper No. 502, p. 42, The World Bank, Washington DC.

3   This phrase was first used by Professor T. Watanabe in his paper 'Heavy and Chemical Industrialisation and Economic Development in the Republic of Korea', *Developing Economies*, Vol. 16, No. 4, pp. 385-407, (1978). Recently the evidence of Professor Watanabe and his co-authors, suggests that the Korean economy has experienced the compressed process compared with the Japanese one. On this subject, see Watanabe, T., Kim, C. N. and Kajwara, H. (1984), 'A Consideration of the Compressed Process of Agricultural Development in the Republic of Korea', *Developing Economies*, Vol. 22, No. 2, pp. 113-36; Watanabe, T., 'Economic Development in Korea: Lessons and Challenge', in Shishido, T. and Sato, R. (eds.) (1985), *Economic Policy and Development: New Perspectives*, pp. 95-111, Auburn House Publishing Company, London.

4   On the subject of causality tests, see Granger, C. W. J. (1969), 'Investigating Causal Relations by Econometric Models and Cross-spectral Methods', *Econometrica*, Vol. 37, No. 3, pp. 424-38; Sims, C. A. (1972), 'Money, Income, and Causality', *American Economic Review*, Vol. 62, No. 4, pp. 540-52; Hsiao, C. (1979), 'Causality Tests in Econometrics', *Journal of Economic Dynamics and Control*, Vol. 1, pp. 321-46; Wu, D. M. (1983), 'Tests of Causality, Predeterminedness and Exogeneity', *International Economic Review*, Vol. 24, No. 3, pp. 547-88.

5   Frankel, E. G. (1987), *The World Shipping Industry*, p. 112, Croom Helm Publishers, London.

Section Two

Dynamic shipping movements in Far East Asia

7 Regional economic co-operation in Far East Asia and maritime transport

Introduction

Access to internationally competitive ocean shipping services is a prerequisite for economic development and integration at national and regional levels. The availability of sea transportation allows markets to grow and economies of scale to be achieved through division of labour and specialisation. The main trading areas of the world, i.e. Europe and North America, have developed into clear regional trading blocs. A similar trading bloc is apparently emerging in East Asia.

The emergence and development of regional trade blocs have an important impact on the requirements for sea transportation. North America, Europe and the Asia Pacific area are the world's dominant trade regions, generating the highest levels of both intra- and inter-regional trade volumes. Of particular interest is the growing economic integration of the Far East Asia region which has already been reflected in the rapid development of regional ocean and air transport networks. The interface between intra- and inter-regional transport systems will most likely continue to favour the development of hub ports or load centres, which are then complemented by feeder services within the region. Such hub ports will require substantial levels of co-operation within the region if an efficient overall system is to be developed.

This chapter focuses upon the current changes within, and the future prospects for, maritime transport, in the context of regional economic co-operation in Far East Asia. The emphasis here is on shipping and port industries involved in sea trade routes between Korea, China and Far East Russia. The initial aim is to illustrate the current problems within these sectors before finally suggesting proposals for solving them.

The rise of maritime power in Far East Asia

South Korea, Hong Kong, Singapore, Taiwan and China have long demonstrated their ability to penetrate world markets. By 1990, they totalled 52.2 million dead-weight tons (dwt.) and accounted for 8.2 per cent of the world's shipping tonnage. (See Table 7.1.) They have become the leaders of the new maritime countries of the East Asian area. As can be seen in Table 7.1, in 1970 the top four Asia Pacific maritime nations, excluding Japan, accounted for only 1.7 per cent of the world's dwt. By 1990, this share had increased to 9.0 per cent, although Japan, whose maritime development is more comparable to that of the traditional maritime nations in Europe, saw its share decline from 12.1 per cent of total dwt. in 1970 to 6.1 per cent in 1990. Encouraged by their governments, the ship-building and shipping companies in this area achieved a remarkable expansion to meet the rise in export volumes. China and Korea are especially good examples.

Table 7.1
Fleet developments of selected Asia Pacific countries

Country	1970 dwt. (mil.)	1970 Composition %	1990 dwt. (mil.)	1990 Composition %
China	1.2	0.4	20.8	3.1
Philippines	1.3	0.4	14.2	2.1
Singapore*	0.6	0.2	13.0	1.9
South Korea	1.3	0.4	12.5	1.9
Hong Kong*	1.0	0.3	11.2	1.9
Taiwan	1.7	0.5	8.7	1.3
Subtotal	7.1	2.1	80.3	12.1
Japan	40.3	12.1	40.8	6.1
East Asia total	47.4		121.1	
World total	334.0	100.0	666.0	100.0

Note: * Data include flag of convenience vessels.

Source: OECD, *Maritime Transport* (1970, 1990).

The maritime sector is one of the main beneficiaries of the high rate of economic growth in East Asia; the East Asian economies are strongly oriented towards international markets, for both imports of raw materials and exports of finished and semi-finished products. This growth of the maritime sector was more significant in the area of regular services, notably for container traffic, and less noticeable for large bulk trades.

Far East Asia has become the foremost world centre for containerised traffic, surpassing both North America and Northern Europe. The share of world traffic handled by ports in the region rose from 19 per cent to 26 per cent during the 1980s, while North America's share declined from 28 per cent to 22 per cent, and Northern Europe's fell from 21 per cent to 18 per cent. At the end of the 1980s the region's traffic was estimated at 20.5 million teu, mostly concentrated in Japan (7.2 million teu), Taiwan (5.3 million teu), Hong Kong (4.5 million teu), and South Korea (2.5 million teu).

During the period from 1985 to 1991, the capacity of container fleets of companies in the main Asian maritime countries increased by 80 per cent, while the world container fleet grew by only 40 per cent.[1]

Table 7.2 shows estimated container throughputs for major East Asian countries in the year 2000 with their historical data. It can be seen that China is forecast to be the leading country with an average growth in aggregate container throughput of 15.1 per cent per annum throughout the 1990s.

Table 7.2
History and forecasts of container throughputs in
major East Asian countries

Country	1985 ('000 teu)	1990 ('000 teu)	Average growth (%) 1985-1990	2000 ('000 teu)	Average growth (%) 1990-2000
Hong Kong	2,289	5,101	17.4	15,176	11.5
Taiwan	3,075	4,869	9.6	9,712	7.1
China	497	1,116	17.6	4,567	15.1
South Korea	1,246	2,508	15.0	5,616	8.4
Japan	5,517	8,063	7.9	16,427	7.4
USSR Pacific	100	80	- 4.4	145	6.1
Total	12,724	21,737	11.3	51,643	9.0

Sources: Containerisation International Yearbook, various issues. Korea Maritime Institute and ESCAP (1994).

Regional container shipping networks

The Far Eastern region includes major container concentrations in Japan - Kobe, Yokohama, Osaka and Nagoya; in Korea at Pusan; the relatively new but growing ports of Dalian, Tianjin and Qingdao on the adjacent coast of The People's Republic of China (PRC); and the much smaller nodes of Vostochny and Nakhodka in Far East Russia. Hong Kong, with a throughput of 9.3 million teu in 1993, dominates the central cluster and its continuing high, though sometimes fluctuating, growth rate - 30 per cent between 1991 and 1992 - reflects rapid economic developments in southern China, as well as its centrality and significance as a major mainline or hub port. New port developments in the Pearl River delta and adjacent areas of southern China are proceeding and, though throughputs were small in the early 1990s, it is likely that in the next decade, new

111

shipping linkages with Hong Kong, Singapore and Kaohsiung will emerge and strengthen. Continuing rapid growth in Shanghai - over 30 per cent between 1991 and 1992 - confirms the port as an emerging focus of container tonnage in the PRC.

Intra-regional shipping operations in the Far East-Southeast Asian area are now carrying significant numbers of containers within a number of sub-systems to and from the Kobe, Pusan, Kaohsiung, Hong Kong and Singapore hubs, as well as to and from regional ports. In these operations, feeder traffic is a component of intra-regional traffic. It is the way in which the region's ports are now linked into shipping networks and, effectively, into port-shipping systems - which is of particular importance in the East Asian area.

Both feeder and regional container traffic provide the basis for intra-Asian shipping networks and it has recently been suggested that it is possible to recognise four sub-systems:[2]

- Japan-Korea-Taiwan-Hong Kong-Singapore Corridor
- East Asia-Southeast Asia Services
- East Asia Short Sea Services: Taiwan-Hong Kong-The Philippines-China
- East Asia-Northeast Asia Services

Table 7.3 shows mainline operators and their fleets, deployed on intra-Asian trades in 1992, a total of 135 vessels with a capacity of 64,238 teu. The China Ocean Shipping Company (COSCO) is the biggest operator in China; transporting 22,860 teu, which represented 35.6 per cent of the total container cargo carried in the year.

Table 7.3
Fleet analysis of mainline operators in 1992:
Vessels deployed on intra-Asian trades*

Operator	No. of ships	teu	Max	Min	Average
APL	6	4,192	1,400	400	699
COSCO	67	22,860	1,140	40	341
Cho Yang Shipping	8	2,929	1,200	108	366
Evergreen Line	4	1,852	510	392	463
Hanjin Shipping	5	5,062	1,184	404	1,012
Hyundai Merchant Marine	1	431	431	431	431
K-Line	15	9,109	1,182	327	607
Maersk Line	6	3,321	650	436	554
NYK	3	2,808	1,500	616	936
Navix Line	5	3,118	1,400	350	624
Neptune Orient Line	2	818	409	409	409
OOCL	4	3,122	1,061	414	781
P&O Containers	2	692	582	110	346
Sea-Land	5	3,044	754	436	609
Yangming Marine	2	880	440	440	440
Total	135	64,238	-	-	476

Sources: Drewry Shipping Consultants (1993), *Feeder and Short Sea Container Shipping*, p. 93, London. *Containerisation International Yearbook*, 1993.

An overview of major container shipping routes, the number of carriers within the Asia Pacific area and links with the wider world market is given in Table 7.4. It suggests the existence of a number of distinct segments in Asia Pacific shipping.

Table 7.4
Major container routes and number of carriers in East Asia

Major trade routes	No. of carriers	Sub-routes
Transpacific	22	Far East - North America East Coast
	28	Far East - North America West Coast
	9	Far East - North America Gulf Coast
	11	Far East - South America East Coast
	10	Far East - North America West Coast
	11	Far East - Caribbean/Central America
Far East - Europe/Mid-east	39	Far East - Europe
	20	Far East - Mediterranean
	23	Far East - Mid-east
	17	Far East - Near East
	17	Far East - Red Sea
Japan/Korea - East Asia	19	Japan - Korea
	23	Japan/Korea - China
	22	Japan/Korea - Australia
	34	Japan/Korea - East Asia
	39	Japan/Korea - Southeast Asia
	9	Japanese Coastal
China - East Asia	14	China - Hong Kong
	23	China - Japan/Korea
	8	China - Southeast Asia
	1	Chinese Coastal

Source: Containerisation International Yearbook (1991).

114

Table 7.5 compares leading container ports in the world. In 1980 the leading container ports were located in North America and Europe. This, however, has changed rapidly. In 1993, four of the top ten container ports were located in East Asia.

Table 7.5
Top ten container ports in the world

	1980		1990		1993	
Port	**Rank**	**teu**	**Rank**	**teu**	**Rank**	**teu**
Hong Kong	3	1.5	2	5.1	1	9.3
Singapore	6	0.9	1	5.2	2	9.0
Kaohsiung	5	1.0	4	3.5	3	4.2
Rotterdam	2	1.9	3	3.7	4	4.0
Pusan	16	0.6	6	2.3	5	2.9
Kobe	4	1.5	5	2.6	6	2.7
Hamburg	9	0.8	6	2.0	7	2.5
Los Angeles	17	0.6	7	2.1	8	2.3
Long Beach (USA)	8	0.8	12	1.6	9	2.0
New York / New Jersey	1	1.9	9	1.9	10	2.2
Keelung	15	0.7	10	1.8	12	2.0
San Juan	7	0.9	16	1.4	14	1.7
Oakland	10	0.8	19	1.1	19	1.4

(unit: million)

Source: Containerisation International Yearbook, various issues.

The impact of regional economic co-operation on maritime transport in Far East Asia

The economic integration of the EC and NAFTA has played a crucial role in triggering discussions on regional economic co-operation in certain zones of Asia; as follows:

- The Growth Triangle
  (Singapore, Johor in Malaysia and Batam Island in Indonesia)

- The BAHT Zone
  (Border of Thailand, Laos, Cambodia and Vietnam)

- The Greater South China Economic Zone
  Hong Kong, Gwandong and Fuchen in China and Taiwan)

115

- The Yellow Sea Economic Zone
  (North and Northeast China, South and North Korea and Japan)

- The East Sea Economic Zone
  (Northeast China, Far East Russia, South and North Korea and Japan)

- Korean Strait Economic Zone
  (Southern Korea, Pusan and Northwest of Japan, Kyushu)

The disintegration of the former USSR and changes within the social system in China were important driving forces in the acceleration of regional economic co-operation in Far East Asia. Three recently suggested economic co-operation zones in the region are the Yellow Sea Economic Zone, the East Sea Economic Zone and the Korean Strait Economic Zone. Their characteristics are summarised in Table 7.6.

The Yellow Sea Economic Zone covers the Northeast coastal provinces of China - the Bohai major economic zone in the broad sense, the Western coastal area of South and North Korea, and Kyushu area of Japan. Specifically, the Bohai zone consists of the Liaoning, Hebei and Shandong provinces and Beijing and Tianjin municipalities; these are situated along the coastline of the Yellow Sea with seaports and a vast hinterland. The distinctive advantages of this region are:

- geographical location;
- rich mineral resources;
- a complex network of land-sea-air communications: the New Euro-Asian Continental Bridge, i.e. Trans-Chinese Railroad (TCR) and Trans-Siberian Railroad (TSR);
- a solid industrial foundation and technological strength;
- sufficient supply of skilled labour;
- ease in raising foreign capital;
- unique tourist resources.

Table 7.6

Summary of characteristics of three economic co-operation zones

	Yellow Sea economic co-operation	East Sea economic co-operation	Korean Strait economic co-operation
Related countries & regions	• Yellow & Bohai Rim regions of China • South & North Korea • Northwest Japan	• Far East Russia, Mongolia • Northeast provinces of China • South & North Korea Northwest Japan	• Southern Korea • Kyushu in Japan
Co-operation model	• information & market oriented, region to region	• multinational plan or oriented country to country	• economic complementary region to region • geographical proximity
Major means of co-operation	• trade, foreign direct investment • free trade zone	• free trade zone • free investment zone	• industrial integration
Stage of development	• increasing trade & investment	• under active discussion & study	• under primary discussion & study

Source: Lim, J-D. (1994), 'Three Models of Regional Co-operation in Northeast Asia: Yellow Sea Economic Co-operation, East Sea Economic Co-operation and Korean Strait Economic Co-operation', Proceedings of International Conference held by Pusan National University, 1-2 September. New information added by the author.

Regional economic co-operation has tended to develop air and shipping routes between major cities of Korea, China, Japan and Far East Russia. With the exception of some regions in China and North Korea, port-centred diversified transportation of these regions has formed a comprehensive and effective system, which plays a very important role in facilitating the development of regional economic co-operation and exchanges.

Investment in communications and transportation in China has, in recent years, increased steadily in response to the need for extensive modernisation. Under the Sixth Five-Year Plan (1981-85) major investments were made in bulk handling facilities for coal, crude oil, grain and timber, and for the construction of the country's first container berths. Fifty four deep-water berths were completed during this period, which increased the annual cargo handling capacity from 200 million tons in 1978 to 370 million tons in 1985.

117

Under the Seventh Five-Year Plan, 96 additional deep-water berths for medium sized ships were completed. In 1990, the total annual cargo handling capacity of all PRC was estimated at 550 million tons; an increase of 180 million tons from 1985.[3] Port expansion and improvements continued to be accorded a high priority during the Eighth Five-Year Plan. Efforts are being made at each port to create the necessary conditions for container berths and energy wharves so as to both co-ordinate the work and enhance the handling capacities of ports in this region. The ports of Tianjin and Dalian will take advantage of having an economic and technical development area in their vicinity and turn themselves into free ports. Other ports such as Quinhuangdao and Qingdao are also endeavouring to develop their own industries and trade inside the harbour limits in order to set up free port, export trade or process areas.

Current problems with the Korean-Chinese shipping route

This section is devoted to the identification of current problems experienced on sea trade routes between China and Korea. A substantial amount of information is required to avoid the drawbacks of national bias in the research of international trade. For this reason, surveys, interviews and questionnaires[4] were carried out to acquire more reliable and systematic data and information, which was then thoroughly cross checked. Although this consisted of rather fragmentary evidence, it was possible to make some observations to achieve the purpose of this section.

General observations on bottlenecks in the shipping sector

Among the Asia-Pacific countries China stands out as having the closest ties between shipping and the state. Its largest shipping company, COSCO, is fully state owned and is *de facto* a national monopoly, although there have been attempts at simulating a form of pseudo-competition by breaking COSCO into several regional companies, ostensibly competing freely with one another. In 1990, mainland China owned 20.8 million dwt. of ocean going tonnage; of these COSCO owned approximately 28 per cent, or 5.8 million dwt.. The remainder were owned by approximately 80 small provincial shipping companies. COSCO has expanded so rapidly in recent years in the liner business that it is now ranked as the fourth largest liner company in the world in terms of capacity; operating a fleet of 70,600 teu. The expansion however, does not stop there.

The China National Foreign Trade Transportation Corporation (SINOTRANS) is the national forwarder in mainland China and used to be the sole cargo supplier to COSCO. In fact 80 per cent of COSCO's cargoes are still derived from it, however the businesses of these two companies are currently overlapping as SINOTRANS now operates its own feeder fleet to Hong Kong. In response to this, COSCO is also expanding its service to include inland transport; a development which is facilitated by the overall growth in containerisation. This indicates that the sea transport policy in mainland China has been decentralised and that competition is now allowed.

Table 7.7
Joint venture shipping companies between China and Korea

	Sinokor	Weidong	Co-Heung	Jinchon	Yellow Ferry[+]
Established	14 Apr '89	14 Aug '90	8 Mar '91	9 Dec '91	29 Aug '94
HQ location	Hong Kong	Weihai	Hong Kong	Seoul	Yantai
Contract parties	Korea: Dongnama Shipping Co	Korea: Dongnama Shipping Co Yukong Line & 5 companies	Korea: Heung-A Shipping Co	Korea: Dae-A Shipping Co	Korea: Zinsung Corporation
	China: SINOTRANS	China: Weihai Shipping Co	China: COSCO	China: Tianjin Shipping Co	China: Qingdao Ocean Shipping Co., Yantai Marine Shipping Co
Equity ratio (Korea:China)	50:50	50:50	50:50	50:50	5:95[++]
Vessel employed	4 containers	2 car ferries	4 containers	1 car ferry	1 car ferry
Operating route	Pusan - Shanghai Tianjin Quindao Dalian	Inchon - Weihai Quindao	Pusan - Shanghai Quindao Dalian Tianjin	Inchon - Tianjin	Pusan - Yantai[+++]

Notes: [+] *This company was taken over by C&K Ferry Lines in October 1995 (See Table 12.2).*
[++] *The equity ratio was changed to 25:75 in October 1995.*
[+++] *Port of Kunsan in Korea was included on the route in October 1995.*

Sources: Korean Foreign Trade Association (1993), Dongnama Shipping Company (1994) and Zinsung Corporation (1995).

Table 7.8
Foreign flag shipping companies operated on shipping routes between Korea and China

	Tranpac Line	EAS Line	TMSC	Bonami Line
Flag	Hong Kong	Hong Kong	China	Hong Kong
Operation start date	June 1989	October 1992	October 1993	January 1988
Local agent	Eagle Shipping Co.	Union Express	Doowoo Shipping Co.	Doowoo Shipping Co.
Vessels employed	Container 387 teu	Container 250 teu	Container 357 teu	Container 320 teu
Operating route	Pusan - Quindao	Pusan - Dalian Quindao	Pusan - Tianjin	Pusan - Shanghai

Source: Dongnama Shipping Company (1994).

Table 7.9
Container cargoes carried by joint venture and foreign flag shipping companies between Korea and China

	1989	1990		1991		1992		Jan-Oct 1993	
	teu	teu	± %	teu	± %	teu	± %	teu	± %
Joint venture shipping company									
Export	1.8	7.9		16.8		49.2		70.2	
Import	2.0	12.8		24.8		43.9		68.6	
Subtotal	3.8	20.7		41.6		93.1		138.8	
Shipment ratio (%)	175	36.7	445	49.9	102	73	124	70.1	69.2
Foreign flag shipping company									
Export	9.1	15.6		13.7		17.3		24.3	
Import	9.4	20.0		28.1		8.0		34.7	
Subtotal	18.5	35.6		41.8		35.3		59.0	
Shipment ratio (%)	83	63.3	92	50.1	17	27	-16	29.9	85.9
Grand Total	22.3	56.3	152	83.4	48	128.4	54	197.8	73.9

Source: Korea Maritime Institute (1994).

Tables 7.7 and 7.8 show four joint venture shipping companies and four shipping companies under foreign flags employed on the China/Korea shipping routes. These link Pusan and Inchon to major ports in China such as Shanghai, Tianjin, Qingdao, Dalian and Weihai. Since the establishment of SINOKOR in 1989, the other three joint venture companies have been established. The types of vessel deployed on these routes are container ships and car ferries.

As can be seen in Table 7.9, eight companies transported total container cargoes of 22,315 teu in 1989 and 128,462 teu in 1992, with a 55.9 per cent annual average growth rate. A striking point drawn from the table is that while the shipment rate of joint ventures was sharply increasing during the period 1989-1993, that of foreign flag shipping companies deteriorated during the same period. The rise of developing maritime countries is mainly based on a combination of national maritime policies and strong competitive advantage. At present China is no exception; however, Korea has been in ascendancy over the last three decades.[5]

There are several forms of Chinese government support for the shipping industry besides straight subsidies. Three of these forms can be summarised as:

- preferential treatment of their own ships in domestic ports;
- cargo reservation and preferences; and
- control of foreign exchange.

Current bottlenecks in the port sector

There are two main types of ports in the PRC: sea ports and river ports. There are over 460 sea ports along 18,400 km of coastline, of which 17 are major ports handling most of China's foreign trade; 76.3 per cent of Korean companies handled their cargoes through four of the top 17 ports in China, i.e. Shanghai, Dalian, Qingdao and Tianjin. There are also approximately 2,000 river ports including those located on major rivers such as the Changjiang, Huanghe, Zhujiang and Heilongjiang (Amur). Because of China's modernisation and economic reform policies there has been a significant increase in foreign trade volume, over 90 per cent of which was transported by sea. Ports and coastal shipping also play an important role for domestic traffic by providing an alternative north-south transport mode thus relieving pressure on the intensively used railway system. With regard to major sea ports, total foreign and domestic cargo grew from 218 million tons in 1980 to 490 million tons in 1989, which is equivalent to an average annual growth rate of 9.4 per cent. In 1990, the volume of cargo handled at these ports declined slightly to 483 million tons following the Government's strict programme to curb inflation and manage aggregate demand, which subsequently resulted in a slowing down of economic growth.

Major ports in the PRC operate on a 24 hour basis with a three-shift system, however operations in some ports are hampered by congestion in the port area. Factors contributing to this congestion include:

121

- aged and outmoded loading and discharging equipment;
- an excessive reliance on break-bulk cargo handling methods;
- a lack of adequate transport infrastructure in the hinterland; and
- untimely or delayed construction of container ports.

Port capacity in China is not sufficient to handle increasing traffic volumes resulting in severe port congestion and an increase in the cost of trade.[6] The failure to provide adequate facilities, therefore, is a crucial factor affecting cargo flows through ports; the effects of port congestion spreads far beyond the port itself. All parties involved in the transportation of goods by sea between trading partners suffer from it. UNCTAD summarised its consequences as follows:

> The port suffers through increased costs of operation and through the possibility of temporary - or permanent - loss of traffic. The shipowner suffers through a drop in the earning power of his ship and from possible incidental harm to the ship, its crew and cargo. ..... The shipper suffers through the direct cost of delays in shipment, the loss of goodwill in his trade and, ultimately, higher shipping charges. Finally, the national economy suffers through delays in obtaining materials for industry or for development projects, the frustration of export activities and higher transportation costs.[7]

The structure and level of port tariffs are determined jointly by the Ministry of Communications, the Ministry of Finance and the State Price Bureau. The following major features of port tariffs in PRC may be detrimental to the promotion of shipping and port developments.

- One overall tariff framework for foreign trade applies to all ports, although there are some variations to reflect differences in port operations (e.g. length of entrance channel, distance from quay to shed, greater freedom for special economic zones).
- Foreign ships pay in US dollars although tariffs are denominated in Chinese currency (Yuan).
- No direct relationship exists between tariffs and the cost of providing services.
- A large difference exists between foreign and domestic tariffs.
- No formal mechanism is in place to adjust tariffs on a regular basis although tariffs are adjusted periodically.

Let us now turn to some problems caused by deficiencies in the operational management of ports in China. While each port has its own individual characteristics, surveys, questionnaires and interviews carried out by the author show that four of the top 17 ports in China have the following operational problems in common:

- a shortage of skilled technical staff; this being one of the major reasons for port congestion;
- crane damage caused by dock labour often being attributed to the ship undergoing cargo work;
- overmanning in port administrative areas; there is a need to introduce measures to extensively retrain and re-deploy manpower - this is complicated by the need to progressively revise accounting and management information systems;
- Chinese parties not tending to abide by despatch agreements;
- procedures of customs clearance being complicated and often delayed, and as a result tending to increase storage costs;
- insufficient road and rail links between ports and their hinterlands; and
- the port system needing to adjust to the change from a labour intensive to a capital intensive industry.

Current problems in container lines between Korea and Far East Russia[8]

The East Sea Economic Zone covers the Northeast coastal area of the Korean peninsular, Far Eastern Russia and the West coast of Japan. With the disintegration of the USSR and the successful nuclear talks between North Korea and USA, economic co-operation is likely to accelerate in the area, including the so-called Golden Triangle, i.e. Tumen River Development Project. This project was initiated by the East-West Centre in Hawaii in 1990. Its development programmes and plans are still being formulated by successive meetings between the UNDP and seven countries; North and South Korea, USA, China, Japan, Russia, and Mongolia. The project covers Hunchun of Jilin in China, Sun-bong and Rajin of North Korea, and Hassan of Far East Russia. From 1991, North Korea began to participate actively in the project and suggested a project developing a free economic zone covering Chong-jin, Ra-jin and Sun-bong.

Two-thirds of Russian territory lies within Far East Asia and, as a result of the development of Siberia and the building of the TSR, the influence of the Russian Federation in the Asian Pacific economy is bound to grow. In the long run, Siberian gas, oil and timber are likely to be important factors in the region's economic dynamism. Here, the benefits of growing trade, enhanced access to capital and advanced technology, and the use of expanded international economic ties are all expected. The motivation for more rapid and comprehensive economic development of the Russian Far East, and its closer integration into the East Sea Economic Zone, was coupled with the Vladivostok Declaration by Gorbachev that Vladivostok itself might become 'a major international centre ..... a seat of trade and culture ..... an open window to the East'.[9]

The impact of the above economic and political developments on foreign trade can easily be identified through various statistical tables published over the last few years. During the period 1987-91, Korean foreign trade with Russia grew from US \$150.5 million to US \$1,202.4 million. As road and rail transportation systems are not available between North and South Korea at the moment, due to political problems, all trade goods in the trading area of Korea/Japan/China/Russia must be carried by sea. Major cargoes transported in the area consist of iron and steel, coal, crude oil, timber, cement, second-hand cars and manufactured goods.

Under such circumstances, a direct shipping line between Korea and Russia was established in July 1991. The line provides a joint service, i.e. two calls per week between the ports of Pusan and Vostochny. This service was formed by both the Korean party; Korea-Soviet Shipping Company Limited (KSSC), which consists of Hyundai Merchant Marine Company Limited and Chun Kyung Shipping Company Limited, and the Russian party; Far-Eastern Shipping Company (FESCO) in Vladivostok.

Each party provides one ship to the joint service. MV Trade Luck (430 teu) was employed by the Korean party from July 1991 until present. FESCO put MV Kapitan Gnezdilov (320 teu) into service from the starting date until March 1992, and replaced her with MV Alexsander Tvardovsky (400 teu) from April 1992. Each party is responsible for operating its own ship at its own expense; they pay all operating expenses of the ship, including wages, fuel, repairs, consumable stores, cargo handling and port charges. In other words, two fully-manned and provisioned ships are employed to ensure two calls weekly at each port in a joint service.   The agents appointed by FESCO and KSSC, Transorient Shipping Company Limited in Seoul, and Asia Merchant Marine Company Limited in Pusan, perform all the normal shipping agent services to the two ships and their masters.

Table 7.10
Container cargo volume in Pusan/Vostochny line

	1991			1992			1993		
	Direct	TSR	Total	Direct	TSR	Total	Direct	TSR	Total
E.bound	5.8	4.0	9.8	3,6	4.6	8.2	8.46	5.7	14.2
W.bound	11.27	5.53	16.8	14.8	6.4	21.3	16.98	6.7	23,7
Total	17.07	9.53	26.6	18.4	11.0	29.5	25.45	12.45	37.9

(unit:'000 teu)

Source: Korea-Soviet Shipping Company Limited (1994).

As can be seen from table 7.10, container cargo volume has increased steadily over the last three years, although there was a sharp decrease of volume from the middle of 1992 due to the temporary disruption of loan agreements between Korea and Russia. However, thanks to the aid policy of the USA for the Commonwealth of Independent States (CIS), transshipment cargo volume through the Sea-Land

Service began to increase from October 1992. It is expected that this trans-shipment trade will keep to a certain level for the time being and support the increasing container cargo volume between the ports of Pusan and Vostochny with direct trade between Korea and far east Russia. While major commodities of the Korean export trade consist of T.V.s, refrigerators, shoes and clothes, Korean import commodities mainly consist of cotton, copper, foodstuffs and fertiliser, amongst others.

A peculiar point can be drawn from Table 7.10 in that an imbalance in container traffic between western and eastern directions arose. That is to say that 14,193 teu were handled east-bound over the last three years, which constitutes only 37.4 per cent of the total transported containers.

Current problems in the container shipping line

Low reliability of service Many liner customers consider some or all of the following aspects of the service as important as ocean freight: frequency of sailings, speed of transit, reliability of service, quality of service and space availability. For these reasons, although customers of the liner service are likely to take a keen interest in ocean freight, this is a situation where the shipper and the liner company are bound to recognise the non-price competitive factors above. In particular, some customers are likely to value the reliability of the service in terms of the adherence to published sailing dates and confidence that the service will continue in depressions as well as in booms.

One of the current problems apparent from the joint shipping line between Pusan and Vostochny was that the reliability of the service was very low during the period between the beginning of December and the end of February, due to the occurrence of high seas near the Port of Vostochny. As a result, ship departure times from the port were often delayed thus causing a delay to the call in the Port of Pusan.

Poor management capacity Within the prerequisites for good service quality we can include safe transit for container cargo, freedom from handling damage and pilferage, prompt and accurate administration, and the provision of a range of through transport services. All operations at the complex are computer controlled. Field surveys and interviews indicated that MV Kapitan Gnezdilov, put into service from July 1991, did not prepare documents in advance for customs cargo clearance before entering the Port of Pusan. The local agent, Asia Merchant Marine Company Limited, therefore collected all information directly from the Russian ship upon calling in at the Port of Pusan and processed it. This caused a considerable time delay for the ship. In response to this kind of situation KSSC installed INMARSAT on her in order to avoid such delays but she was replaced with MV Aleksander Tvardovsky (400 teu) from April 1992.

Poor port management information system and the lack of a cargo tracking system An automated management information system is designed to control the transhipment of ISO containers and allows for advanced planning of cargo operations before the arrival of the shipment at the port. Additionally, it can be utilised to prepare cargo papers, charge payments for the transhipment and storage of cargoes and provide all necessary information on the transportation process. Such a system is not yet completely in operation at the Port of Vostochny. It is felt that uncomputerised services and lack of cargo tracking systems are, in addition to the length of transit time, the main reasons for the reduction in Trans-Siberian Rail cargoes, against the general trend of growth in cargo volumes on Far East Europe trade routes.

Highly bureaucratic system at Port of Vostochny Cargo customs clearance has become a very complicated procedure. This has been due to the existence of five major factors, which include: strict governmental control of exports and imports; the licensing of exports and imports; financial considerations for revenue purposes embracing hard currency; statistical requirements for the export and import trades; and finally, the documentation requirements for all exports and imports arising out of the other four factors. It would appear that these factors are commonplace in Russia.

Field surveys and interviews revealed that it necessitated approximately one week to transfer containers from a container ship to a train ready to depart for the TSR network. Thus, coupled with the extraordinary delay experienced in cargo handling in Vostochny, the main advantage of utilising the TSR is somewhat diminished.[10]

Substandard work attitude of Russian crews After a bewildering change at a political level, the countries of the CIS are now adjusting to fundamental economic reforms. Since 2 January 1992, the Russian government, newly committed to capitalism's values and methods, has set both Russia and the other former republics on course for integration into the world market. Free prices, privatisation and rouble convertibility are no longer just concepts on the lips of politicians, they are quickly becoming reality.

It would seem however, that Russian crews are generally less oriented towards capitalism and have no cost and time consciousness in operating ships, despite the fact that time and cost are very important factors in liner shipping. Motivation is often a problem; the interviewees remarked that crews are often much more interested in personal trading than in their own ship-board role. In addition, frequent crew changes on Russian vessels have caused personnel to lose the opportunity to accumulate know-how in both handling container cargoes and in operating ships on the Pusan/Vostochny liner route.[11]

Difficulties in the collection of empty containers As shown in Table 7.10, 23,704 teu were handled outbound compared with 14,193 teu inbound, from 1991 to

126

1993. Container transportation eastward is highly limited in the TSR and the proportion of containers carried westward to those carried eastward is approximately 2:1. As a result of the eastbound-westbound traffic imbalance, serious problems arise in organising empty containers for export from Korea. Leaving aside the time lag inherent in the collection of empty containers, the rate of collection here is especially low when compared to other liner routes.

Proposals for solving the problems

Some of the current problems facing the joint shipping line between Korea and Russia have been illustrated above. Some ideas and proposals for solving them are suggested as follows:

Establishment of a port management information system and cargo tracking system at Port of Vostochny To increase the quality of service and reduce vessel time in port, it is necessary to establish a port management information system at the Port of Vostochny. This system must be designed to track cargo and also provide customers with cargo status and other relevant information. It should be also linked to the TSR system, which is directly related to the joint shipping line. Technical assistance and financial support from the Korean side, with the co-operation of other shippers, can be provided for this system.

Increase the strength of the transshipment function As one way to secure considerable container cargo volume in the joint shipping line, the Port of Pusan needs to strengthen the function of transshipment. The transshipment of container cargo from the Sea-Land service and from Chinese trade both suggest implications for the direction of development for joint shipping lines.

Advance of ability of ship management The Korean party must be active in the education of the Russian party, including crew training, and provide an insight into advanced management techniques in order to increase efficiency in ship operations and to maintain a good level of service reliability. To allow Russian crews to acquire know-how on ship operations and business practices in capitalistic conditions, the Korean party must persuade the Russian party to change crews less frequently than at present. The development of ship management know-how will play a crucial role in reducing the idle time of ship operations both at sea and in port.

Introduction of an incentive system The introduction of a reward and penalty system into the joint service may be beneficial in order to enforce each party to adhere to the published time schedules and prescribed service levels, as agreed between the two parties. This would obviously provide mutual benefits to both participants.

Port development and the modernisation of cargo handling equipment The main purpose of the Port of Vostochny is to handle import-export transit cargo in the Far East. Cargo turnover of the port increased rapidly in spurts between 1985 and 1989 and increased again after 1993, after a temporary decrease from 1989 to 1992. In such circumstances, it is necessary to construct special new container berths to secure the on-dock container yard and to modernise container cargo handling equipment, in order to meet the increase of container cargo volumes.

Establishment of an efficient intermodal transportation system As mentioned above, it required approximately one week to tranship a container, from a vessel alongside, at the Port of Vostochny to a railcar at the starting point of the TSR; the rail station at Vostochny-Nakhodka. This is one of the main reasons for the deterioration of the inherent spatial advantages of the TSR. It is necessary to establish an efficient intermodal transportation system in order to solve the problem.

Conclusion: Some considerations for the development of maritime transport

Some observations relating to sea transport between China and Korea, and between Far East Russia and Korea in this chapter, illustrate that shipping and port services contribute to the growth of structural interdependencies which are imperative for regional and international economic co-operation. Furthermore, shipping as a component of an intermodal transportation system has played a particularly critical role in Far East Asia as well as in the development of transpacific trade; and finally, that numerous bottlenecks exist in both port and shipping sectors.

Considering the fact that sea transport plays such a key role in supporting the development of efficient regional, national and international intermodal trans-portation systems, solutions must be found to remove bottlenecks in ports and shipping. First of all, it is essential to identify and implement administrative and policy measures to create adequate competition and remove inefficient procedures via pressures of the market.

Five directions for the general improvement of the port sector can be identified when considering the Korea-China and Korea-Far East Russia shipping routes. Firstly, because the role of transport infrastructure changes over time, physical investment in infrastructure is essential and this requires a high proportion of national investment. Secondly, the efficiency of port operations must be increased by greater use of containers, palletisation and the use of modern bulk cargo handling methods. Thirdly, in addition to improving port facilities and intermodal transport systems, all countries concerned in the three economic zones in Far East Asia must continue to invest in road, rail and inland waterway networks linking ports to their hinterlands. Fourthly, greater emphasis must be placed on soft investments such as facilities management and the integration of various forms of transport into a total logistics system. Fifthly, because pressure on ports is often even tougher, as in many cases they themselves face competition, ports must be able to offer their clients, that is the shipowners and forwarders, the equipment and organisational characteristics which best meet their needs.

In the shipping sector, it again appears to be necessary to highlight the worsening of relations between shippers and maritime transporters. This is basically caused by the respective economic and commercial situations confronting each of these interested parties, i.e.:

- Shippers, who have become more and more demanding in terms of costs and quality of service. The liberalisation of world markets has caused an increase in the competition which they face, i.e. shippers and transporters.

- Shipping companies, whose activity is not sufficiently profitable on a global level, due to the pressure on freight rates as well as port congestion, and who are seeking to reduce costs which they bear, including port costs.[12]

Co-ordination and co-operation within shipping and port sectors in the Yellow Sea and East Sea economic zone and, of course, other East Asian countries, will contribute to the promotion and development of shipping trade routes and will enhance the level of understanding amongst them. This in turn, of course, will aid the development of their economies as a whole.

The greatest challenges to the future of transportation services in East Asia are those relating to the development and co-ordination of infrastructure suited to the needs of the ever-increasing intra-regional trade. Without appropriate inter-governmental co-operation and policy measures for transport infrastructure, severe bottlenecks will co-exist with localised under-investment or over-investment in ports and shipping.

In the near future, discussions on the following are required among countries in the Yellow Sea and East Sea economic areas, in order to promote and develop maritime transport and to meet the demands of a constantly changing environment.[13]

- Activation of the functions of Port State Control (PSC) for preventing oil pollution.
- Establishment of the Trans-Korean Railroad (TKR) between North and South Korea, and its link to TCR and TSR when Korea is reunified.
- Promotion of an intermodal transportation system with TSR, TCR and TKR.
- Establishment of a co-exchangeable system of Electronic Data Interchange (EDI).
- Establishment of a Search and Rescue (SAR) system.

129

- Development of cruise routes and the promotion of a cruise industry with water-jet vessels.
- Removal of inefficiency in port operations and management.
- Deregulation of discriminatory policies in shipping and ports.
- Development of exchange and education programmes of specialists and technicians in port and shipping sectors.

Notes and references

1   Kim, J. H. (1994), 'Increasing Intra-Asian Trade and Liner Shipping Networks: the structure and dynamics of change', Proceedings of KMI/IAME Joint Conference in Seoul, Korea, 8-10 June.

2   Robinson, R. (1994), 'Regional Container Shipping Networks; the structure and dynamics of change', Proceedings of KMI/IAME Joint Conference in Seoul, Korea, 8-10 June.

3   Brooks, J. F. (1994), 'The People's Republic of China: the context of foreign capital investment in the port sector', Proceedings of KMI/IAME joint conference in Seoul, Korea, 8-10 June.

4   A survey was carried out by Korea Shippers' Association in 1993, sampling 600 import/export companies in Korea. The questionnaires and interviews to major shipping companies involved in Korea/China routes were made by the authors in 1994. See Lee, T-W. and Cho, S-H. (1994), 'Promotion and Development of Sea Trade Routes between Korea and China', The 4th Conference of the Society for East Asian Studies in Tianjin, China, 25-26 July.

5   See Lee, T-W. (1990), 'Korean Shipping Policy: The Role of Government', *Marine Policy*, Vol. 14, No. 5, pp. 421-437.

6   Recently a Hong Kong based charterer has warned that China risks distorting world shipping markets unless she acts to relieve congestion at her ports. During the first half of 1993, charter rates for ships carrying cargoes related to the steel industry and raw materials increased sharply, mainly because of the surge in imports by China of steel-related commodities. Waiting times of ships for unloading steel at ports such as Huangpu, Xingang and Haikou increased to 30 days from only three or four. Likewise, vessels unloading iron ore at Dalian and Qingdao had to wait up to 15 days to clear port. *Asian Shipping*, May 1994, p. 3.

7   UNCTAD (1976), *Port Congestion*, United Nations, TD/B/C.4/152. On the discussion of the shipper's cost, see Jansson, J. O. and Shneerson, D. (1987), *Liner Shipping Economics*, Chapter 7, Chapman & Hall, London.

8   Lee, T-W. (1994), 'Current problems in transportation activities of joint Korean-Far Eastern Shipping Line and some proposals for solving them', *Journal of Social Science Study*, Vol. 1, Korea Maritime University.

9   *Far Eastern Economic Review*, 11 September 1986.

10 Levikov, G. A. (1991), 'Trans-Siberian Container System: some problems, ways of solution', in *Current Issues in Maritime Economics*, p. 2, International Conference at the Erasmus University, Rotterdam, 20-22 June.

11 The operational needs of a container line are assessed on an assumed number of voyages and cargo operations in a given period. The support services activities are based on experience and observations, being largely of a routine nature. Downard, J. H. (1984), *Managing Ships*, p. 120, Fairplay Publications, London.

12 For example, recognising the above worsening situation and based on the agreement of shipping conference made between Korean and Chinese governments in Seoul in July 1994, it was stressed that China must open her shipping market more to Korea and thus allow Korean shipping companies to carry out their own shipping agent service, cargo booking business, etc., within China and that Korea must allow mother container vessels of COSCO to call in at the Port of Pusan.

13 Some of these have already been suggested to the author at 'The Forum on the Future of Coastal Area of the Straits between Korea and Japan', held in Pusan on 21 October 1994.

8 The emergence of private shipping companies in Far East Russia and their impact on Korean shortsea shipping

Introduction

The liquidation of three Korean shortsea shipping companies, engaged mainly in the Korea, China and Japan trading area, within the first half of 1992, disturbed Korean shipping interests to such an extent that questions were asked as to how it could possibly have happened. There are many different reasons for the failure of shipping businesses but they may be categorised simply as either internal or external factors. It would seem that most shipowners tend to blame failures on external factors such as a lack of government subsidies, protectionism within their competing countries, an increase in shipping costs or excessive tonnage on certain routes. Korean shipowners were no different. We can observe many similar examples in foreign countries from surveys of their literature, however, the Koreans added a factor which has never been considered prior to 1988 in that country; the dumping freight rates of Russian and disguised ships. In Korea the term 'disguised ship' is commonly used to describe the flags of such countries as Panama, Liberia and Honduras, whose laws allow ships owned by Korean nationals, shipping companies or shipping agents to fly these flags in the Korea/Japan/China/Russia trading area.

Many Korean shipowners maintained that such ships disturbed a stable and protected shipping market in Korea and played a major role in their resulting business failures. It was felt that the validity of this argument should be tested by a field survey and by the provision of reliable evidence. It is difficult to make a precise assessment of the impact of Russian and disguised ships on the Korean shipping market since firstly it is impossible to acquire a comprehensive set of statistics relating to each line. Secondly, it would seem that the argument which Korean shipowners made was not open to the general public for inspection and, in addition, was not based on reliable data. Consequently, we are forced to rely almost entirely on national and international interviews, mostly contemporary, to acquire sources for information about the operation of such ships.

The author held interviews between April and July 1992 with the following organisations:

- Far Eastern Shipping Company in Vladivostok
- Amur River Shipping Company in Khabarovsk
- Primorsk Shipping Company in Nakhodka
- Lena River Shipping Company in Yakutsk
- Arctic Shipping Company in Tiksi
- Department of Merchant Marine under the Ministry of Transportation of the Russian Federation in Moscow
- Seven private shipping companies in the region of Primorsk, including Vladivostok, Nakhodka, and Khabarovsk
- Japan Maritime Research Institute in Tokyo
- United Orient Shipping and Agency Company Limited in Tokyo
- Four shortsea shipping companies and three shipping agents in Korea

Much of the information acquired by interviews consists of very fragmentary evidence and, except in a few cases, it was virtually impossible to construct a reasonably reliable series of data which could be used to test the argument posed by the Korean shipowners. Nevertheless, despite the unsystematic nature of the data, it is possible to make one or two observations, although the reader should be warned against placing too much reliance upon them. Although the primary purpose of this chapter is to test the argument by using the information and data acquired by interviews, there is a secondary objective, namely to examine the implications for Korean shipping policy as a whole, within the context of changing circumstances.

Economic co-operation in Northeast China, Russian Asia, and North and South Korea

After the disintegration of the USSR, economic co-operation tends to have been strengthened in Far East Asia and in its cross border transactions in the so-called 'Golden Triangle'. The importance of the Russian Federation in the Asian Pacific economy was outlined in the previous chapter. In 1991 an organisation dedicated to the exchange of human and physical resources between the cities of Pusan and Vladivostok was established and named the Pusan-Vladivostok Friendship Association. Its members consist of mayors, businessmen, politician and scholars from both cities, for example, members of the National Assembly of Korea, City Congressmen and key figures from the Pusan Commerce and Industry Chamber. Following this progress, on the 30 June 1992, the city of Pusan, one of the largest container ports in Asia, signed a sister-city agreement with the city of Vladivostok[1] which was changed from a military port to a commercial one in January 1992 and is an open window to the Pacific for the Russians. There is little doubt that these movements will contribute to the promotion and acceleration of economic co-operation. As outlined in the previous chapter, in the long run Siberian primary products are likely to be important factors in the region's economic dynamism.

The progress made in talks and the restoration of full diplomatic relations between China and Russia recently created a relaxation of tensions along their borders, with a resulting increase in trade, tourism and cultural exchanges. More importantly, China is eager to establish a special free trade zone within the area of Northeast China with the co-operation of Korea and Japan, and has been active in the implementation of that plan.

Meanwhile, there are some signs that might signal the possible opening up of North Korea. First, North Korea appears to be in the middle of a severe foreign exchange crises as well as crisis's of rationality, legitimisation, and motivation. Second, North Korea seems to be under pressure from its allies, mainly China and Russia, to open its society and to improve its economic performance. Third, relations between North and South Korea have improved tremendously in recent years even though major political differences remain. Recently, presenting its own development plan in co-operation with UNDP, North Korea declared that it would give an opportunity to invest within the framework of the Golden Triangle to South Korea. Moreover, South Korea is also promoting its own economy which has been depressed since 1990 and ensuring its own survival by becoming an indispensable economic partner of its neighbouring countries. South Korea believes that it is very much in Korea's interest, in both the short and the long term, to promote regional economic co-operation and to secure political stability.

The impact of the above economic and political developments on foreign trade can easily be identified through published statistical tables. In the period 1985-1989, Korean foreign trade with China grew from US $1,161 million to US $3,143 million, i.e. an increase at an annual rate of 28.3 per cent. In the same period, the value of Korea's trade with Russia grew six fold, i.e. from US $102 million to US $600 million at an annual rate of 55.7 per cent. The value of trade between North and South Korea has increased from US $22 million in 1989 to US $25 million in 1990. Although its size is small and most of it consisted of South Korea's import goods, this is a remarkable event when we consider that no direct and indirect trade was apparently transacted before. Unfortunately, it was not possible to acquire consistent data concerned with the volume of seaborne trade in Korea. In the case of quantum data of principal cargoes being unavailable, the data of their value as an alternative can be used to estimate their quantity indirectly.

Employment of shipping is mainly dependent upon the volume and pattern of seaborne trade. The size of shipping tonnage is therefore, ultimately governed by the volume of seaborne trade, the distances over which it is transported and the efficiency of seaports. The scope for employment of tramp shipping and its growth are dependent upon the volume of bulk cargoes in import and export trades of a country apart from international cross trades in which it can participate. Since road and rail transportation links are not currently available between North and South Korea, all Korean trade goods in the trading area of Korea, Japan, China and Russia must be carried by sea. The major bulk cargoes transported in the area consist of iron and steel, coal, crude oil, timber, and cement.

Creation of private shipping companies in Russian Asia and their impacts on Korean shortsea shipping

When focusing attention on the arguments posed by some Korean shipowners, centering on Russian as well as disguised ships, it is worthwhile to discuss how they have entered and made inroads into the Korean shipping market. Furthermore, consideration should be given to their competitive factors in comparison to those of the Korean fleet. As a preparatory stage to this, it is necessary to note that regardless of their size and business performance, more than ten private shipping companies were established in the Russian Asia area between 1990 and 1992.   These have centred in Vladivostok, Khabarovsk, Nakhodka, and Yuzhno-Sakhalinsk with the most notable ones being located in Vladivostok and Khabarovsk.[2] (For an overview of the restructuring of the FSU merchant marine compare Appendices 8.1 and 8.2)[3]

For Russia, where sufficient ship finance cannot be raised at home and capital in hard currency is scarce, the investment barrier is one of the most serious obstacles to the development of a private shipping company. Moreover, in Russia, finance for the purchase of second-hand ships is even more difficult to obtain from abroad and there was no original accumulation of capital in the private shipping sector.[4] However, it should be noted that a peculiar mechanism was generated in Russian Asia as illustrated in Figure 8.1.

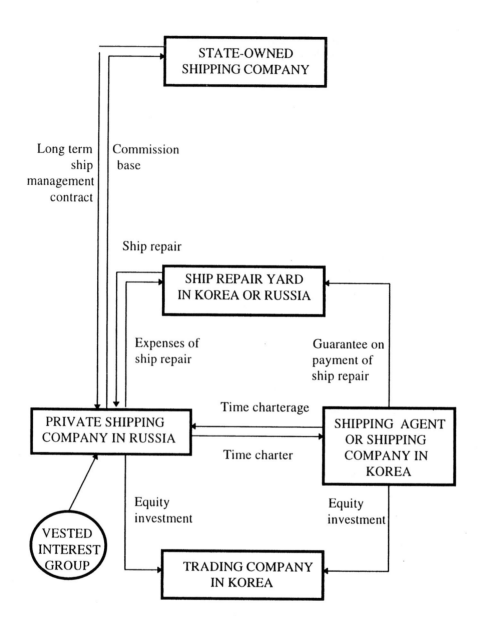

Source: depicted by the author.

Figure 8.1 **Joint ventures and joint operations in shipping between Korea and Russia**

Figure 8.1 shows the parties as they stand in legal and financial relationships to each other in a typical mechanism of ship acquisition. Its events may be described as follows:

(1) The long term management of ships, in which a State-owned shipping company gives a title to a private shipping company in exchange for the coverage of maintenance and repair costs Owing to the deteriorated position of the economy in Russia, most State-owned shipping companies in Russian Asia had a sizeable overcapacity of merchant ships. In addition to this, they have periodically idle tonnage during winter months. As a result, they could not generate enough earnings to even maintain and repair their retained tonnage, hence, some vessels are committed to private shipping companies to cover their maintenance and repair costs.

(2) The private Russian shipping company charters the ship to a foreign shipping company or agent under the conditions of a time charter with very low charterage In a time charter, a fully-manned and provisioned ship is hired by the shipowner to the charterer for a fixed period at agreed rates per dead-weight ton. In the customary time charter provisions, the shipowner pays the insurance premium, crew wages, cost of stores and repairs, but not fuel costs. The charterer pays fuel, port charges, some crew overtime and loading and unloading expenses. However, it was confirmed by the field survey that even fuel costs were on the Russian shipowner's account in some chartering contracts with Korean partners. In this case, 48 hours are exempted from the off-hire clause for him. This arrangement may be caused by the relatively cheaper bunker costs in Russia compared to Korea.

(3) When an old ship is in need of repair in a Russian or foreign shipyard to reactivate her, repair costs were sometimes covered by loans secured by the time charters between Russian and foreign parties.

(4) The accumulation of capital by net revenue after operating and other costs were deducted from time charterage, which provides a major source of finance for the purchase the ships from the State-owned shipping company A simple calculation indicated that a Russian shipowner could purchase a 15 years old river/sea type bulk cargo vessel of 4,000 dwt. within two years, given the present contract conditions made between the Russian and Korean partners.

(5) The execution of maintenance and repair by the private shipping company, which promises to keep the ship at a certain level, and/or a commission charge is paid to the State-owned shipping company as a type of dividend when the private shipping company made net profits through the operation of the ship It was found that although it made a considerable net income through this mechanism, so far private shipping companies have never paid part of their profits to the

State-owned shipping company. They normally open bank accounts in third countries with the help of the charterer and make their net income nearly zero. This is achieved through internal transfer pricing procedures or the manipulation of its financial statements with respect, for example, to accounts of maintenance and repair expenditure, agents charges and crew's provisions.

It was also confirmed by the field survey, that some private shipping companies imported consumer and industrial goods from foreign countries with the capital saved in third country accounts and made substantial commercial profits. They were mainly carried by a ship chartered under the mechanism, which was supplied with bunkers on the Russian shipowner's account, as mentioned in (2). This means that the private shipping company first accumulates capital through shipping business and then, in turn, changes the shipping capital into commercial capital and speeds up it's turnover rate.

(6) The execution of the time charter party by a foreign shipping company or agent as the charterer, whereby the charterer promises to make periodic time charter payments According to surveys made in 1992, under this general mechanism, with some differences on an individual case basis, the Russian fleet totalled 21 vessels of 73,500 dwt. (an average size of 3,500 dwt.). For our reference, it is interesting to note that numbers of Russian ships calling at Port of Pusan are sharply increasing. (See Appendix 8.3.)

Some implications can be drawn from the mechanism of ship acquisition described above. Above all, a Korean charterer can employ a Russian manned ship without any trouble caused by crew nationality in the trading area of China and North Korea, unlike a Korean national flagged ship. Moreover, a Korean shipping company or agent could enjoy very low time charterage, compared to a competitor, whereby, for half of the normal time charterage in the Korean market a ship can be chartered from a Russian partner under this mechanism.

This major difference in time charterage handed competitive power to the Korean charterer rather than Korean national shipowners and thus, for the initial period, the charterer was able to make a profit through this mechanism. However, owing to an economic depression, which included a contraction of construction activity in Korea since 1990, the volume of seaborne trade declined considerably in such trades as cement between China and Korea, and timber between Korea and Russia, for example. As a result, it is reported that there is a sizeable overcapacity of bulk cargo ships and trade growth is unlikely to be vigorous enough to absorb the surplus within two years in Korea. Cheap time charterages in themselves do not guarantee success from the charterer's point of view as profits can be made only when the freight rate is higher than time charter hire base.

Meanwhile, the Pacific Ocean Transportation Conference (POTC), was established in 1990 and consisted of five State-owned shipping companies, i.e. Arctic Shipping Company, Far Eastern Shipping Company, Sakhalin Shipping Company, Kamchatka Shipping Company, and the Primorsk Shipping Company.

This organisation aims to co-operate both in the promotion of their shipping business and to remove unfair transactions and discriminatory practices imposed on their ships by other organisations in Russia as well as abroad. A priority of the POTC concerned the practice of dumping time charterage. For example, regulatory procedures on dumping time charterage by private shipping companies were included in the main agenda of the 14th Conference, held in Vladivostok. A key member of POTC said that

> ... many data of some concrete cases of dumping time charterage were collected with reliable evidence by a special committee, and we will urge the State-owned shipping companies concerned with this matter to restitute their ships from the private shipping companies, otherwise we will impose various powerful restrictions on them.

The four suggested methods to restrict them are (1) to prevent the ships concerned from using Russian ports, (2) to stop them bunkering in Russian territory, (3) to prohibit them from using repair yards in Russia, and (4) to reject their request for certificates of Russian ship classification. It is unlikely however, that these measures are workable in reality. The reason for this is that the ships can be not only registered in open registry countries but also repaired in third countries with the help of their charterers or agents. In addition, since prices of bunker are sharply increasing in Russia, much of the advantage gained by utilising Russian facilities is diminishing.

Meanwhile, thanks to the widespread availability of information on the river/sea chartering market in question, the State-owned shipping company which had previously delivered their vessels to private shipping companies, began to find their own chartering partners. It made profits in a similar way to the mechanism presented in Figure 8.1, in a trading area with an increasing demand for such vessels at low charterage. Time charterage therefore, has begun to increase relatively in recent years and amounted to two-thirds of its normal level in the Korean shipping market.

It can be concluded then, that Russian ships have had a decreasing impact on the Korean shortsea shipping market. This is partly because both their tonnage and the volume carried by them are small enough to be disregarded when compared to those of Korean national ships and partly because the discrepancy in the time charterage between the two countries is rapidly narrowing.

The impact of disguised ships on the Korean shipping market

Before the impacts of disguised ships on the Korean shortsea shipping market are discussed, it is worthwhile to investigate why such ships have appeared. The following factors are of prime concern for Korea's shortsea shipping interests.[5]

First, Korea's shortsea shipping market is protected and severely regulated by the government. It is not easy, even for a Korean national, to freely enter the market. Those who wish to initiate a shortsea shipping company should purchase more than one existing ship with a license for shortsea business. Thus, the value of the ship is higher in absolute terms than its market value because it includes the price of goodwill operating license. The government fixes the number of licensed ships by ship type at a certain period. Therefore, when a shipowner meets a large cargo owner with the contract of affreightment (COA) and wants to carry cargoes with his own vessel, he can utilise one of three alternatives to secure shipping tonnage: (1) time charter, (2) additional purchase of a proper sized vessel with a license, and (3) buy any vessel with a license, when a proper vessel with a license is not found, and substitute it with a proper sized ship. In the third case, the shipowner has to buy two ships, the license for shortsea business is taken from the former and is transferred to the latter, thus the value of the former sharply declines to scrap price. It is allowable to transfer a ship license to a substitute ship on a one to one basis, regardless of the size of the substitute shipping tonnage.

When there is insufficient capital to purchase a ship with a license and/or a ship substitutor, a shipowner is forced to rely on either a time chartered vessel or a disguised ship to fulfil any long term COA. If the shipowner is not satisfied with the charterage of the former, then probably the latter will be considered as an alternative. In such circumstances an old vessel at a lower price than a ship with the license can be bought and registered in Panama, Liberia or Honduras for example, whose laws allow ships owned by him to fly these flags.[6] That is to say, a disguised ship is created. As far as shipping costs and the flexibility of shipping management are concerned, it enables the owner to compete with a time charterer or Korean national shipowner.

Second, the competitive power of Korean flagged merchant ships has deteriorated rapidly owing to the sharp increase of crew wages and a lack of seafaring labour. When coupled with the first reason above, the emergence of disguised ships, which can benefit from lower crew costs and fewer regulations than Korean national ones, was accelerated.

Third, disguised ships could ply freely to and from China or North Korea without any obstacles caused by flag, unlike the Korean flagged ships.

Fourth, the financial condition of shortsea shipping companies has deteriorated and their know-how in business management is relatively both low and un-systematic.

Fifth, the Korean shortsea market is characterised by a plethora of smaller sized shipping companies, none of which individually are in a position to significantly influence the market. Both fleet size and the size of management power within these companies, are on a predominantly small scale.

Sixth, the reorganisation programme for the Korean shipping industry launched in 1983 has led the government to impose detailed regulations on shipping management and in turn, has resulted in the weakening of the capacity or ability of shipping companies to rapidly and flexibly respond to changing circumstances.

A disguised ship can, therefore, be used not only for the avoidance of government regulations but also for saving shipping costs. However, it seems that many disguised ships owned by Korean shipowners are sub-standard ones on the basis of IMO regulations. The use of these vessels must be controlled by the port state control system.

It was reported by one organisation that approximately 80 disguised ships were employed in the Korean shortsea shipping market in April 1992. At this point, it is difficult to scientifically and systematically quantify their impact on the Korean shortsea shipping market. However, it is certain that they played a leading role firstly, in highlighting the advantages of opening Korean ship registration; secondly, in triggering discussions on its possibility and the economic consequences thereof; and finally, in disturbing, to some extent, the Korean shortsea shipping market.

Conclusion

This chapter tried to evaluate the argument that Russian and disguised ships played a major role in disturbing the Korean shipping market. Although the test was not satisfactorily carried out owing to the unsystematic data and the fragmentary information acquired by interviews, it is hoped that some useful observations have been made. These observations are not only on the mechanism of the emergence of private shipping companies in Russian Asia and their management behaviour, but also on the causes of the creation of disguised ships in Korea and their implications for Korean shipping policy.

It would appear that since the First Five Year Economic Development Plan in 1962, the government has paid much greater attention to the ocean-going sector of Korean shipping policy rather than to the shortsea shipping sector, until recent years. In other words, in spite of its importance, Korean shortsea shipping has attracted relatively little attention from the government and maritime researchers. As discussed earlier in this chapter, economic and political co-operation between China, Russia and North and South Korea tends to increase seaborne trade volumes and thus causes shortsea shipping to develop between these countries. This obviously means that Korean shortsea shipping has become a more important sector than before.

Under these circumstances it can be argued that Korean shipping policy is now located at a turning point. It is argued here that it should proceed by letting the shipping companies acquire enough competitive power to be able to cope with Russian and disguised ships by, for example, the introduction of a Korean International Ship Register (See Chapter 13). Moreover, the government must make more of an effort to encourage and promote the shortsea shipping sector than before. This should be based on the philosophy of removing any unnecessary intervention which distorts capital market principles and on the recognition of the peculiarities and characteristics of the shipping industry. Ultimately, the government must abolish or deregulate inefficient and unnecessary governmental regulations so that shipping companies can restore vigour and vitality to their self-management.

Notes and references

1   On further information on the port, see Fraser, Jnr., R. J. (1994), 'The Ports of the Russian Far East: A Management Strategy', *Maritime Policy and Management*, Vol. 21, No. 1, pp. 37-44.

2   This was confirmed by the author's field surveys in Russia and Japan.

3   Bergstrand, S. and Doganis, R. (1987), *The Impact of Soviet Shipping*, Allen & Unwin, London.

4   Long, D. M. (1986), *The Soviet Merchant Fleet: Its Growth, Strategy, Strength and Weakness, 1920-1999*, Lloyd's of London Press, London; and The MRC Business Information Group (1990), 'Soviet Shipping 1991', Special Report from the MRC Business Information Group, Oxford.

5   Lee, T-W. (1992), 'Turning Point of Korean Shipping Policy', a paper presented to the International Association of Maritime Economists in Lyons, France, 3 July.

6   Sturmey, S. G. (1962), *British Shipping and World Competition*, The Athlone Press, London.

Appendix 8.1
USSR shipping organisation

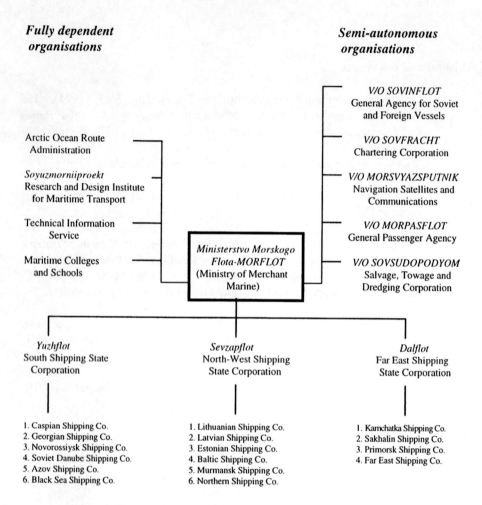

Fully dependent organisations

Semi-autonomous organisations

V/O SOVINFLOT
General Agency for Soviet and Foreign Vessels

V/O SOVFRACHT
Chartering Corporation

Arctic Ocean Route Administration

Soyuzmorniiproekt
Research and Design Institute for Maritime Transport

V/O MORSVYAZSPUTNIK
Navigation Satellites and Communications

Technical Information Service

V/O MORPASFLOT
General Passenger Agency

Maritime Colleges and Schools

Ministerstvo Morskogo Flota-MORFLOT
(Ministry of Merchant Marine)

V/O SOVSUDOPODYOM
Salvage, Towage and Dredging Corporation

Yuzhflot
South Shipping State Corporation

Sevzapflot
North-West Shipping State Corporation

Dalflot
Far East Shipping State Corporation

1. Caspian Shipping Co.
2. Georgian Shipping Co.
3. Novorossiysk Shipping Co.
4. Soviet Danube Shipping Co.
5. Azov Shipping Co.
6. Black Sea Shipping Co.

1. Lithuanian Shipping Co.
2. Latvian Shipping Co.
3. Estonian Shipping Co.
4. Baltic Shipping Co.
5. Murmansk Shipping Co.
6. Northern Shipping Co.

1. Kamchatka Shipping Co.
2. Sakhalin Shipping Co.
3. Primorsk Shipping Co.
4. Far East Shipping Co.

Source: Bergstrand, S. and Doganis, R. (1987), *The Impact of Soviet Shipping*, p. 2, Allen & Unwin, London.

Appendix 8.2
New shipping organisation in Russia

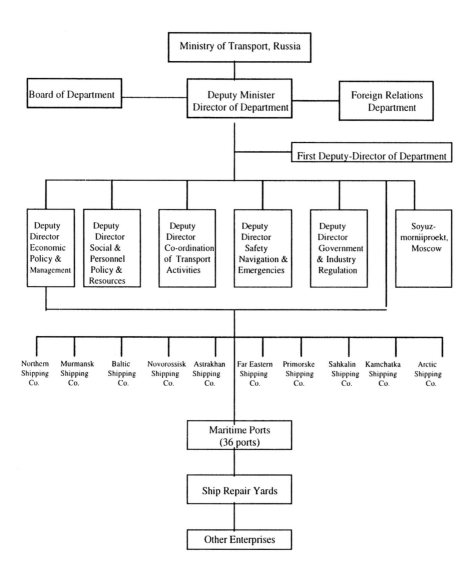

Note: This chart was acquired by the author in Moscow in July 1992 and was translated into English by Mr Vitali Serebriakov of Soyuzmorniiproekt.

Appendix 8.3
Number of Russian ships calling into the Port of Pusan

Year	Number of ships
1989	100
1990	263
1991	657
1992	1,066
1993	1,270
1994	1,660

Source: Korea Maritime and Port Administration (1995).

Appendix 8.4
Total expenses paid by Russian ships and seamen

Item	Amount in Bn. Won	(US $ in Mil.)
Ship agent fee	1.0	(1.3)
Port charge	2.5	(3.2)
Loading and discharging	3.1	(3.9)
Ship repair	15.6	(19.5)
Communications	0.2	(0.3)
General expenses	25.7	(36.1)
Others	0.8	(1.0)
Total in 1992	**48.9**	**(65.3)**
Total in 1994	**100.0**	**(125.0)**

Source: collected by the author.

Appendix 8.5
Russian ship repair in Port of Pusan

Year	No. of ship repair	Repair costs (US $ mil.)
1989	10	101.0
1990	12	8.0
1991	34	22.3
1992	43	19.5
1993*	33	13.2
Total	**132**	**165.0**

*Note: * until April of 1993.*

Source: collected by the author.

9 A challenge to the Far Eastern Shipping Company (FESCO) in the Russian privatisation period

Introduction

The management of sea transport in the former Soviet Union was based on the principles of direct supervision by the Ministry of Merchant Marine, which combined the functions of state control of the industry. A development project for sea transport was prepared under the supervision of the Ministry in Moscow. All purchases of new buildings from shipyards, imported handling equipment, spare parts, automatic operating systems and material supplies, had to be authorised by the Ministry, as had their distribution among the enterprises.[1] The management of the merchant fleet and port operations was also within the scope of the Ministry. All revenues from fleet, ports, factories and other complementary enterprises were transferred to the Ministry.

The disintegration of the Soviet Union into independent countries has caused a considerable disproportion in the distribution and quality of the merchant fleet and transhipment complexes. In addition, the promulgation of the privatisation programme has made shipping companies, sea transport infrastructure and other enterprises administratively and financially more independent than before.

The fundamental objective of the privatisation programme is to create private owners who will facilitate the development of the market economy by increasing the efficiency of former federal, regional and municipally-owned enterprises. The other important objectives of the programme are to contribute to the financial stabilisation of the economy, promote competition, attract foreign investment, and create a safety net and social infrastructure. In general, the State Committee of the Russian Federation for the Management of State Property (Goskomimustchestvo, GKI), a special governmental body set up to manage the privatisation process, is following separate tracks for privatisation, which are dependant on the size and nature of the enterprises concerned.

Most enterprises, other than very small ones such as shops and restaurants, are sold largely through share issues after the companies have been transformed into joint stock companies. The specific requirement with regard to corporatisation is that large enterprises with more than 1,000 employees, or of book value of more

147

than 50 million roubles, are to be transformed into joint stock companies before they can be privatised. For example, the FESCO and the Black Sea Shipping Company (BLASCO) belong to this category of very large enterprises with the above characteristics, and thus have been subject to corporatisation.

The process of privatising FESCO was carried out in compliance with the special industry privatisation programme, and it became a number of joint stock entities in December 1992. In the Russian Federation the company is second only to the Baltic Shipping Company and has a well established fleet with a diversified organisation and service network.[2]

This chapter aims to investigate the current and future situation of FESCO before and after the privatisation process, partly by the analysis and observation of its financial statements, and account for the company's emergence as a key company in the Pacific-Rim region.

The privatisation programme in the Russian Federation

This section provides a brief description and explanation of the programme[3] in order to improve understanding of how shipping companies in the former Soviet Union are being privatised.

The Government of the Russian Federation has begun to establish a programme for the privatisation of federal and municipally-owned enterprises (hereinafter these enterprises are referred to collectively as state enterprises) on the basis of the 'Law of the RSFSR on the Privatisation of State and Municipal enterprises in the RSFSR', 3 July 1991. Privatisation means the transfer of ownership and, thus, the control of these enterprises to citizens, institutions, and other legal entities, both domestic and foreign. The programme does not permit ownership to be transferred to another enterprise or entity of which more than 25 per cent is owned by federal, regional or municipal governments.

Upon corporatisation, workers and managers are entitled to receive various benefits depending on which privatisation option is selected for the enterprise.

The Government devised a model for the corporate charter which each new joint stock company should follow, specifying how the company should be organised and managed. Moreover, it specifies that the Council of Directors of the company should initially include the Director General of the company, the representatives of the appropriate Fund (or Committee)[4], the representatives of the workers' collective and those of the local government. The composition of the Council of Directors can be changed after the stock has passed into private ownership through a vote by the holders of common stock. Council members may then be changed by a majority vote. Depending on the privatisation option chosen, the workers and the Fund (or Committee) may own a large number of stock in the enterprise. Most of the stock held by the workers is likely to be non-voting preferred stock. Workers may sell this stock without restrictions, but it will remain non-voting preferred stock.

The Government has given away a portion of the state's assets to all of its citizens through 'vouchers', also referred to as 'privatisation checks'. The process for distributing these vouchers began 1 October 1992. They entitle their holders to exchange them for stock in state enterprises that are undergoing privatisation. Each citizen received a voucher with a face value of 10,000 roubles. It is anticipated that a minimum of 10 per cent of the stock in each enterprise will be sold exclusively to voucher holders. Other blocks of stock can be purchased with a combination of vouchers and cash. The objective is to sell 35 per cent of the stock in each enterprise with vouchers.

Though vouchers are initially distributed only to Russians, they can be freely resold to anyone, including non-Russians. In some cases, it may be necessary to purchase vouchers on the resale market and use them together with cash to purchase stock in an enterprise. The GKI and the local committees for privatisation positively encourage the development of financial institutions which can assist the general public in purchasing or exchanging vouchers for state enterprises.

The Russian government gave managers and workers the primary responsibility of corporatising and developing a privatisation plan, following guidelines and procedures laid down by the GKI. The privatisation committee of each company, which was subject to mandatory corporatisation, was required to submit this plan to the appropriate committee by 1 October 1992. The managers and workers of each state enterprise had been given important responsibilities in the corporatisation and privatisation processes of their enterprise. In return for this, they received various benefits in addition to the vouchers they received as Russian citizens. They can also choose to become the owners of their enterprise and will be given, or can buy, some stock on preferential terms. Furthermore, they can buy more stock, if they so wish, without limit on the same conditions as other citizens.

In the case of joint stock companies, three privatisation options were set up for managers and workers. The first option is considered to have been accepted by a workers' collective unless the second or third option is chosen by a two-thirds majority vote of the collective. In all three options, 10 per cent of the proceeds of the sale of stock to non-employees will be contributed to the personal privatisation accounts of the employees. The three options are outlined below.

Option 1: Non-employees buy control

Under the first option, the bulk of the stock may be sold to investors other than employees. This option is particularly relevant to foreign investors who can purchase shares through a voucher auction or by competitive tenders.[5] In this case, employees will still retain the right to receive stock representing 25 per cent of the authorised capital of the enterprise without charge. Each employee however, may not receive shares with an authorised value (book value) of more than 20 minimum monthly salaries. These shares will be of non-voting preferred stock with a minimum dividend. There are no special restrictions on employees selling them except for those general restrictions which apply to the sale of all other stock in corporations.

In addition to the above allocation, employees also receive a sum equal to 10 per cent of the proceeds from the sale of the enterprise, deposited in a special privatisation account. This can then be used to purchase 10 per cent of the voting common stock under the following terms:

- 30 per cent discount from the book value;
- payment in instalments, but the first instalment has to be at least 20 per cent;
- down payment of not less than 15 per cent of the book value;
- privatisation vouchers may be used as down payment;
- the total stock offered for purchase to employees on these favourable terms may not exceed the total of six minimum monthly salaries multiplied by the number of employees.

Executive managers of state enterprises are also given the option to buy voting common stock at the book value, and may use vouchers as payment. The total stock bought on these preferential terms by managers may not exceed 5 per cent of the authorised capital value.

Option 2: Employees buy control

Under the second option, employees of an enterprise may choose to buy voting common stock representing 51 per cent of the authorised capital through closed subscription. In this way, they can buy a controlling interest in the state enterprise where they work. A preferential price for stock is set equal to the book value of the stock multiplied by 1.7. This price, which is higher than in Options 1 and 3, reflects the fact that employees can obtain control of the enterprise.

As with the other options, employees may buy more stock without limit, but no preferential terms exist. The balance of the stock will be sold as a block to small investors. A minimum of 10 per cent of the stock is reserved for purchase using only vouchers.

Option 3: Employees enter into a restructuring agreement

This option may only be used by state enterprises with a work force of more than 200 employees and a book value of fixed assets between 1 and 50 million roubles. A group of workers may enter into an agreement with an appropriate Property Fund (or Committee) in order to restructure the enterprises.

One possibility for a foreign investor to join in this option is for them to prepare a restructuring plan. Such a plan requires the approval of the workers' collective and has a term of only one year. It must specify the obligations of the group to restructure the enterprise, including the requirement that its members shall pledge as collateral their own personal assets of an amount of no less than 200 minimum salaries each.

The workers in the restructuring group have an option, to purchase 20 per cent of enterprise shares at the book value. Vouchers cannot be used to purchase this stock. In addition, all workers of the enterprise, including those in the group, have the right to buy another 20 per cent of the stock of the enterprise under the following terms:

- 30 per cent discount from the book value;
- payment in instalments for a period of 3 years;
- down payment of not less than 20 per cent of the book value;
- privatisation vouchers may be used as down payment;
- the total stock purchased by each employee can not exceed 20 minimum monthly salaries.

During the privatisation process the following major shipping companies within the Russian Federation have progressed through the corporatisation stage and onto their respective choice of privatisation scheme, which are listed in Table 9.1.

Table 9.1
Privatisation options chosen by major shipping companies in Russia

Option	Company name
Option 1: Non-employees buy control	Northern Shipping Company Novorossiysk Shipping Company
Option 2: Employees buy control	Arctic Shipping Company Baltic Shipping Company Far Eastern Shipping Company Kamchatka Shipping Company Murmansk Shipping Company Primorsk Shipping Company Sakhalin Shipping Company
Option 3: Employees control in restructuring	None

Source: collected by the author.

As can be seen in Table 9.1, only two Russian shipping companies, the Northern and Novorossiysk, chose Option 1. According to this scheme 25 per cent of stock are preferred, non-voting stock given to workers; 0-10 per cent common stock sold to workers in closed subscription; 0-5 per cent common stock sold to

151

managers in closed subscription; 60-75 per cent common shares available to foreign investors. The remainder of the shipping companies were agreeable to Option 2 under which working staff buy out 51 per cent of the shares of the statutory fund in closed subscription. On average, the state has the right to 20-25 per cent of the total, the rest are sold outside.

Privatisation of individual objects, mainly ocean-going and sea/river-going vessels, has created a number of small private shipping companies. The main bulk of vessels originates from inland waterway, fishing and navy fleets. A recent field survey has shown that more than ten private shipping companies have been established in Vladivostok, Nakhodka and Yuzhno-Sakhalinsk during the period 1991-92, although their business size is generally small.[6]

FESCO - before and after privatisation

The FESCO, like most Russian shipping companies, selected the second option of privatisation in December 1992. After corporatisation, the meeting of FESCO's shareholders voted for the following allotment of shares in September 1993: 51 per cent of stock for FESCO's ownership; 20 per cent for state ownership; and the remaining 29 per cent for voucher auction. It is pertinent to note that in line with the privatisation programme, the appropriate mechanism of state control over state-owned shares has been elaborated.

Table 9.2
FESCO merchant fleet performance (1992-93)

Performance	1992	1993	% change 1992-93
a) Cabotage (tons)	3,180,000	2,439,000	- 23.3
b) Overseas transportation (tons)	8,279,000	7,975,000	- 3.7
c) Total cargo carried (a + b) (tons)	11,459,000	10,414,000	- 9.1
dwt. / day of (c) (tons)	574,311	583,709	+ 1.6
dwt. / day of (b) (tons)	443,882	486,195	+ 9.5
Net currency earnings (US $)	137,110,000	168,072,000	+ 22.6

Source: Soyuzmorniiproekt (1994).

The Department of Marine Transport (DMT),[7] as agreed with the GKI, nominated an authorised representative at FESCO to participate in shareholders' meetings and have the right to vote, based on the number of shares owned by the state.

So far the organisational structure of FESCO after privatisation has remained practically unchanged. The most recent innovation is the establishment of the Board of Directors headed by Victor Miskov, FESCO's ex-top executive. However, it is planned to alter the organisational structure of administration as well as the management system itself. The performance of FESCO's merchant fleet in the period 1992-93 is presented in Table 9.2.

A major problem faced by shipping companies in the CIS is the significant drop in net revenues due to reduced cargo volumes, coupled with increases in the expense of bunkering and repairs abroad. By contrast, the operation of the FESCO fleet in both national and international trade in 1993, earned more than US $168 million in net profit; a 22.6 per cent increase over the same period in 1992, despite the fact that the total volume of cargo carried in 1993 decreased by 9 per cent compared to that in 1992. This is attributable to an increase in the overall efficiency of ship performance at any given service in association with a rise in freight rates in international trade.

The problem of the ageing FESCO fleet and the replenishment plan

Table 9.3 shows dead-weight tonnage (dwt.), average ship age, and the number of ships by type in the FESCO fleet in 1993. The company has 175 vessels totalling approximately 1.8 million dwt., mainly composed of 55 general purpose ships and bulk carriers, together accounting for 43.7 per cent of total tonnage. It is a striking feature that FESCO has no tanker fleet.

Table 9.3 also reveals that the ageing fleet is one of the examples of large scale obsolescence and structural shortcomings which have characterised the difficult conditions under which FESCO operates. The average age of the FESCO fleet is 16.2 years, compared with the Russian average of 18.3 years.[8] Its dry bulk fleet is relatively new with 20.6 per cent being under 10 years, compared with the average 14.4 years of the total world fleet. However, its general-purpose ships are particularly old, over 19 years compared with 16.5 years of the total world fleet,[9] and in effect about 50 per cent of the FESCO fleet is over 16 years old.

With its rapidly ageing fleet FESCO is presently confronted with the problem of finding various ways to replenish tonnage. After the promulgation of 'Mortgage Law', they began to both mortgage their vessels as security for credit, and change Russian registry and flag.

When mortgaging their vessels, they widely use joint ventures based on old ships which should have been long since decommissioned. After repairs or refits at shipyards abroad, at the expense of foreign investors, the ships, as a rule, are registered under a flag of convenience.

Table 9.3
FESCO fleet on 1 December 1993

Type of ship	Number of ships	Dwt. '000 tons	%	Average age
General-purpose ships	55	415.7	23.1	19.7
Container ships	21	223.1	12.4	15.8
Palletised timber carriers	20	224.6	12.5	13.7
Timber carriers	12	59.0	3.2	25.2
Bulk carriers	13	368.6	20.6	9.3
Timber/pulp carriers	2	47.2	2.6	18.0
Ro-Ro ships	2	10.2	0.6	12.3
LASH ships	1	40.9	2.3	10.0
Reefer ships	17	81.9	4.6	15.1
Passenger ships	8	9.6	0.5	11.8
Ice-breaking ships	17	249.5	13.9	11.0
Tug/barge trains	7	66.7	3.7	15.7
Total	**175**	**1,796.9**	**100**	**16.2**

Source: Institute of Shipping Economics and Logistics (1994), *Shipping Statistics Yearbook.*

Bareboat charter financing as a way to acquire tonnage is also utilised by FESCO. For example, they set up a special department to manage 12 general purpose ships of the 'Nikolay Morozov' type (10,000 dwt.) leased to Japan on terms of bareboat charter in 1991.

Another promising approach to renew tonnage is used. Here joint ventures are established with foreign firms for new buildings and joint operations. Evidence of this can be found from three developments which occurred between 1991 and 1994. Firstly, MV Shantar was replaced by a larger 570 teu ro-ro container ship on the FESCO Australia Ro-Ro Line (FAROL), which is also operated by FESCO. Secondly, among the latest changes in the FESCO fleet on its own is the replacement on the FESCO Australia Line (FAL) of three small container vessels by two larger and more modern ships.[10] MV Novicov Priboy, Constantin Paustovski and Gamzat Tzadasa, originally built as conventional general cargo vessels in 1968, 1970 and 1971 respectively, and later converted into container carriers, are giving way to MV Capitan Kurov and Capitan Seryh. Both ships (19,479 dwt., capacity 1,300 teu, each) were built in Germany in 1986.

The plan of FESCO's fleet development in accordance with the State Programme of Revitalisation of the Russian Merchant Fleet and Ports is shown in Table 9.4. This plan is very much in line with the recommendations made by MORFLOT since the 1980s, which aim to improve the fleet in terms of quality and efficiency rather than quantity. The proposed changes in the FESCO fleet tonnage and its composition during the period 1993-2000 are to be achieved through the new building of 79 dry cargo ships and 7 passenger vessels. This plan will require an estimated US $22 billion based on 1992 average world shipbuilding prices.

Under this plan the company has ordered the new building of 15 timber carriers of 5,300 dwt. from Amur shipbuilding yard, Komsomolsk-on-Amur in 1993. Two of them, called MV Amur and Ussuri, were delivered in 1995 and the delivery of two more vessels is expected in 1996.[11] Moreover, contracts were signed for the delivery of two 1,200 teu container ships from Poland in 1994 and five 1,400 teu container ships from Germany in 1995. Because one of the main tasks of FESCO is the provision of passenger services in the Far East,[12] the plan includes the expansion of the FESCO fleet by seven new passenger ships.

All the above-mentioned contracts have been financed by FESCO (since subsidies for replenishing old vessels from central funds have practically terminated over the last five years), although, in the case of timber carriers, some 15-20 per cent of total new building price is being financed from the fund for the revival of Russia's merchant fleet. In this case, the company considers it necessary to attract capital from Russian cargo owners. It is noteworthy that FESCO obtained confirmation from the Norwegian Guarantee Institute giving the credit required by the company. The Export-Credit Fund of Norway, the Trade Union Bank, and the Norwegian Guarantee Institute are now elaborating the terms and conditions of credit to be submitted to FESCO. It has also managed to arrange additional financing with western shipping financial institutions, such as the Christiania Bank og Kreditkasse in Norway, the Hill Samuel Bank Limited in the UK, and the Westdeutsche Landesbank in Germany; reaching preliminary agreements on the allocation in 1995 of long term credit worth more than US $100 million. Furthermore, FESCO has raised US $32.7 million from the European Bank for Reconstruction and Development for its replenishment programme involving two Polish container ships mentioned above.[13] In the meantime, FESCO is preparing ships of the 'Pioneer' and 'Belolorskles' types and passenger ships of 'Maria Ermolova' type, for decommissioning from the year 2001.

Table 9.4
Plan of FESCO's fleet development (1993-2000)

Ship type	dwt. ('000 tons)	Number of ships	Est. cost* per ship (US $ million)	Total est. cost* (US $ million)
a) Dry cargo fleet		79		1,543.5
Container ships		7		214.0
capacity of :				
500 teu	9.0	4	16.0	64.0
1,500 teu	28.0	3	50.0	150.0
General purpose ships		37		672.0
Timber carriers		15		127.5
Reefer ships		8		189.0
Bulk carriers		12		341.0
b) Passenger fleet		7		
Cruise liners				
400-500 beds	1.5	5	90.0	
500-700 beds	2.1	1	100.0	
700-800 beds	3.5	1	120.0	
Merchant fleet total				
(a + b)		**86**		**2,213.5**

Note: * *Average world shipbuilding prices as of November 1992.*

Source: Soyuzmorniiproekt (1994).

An analysis of FESCO's financial situation since privatisation

One can assess the financial standing of FESCO by its balance sheet for the first half of 1993, referring to its privatisation plans. An analysis of its financial position is summarised in Table 9.5. This shows a set of specific and consolidated indicators relative to FESCO's financial position.

Table 9.5
Major indicators of financial analysis of FESCO (1993)

Indicators	1 January	1 July
1. Working capital/total assets	0.12	0.15
2. Retained earnings/total assets	0.00	0.00
3. EBIT/total assets		0.88
4. Market value of equity/total debts	1.18	1.35
5. Sales/total assets		(1.60)
6. Current assets/current liabilities	1.30	1.36
7. Total debt/total assets	0.46	0.43
8. EBIT/market value of equity		1.53
9. Z-score (Zeta analysis)		3.89
10. EBIT per share (roubles)		112,884
11. Assets per share (roubles)	57.9	128,500
12. Market value of equity per share (roubles)	31.4	73,900
13. Market value of shares (roubles)		479,400

Source: Soyuzmorniiproekt and FESCO (1994).

As can be seen in Table 9.5, the first five indicators are used to predict possible bankruptcy of FESCO. They include the following:

- Indicator 1, frequently found in studies of corporate problems, is a measure of the net liquid assets of the joint stock company relative to the total capitalisation.
- Indicator 2 features the efficiency of the joint stock company in the past. As FESCO is still in the starting phase, this indicator is zero for the time being.
- Indicator 3 is calculated by dividing the total assets of FESCO into its earnings before interest and tax (EBIT) deductions. In essence, it is a measure of the true productivity of the company's assets, abstracting from any tax or leverage factors. Since a company's ultimate existence is based on the earning power of its assets, this ratio appears to be particularly appropriate for studies dealing with corporate failure.
- Indicator 4 shows how much the assets of a company can decline in value, where the market value of equity plus debt before liabilities exceeds the assets and the company becomes insolvent. Equity is measured by the combined market value of all shares of stock, preferred and common, while total debts include both current and long term ones.
- Indicator 5, or the capital-turnover ratio, is a standard financial ratio illustrating the sales generating ability of the company's assets.

The other eight indicators in Table 9.5 characterise the other aspects of FESCO's financial situation:

- Indicator 6 is the most commonly used measure of short term solvency, since it provides the best single indicator of the extent to which claims of short term creditors are covered by assets that are expected to be converted to cash in a period roughly corresponding to the maturity of the claims.
- Indicator 7, or debt ratio, measures the percentage of total funds provided by creditors. Creditors prefer a low debt ratio, since the lower the ratio, the greater the cushion against creditors' losses in the event of liquidation.
- Indicator 8 features supplementary characteristics of the company's profitability.
- Indicator 9 is used to predict bankruptcy of joint stock companies as a consolidated index of financial stability. Z-score is calculated on the basis of the first five indicators, which are indicative of liquidity, cumulative profitability, current profitability, leverage and turnover, respectively. Discriminant analysis can examine these ratios simultaneously, and the overall score or profile is the essence rather than any one ratio or group of ratios. It is generally agreed that all firms having a Z-score of greater than 2.99 clearly fall into the 'non-bankrupt sector', while those firms having a Z-score below 1.81 will all go bankrupt. The area between 1.81 and 2.99 is defined as the 'zone of ignorance'.[14]

The Values of some specific indicators in positions 10-12 of Table 9.5 are given in terms of roubles per share. These are EBIT, values of total assets, and market value of equity of FESCO. Finally, the last indicator gives the value of shares corresponding to the financial standing of the company.

It is now evident from Indicators 3 and 8 that FESCO's profitability is exceptionally high; recording 88% in annual terms, whereas other Russian enterprises on the whole averaged only 15%. This extraordinarily high profit rate is partly attributable to the hyper increase in the exchange rate of US dollar to rouble. Moreover, on the basis of Indicators 1, 4, 6 and 7, it can be said that the company remarkably improved its financial position in the first half of 1993. This case is not typical of other Russian enterprises - their financial performance in the current economic situation has been deteriorating since the break-up of the Soviet Union. The assets of FESCO, which are evaluated by foreign auditors, are approximately US $1 billion.[15] The liquidity, efficiency and leverage ratios in Table 9.5 suggest that the company is in very good condition; enough to justify the increase of external long term debt for speeding up the fleet replenishment programme.

Furthermore, FESCO achieved a high rate of return on investment. As of January 1993, the value of FESCO's assets per share amounted to 57,900 roubles and the market value of equity per share to 31,400 roubles. During a period of six months, these shares increased to 128,500 and 73,900 roubles, respectively. The market value of the shares was approximately 480,000 roubles at the price in the first half of 1993.

Since FESCO's Z-score of 3.89 is well above the 2.99 upper limit of Altman's zone of ignorance, it indicates that there is virtually no chance that the company will go bankrupt within the next two years, assuming that macroeconomic conditions during this period do not substantially change.

In summary, despite the question of quality regarding the financial statement in the analysis provided here[16] and the very short time allowed for the analysis, the examination of FESCO's financial statements and the observations on its financial situation allow the conclusion to be made that, since privatisation, not only has the financial standing of the company been improved, but also the company has a sound creditworthiness to raise foreign capital.

Policy and perspective of the Far Eastern Shipping Company

A modern mechanism to develop a market economy in Russia has been established, supported by legislative and regulatory documents. In the shipping context the main aim is the granting of full autonomy for sea-going transport. Russia represents the vast majority of the Commonwealth of Independent State's shipping interests. Drastic changes in the structural pattern of the shipping sector have taken place recently. The functions of the transport departments have also been transformed.

The main tendency in FESCO policy after privatisation is the aspiration for autonomy and independence from state machinery and the DMT in all matters concerning industrial activity, administration, management and finance. In so doing, FESCO has been reorganised and privatised as an 'open face' to the world market, in particular to the Asian Pacific Rim, which demonstrates its commitments for the next century. It should be emphasised that FESCO has already been transformed into a joint stock company and to some extent has been commercialised.

The policy directions of FESCO are:

- to pursue an independent policy in industrial activities and to seek new cargo resources and customers;
- to increase the carriage of goods for foreign affreighters and to maximise the hard currency inflow;
- to expand geographic areas of operation and intensify operations on existing services;
- to renew fleet tonnage with capital raised from foreign and domestic capital markets;
- to set joint ventures;
- to open container and passenger lines on the routes in the Asian Pacific Rim, and increase the rate of ship utilisation.

A striking problem currently being faced by FESCO arises from the ageing fleet, therefore, for the company, new or younger vessel acquisition is the most crucial area of investment and planning. The fleet replenishment plan (see Table 9.4) has been devised by the company and the DMT and it seems that, so far, it has been well implemented in the hands of the company itself. The question of financing construction of new ships has been partly solved by: direct import of foreign capital from western financial institutions; investments from its foreign partners with mutually profitable joint operations of ships; and, although the amount is small, self-financing through retained earnings and the proceeds of privatisation.

The analysis of FESCO's financial statements (see Table 9.5) and other observations enable the conclusion to be drawn that the company is making good progress in the transition period, taking benefits from and overcoming the side effects of privatisation. Consequently, FESCO can potentially make a notable impact on the Pacific Rim shipping market.

Notes and references

1   On the organisational framework of former Soviet merchant shipping and the new shipping organisation chart of the Russian Federation, see Appendices 8.1 and 8.2.

2   On Russia's principal shipping companies, their fleets and trading patterns, see Peters, H. J. (1993), 'Russia's Waterborne Trade and Transport: Issues in Market Transformation', *Maritime Policy and Management*, Vol. 20, No. 4, pp. 265-92.

3   The State Committee of the Russian Federation for the Management of State Property (1992), *The Russian Privatisation Programme*, 20 August 1992, Moscow, Russia.

4   After corporatisation and before privatisation, the appropriate Fund (or Committee) represents the State as the owner of stock at State enterprises.

5   Ash, T. N. and Hare, P. G. (1994), 'Privatisation in the Russian Federation: Changing Enterprise Behaviour in the Transition Period', *Cambridge Journal of Economics*, Vol. 18, pp. 622-3.

6   On the mechanism of emergence of private shipping enterprises in Far Eastern Russia, see Chapter 7 of this book.

7   The former Ministry of Merchant Marine (MORFLOT) has been integrated into the new Russian Ministry of Transport as the Department of Marine

Transport. Holt, J. (1993), *Transport Strategies for the Russian Federation*, The World Bank, Washington D.C., Chapter 7.

8   *Lloyd's List*, 8 June 1995, p. 1.

9   Institute of Shipping Economics and Logistics (1994), *Shipping Statistics Yearbook*.

10   On an example of joint container service between Korea and FESCO, see Chapter 8 of this book and Lee, T-W. (1994), 'Current Problems in Transportation Activities of Joint Korean-FESCO Line and Some Proposals for Solving Them', *Journal of Social Science*, Korea Maritime University, Vol. 1, pp. 197-206.

11   Marine Publications International Limited (1995), *Soviet Maritime*, No. 39, pp. 1-2.

12   On FESCO's joint activities in passenger operation, see Chapter 12 of this book and Lee, T-W. and Song, D-W. (1995), 'Current Situation and Prospect for Ferry Lines between Korea, China and Far East Russia', *Cruise & Ferry '95 Conference Papers*, Vol. 1, London.

13   Marine Publications International Limited (1995), op. cit., p. 1.

14   Altman, E. I. (1968), 'Financial Ratios, Discriminant Analysis and the Prediction of Corporate Bankruptcy', *Journal of Finance*, Vol. 23, No. 4, p. 606. See also Altman, E. I. et al. (1977), 'Zeta Analysis: A new model to identify bankruptcy risk of corporations', *Journal of Banking and Finance*, Vol. 1, pp. 29-54.

15   Marine Publications International Limited (1995), op. cit., p. 1.

16   The quality of financial statements depends on the information that is disclosed in the financial statements, the accounting principles used, the knowledge of financial statements possessed by the user, and the ingenuity of the individual who is performing the analysis. Although there is no available way to check whether they are 'true and fair', it is reported that a western accounting auditing company analysed FESCO's financial statements. On the view of true and fair accounting, see Parker, R. H. and Nobes, C. W. (1994), *An International View of True and Fair Accounting*, Routledge, London.

10 Factors concerning the success and failure of shipping joint ventures and joint operations: With reference to Korean-Russian co-operation

Introduction

Joint ventures have been studied extensively by researchers in business administration, however, the focus of past research has, unfortunately, been rather limited to the manufacturing industry. Moreover, although the literature on maritime joint ventures[1] has dealt with an extensive number of issues, including among others, the conceptual, economic, financial, legal, technological and organisational management aspects of joint ventures, very limited attention has been given to the key role that effective implementation and management plays in determining joint venture success. Furthermore, they tend to be rather fragmented, which is explained by the fact that no comprehensive framework currently exists for the study of maritime joint ventures. Additionally, in such literature, research on the factors determining the success and failure of joint ventures is still in its infancy.

Since 1990, Korean shipping and fishery companies and their counterparts in Russia have been developing shipping joint ventures and joint operations, and other co-operative arrangements in the shipbuilding and ship repair businesses. They have offered many opportunities and benefits to both Korea and Russia as the two countries currently have many complementary needs. They also pose many problems which require close scrutiny, particularly in the operation and management areas of joint ventures. If joint ventures and joint operations are to develop and prosper as mutually beneficial forms of co-operation on a long term basis, the problems faced by the two countries must be clearly understood and analysed.

A major objective of this chapter is to highlight the problems which have occurred in formalising joint agreements, in addition to those found in the management of shipping joint ventures between Russia and Korea. It seeks to examine the joint ventures and joint operations from a global perspective, namely to identify which problems are unique to joint ventures and joint operations between the two countries and which are merely replicas of similar problems encountered in joint ventures world-wide. The use of such a global perspective can be helpful, not only for putting the managerial problems of joint ventures into perspective, but it can also assist in identifying solutions to problems existing between Korean and Russian concerns, based on the cumulative experience in joint ventures around the globe.

Research approach and data sources

In recent years, the author has actively studied the significant environmental change in which the Russian shipping business operates and has helped to facilitate the development of both shipping enterprises and individual managers in Russia. He has developed good working relationships with both the academic community in Moscow and the Russian Far East, and many shipping companies in Russia. Since 1989, the author has conducted and/or participated in several multi-day shipping joint venture meetings and field trips in Russia, and has interviewed managers from different types of organisations in the former Soviet Union and present-day Russia. Of these, several are from state-owned shipping companies, with others from private shipping companies and four from joint ventures themselves. Included in these were general managing directors and middle level management of the Far Eastern Shipping Company (FESCO), Sakhalin Shipping Company (SASCO), Lena River Shipping Company (Lenarechflot) and Amur Shipping Company (AMUR). Interviews with the managing directors also provided the opportunity to collect and supplement background information and to explore their role as founders and managers of joint ventures and joint operations. Following field trips and interviews, it is felt that a questionnaire should have been designed to consolidate the findings in this study, however, this was felt to be of little value owing to the extremely limited number of samples employed.

This chapter uses an interpretative research methodology in order to utilise previous field work and management consultancy experience in Russia and Korea. Such a methodology, which was most clearly represented by the works of Max Weber,[2] allows contextual conditions, as well as focal phenomena of joint ventures, to be considered by employing multiple sources of both primary and secondary data.

Because the complexities of shipping joint ventures and joint operations have been a major obstacle for researchers, the author has utilised multiple sources of data as a means of gaining a more complete picture of joint ventures and joint operations. The primary sources of data were the in-depth case studies of FESCO, Lenarechflot and AMUR, and their relationships with Korean shipping companies. In these case studies, those factors that determine the degree of success experienced in the management of joint ventures and joint operations have been isolated and highlighted. Valid and reliable data were available for this study as the author had been involved in the establishment of joint ventures and joint operations between Russia and Korea, for which he has subsequently acted as a consultant and advisor.

The secondary source of data here is derived from a longitudinal literature survey. This data collection was largely concerned with the manufacturing industry as literature on the shipping industry concerning joint ventures and joint operations, although fully utilised here, was very restricted.

The background of joint ventures and joint operations

Following Mikhail Gorbachev's rise to power in 1985 and dating back to his *perestroika* (restructuring) and *glasnost* (openness) movements of the late 1980s, the Soviet government began a major drive to place all domestic industries, including the shipping industry, on a more rational and cost-effective basis. These trends resulted in greater financial needs for industries of the former USSR. Additionally, the deteriorating financial condition of the shipping industry forced it to pursue solutions from abroad.

In January 1987, the Presidium of the USSR Supreme Soviet issued an edict authorising joint ventures between Soviet entities and foreign companies. In accordance with this edict, the USSR Council of Ministers adopted the so-called 'Joint Venture Decree' in the Soviet Union. Since the Decree, numerous other decrees governing joint ventures have been issued.[3] On 24 September 1990, the USSR Parliament gave President Gorbachev emergency powers to lead the country towards a free market economy, including the mandate to privatise state assets and factories by transforming them into joint stock companies with shares to be traded on a stock exchange. Thanks to the series of events briefly mentioned above, joint ventures are becoming increasingly popular in Russia as we enter the mid-1990s.

There were two major incentives for Korean companies to become involved in joint ventures and joint operations; firstly, to develop and exploit a new shipping business market; and secondly, to contribute to the important improvement of diplomatic relations between the two countries. Russian partners were interested in both gaining access to capital resources and claiming the right to load container cargoes in Pusan and carry them to third countries.

As of October 1995, there were four shipping joint ventures and four joint operations between Russia and Korea, as can be seen in Tables 10.1 and 10.2. (However, this does not include the numerous joint fishing ventures between the two nations.[4]) Apparently, they are all private arrangements, but the industry and the Korean government are often closely consulted on their establishment. In particular, Korea Maritime and Port Administration has influenced such establishments on the basis of certain fundamental principles: (i) private level arrangements should have no adverse effect on the existing government-to-government relations or on Korean shipping policy; (ii) bilateral private arrangements should be fair.

165

Korean-Russian joint ventures and joint operations can be divided broadly into two categories depending on the size of the Korean participants, their main objectives and the degree of Korean government involvement in the arrangements. Firstly, there are ventures in which medium-large shipping companies participate under the general guidance of the two governments. The Transorient and SASCO International Shipping Company are good examples here. Incentives for the Korean partner of the former joint venture is to gain access to container cargoes to and from Europe through the Trans-Siberia Railway and for the conglomerate, Hyundai, to find new markets for shipbuilding, ship repair, port construction and natural resources from Siberia. With the inherent lack of central funds forcing Moscow to cease its provision of supplies and capital to former state-owned shipping companies, Russian concerns have had to seek ways of becoming financially independent and self-sufficient. Therefore, from FESCO's point of view, container operation has played a crucial role in earning hard currency. In addition to hard currency, joint ventures of this type offer the Russian side experience in highly advanced container operation techniques, as well as access to Korean cargoes and capital.

Table 10.1
Korean-Russian shipping joint ventures as of 31 October 1995

Joint venture name	Korean party	Russian party	Established	Remarks
Transorient Shipping Co.	Hyundai Shipping Co. & Chun Kyung Shipping Co.	SOVFRACHT & FESCO	1991	
SAMUR Shipping Co.	Samsun Shipping Co.	AMUR	1991	Taken over by CHAMUR
CHAMUR Shipping Co.	Changwoo Shipping Co.	AMUR	1992	Taken over by Sunwoo Shipping Co.
SASCO International Shipping Co.	Heung-A Shipping Co.	SASCO	1994	

Source: collected by the author.

The second type of Korean-Russian joint ventures calls for the participation of Korean shipping agencies. They have developed private-level joint operation arrangements with Russian partners in order to access agency services. The earliest of this type of joint venture began in 1991. At the initial stage the Korean agency carried out technical ship management for Russian partners and arranged the repair of Russian ships at Korean yards. At the next stage, the Korean partner became involved in joint operations with vessels time- and/or voyage-chartered from the Russian partner. A good example here is the anonymous company shown in Table 10.2.

Table 10.2
Korean-Russian shipping joint operations as of 31 October 1995

Korean party	Russian party	Starting year	Remarks
Hyundai Shipping Co. & Chun Kyung Shipping Co.	FESCO	1991	
anonymous co.[+]	Lenarechflot	1993	
Tae-Keum Shipping Co.	Centaur Shipping	1992	Russian party bankrupted in 1993
Sunwoo Shipping Co.	AMUR	1993	See Table 10.1

Note: [+] *The author was requested by the company not to disclose its name.*

Source: collected by the author.

Following this stage, Korean and Russian partners set up a joint venture with Russian flagged vessels. Good examples here are SAMUR and CHAMUR. (See Table 10.1.) However, it must be noted that ultimately, the former was taken over by the latter. The Korean partnership with CHAMUR was taken over by the Sunwoo Shipping Company in 1993, owing to frequent conflicts of management control among the Korean managers of CHAMUR. At the latest stage, the two partners set up a joint venture paper company with vessels registered in flags of convenience countries.[5] A good example is the paper company, Link Vest Limited in Hong Kong, which was established by both the Sunwoo Shipping Company and AMUR in 1994. Not only does it handle shipping business but it also indirectly engages in the trading business through either the establishment of a subsidiary or an independent trading company formed between the Russian partner and the other Korean partner.

The benefits of this kind of joint venture for Korean enterprises include the acquisition of ships for agency services and the development of shipping businesses associated with chartering and cargo broking. In recent years Russian partners have been anxious to generate hard currency by readily accepting requests for the chartering of many vessels to Korea. In so doing, in addition to forming and managing the joint venture, they have developed a trading company in association with Korean partners in order to increase their revenue sources. Currently, the Russian side is showing a preference for joint operations over joint ventures, partly because the establishment and operation of joint ventures require more costly financial arrangements, and partly because they incur more cumbersome procedures. Moreover, joint operations are not based on governmental treaties. Having said that, FESCO has been increasingly involved in exploiting joint operation opportunities in passenger shipping between Pusan and Vladivostok as a means of generating additional hard currency. It has responded to these changes by exploring the various revenue-raising activities described above.

Problems with joint ventures

Joint ventures are rather unique and problematic in their combination of two major hurdles: multiple national affiliation and multiple ownership. The former means that joint ventures bring together parent companies which are anchored in environments differentiated by culture and political, economic and legal systems. The latter means that joint ventures are owned, and often managed, by at least two parent firms. Because of this combination, joint ventures are probably more problematic to manage than other forms of foreign direct investment.

Foreign investors in Russia can face five unfamiliar obstacles to success. The first is the lack of a modern banking system. The Russian business infrastructure presents additional problems; it is almost impossible to expect a Russian buyer to insure a letter of credit. In addition to this, currency convertibility is extremely low. The second obstacle arises from the incumbent insurance services. Foreign investors face many problems even when using their own insurance companies, because Russian insurance law does not recognise foreign insurers on Russian territory. The third is supply shortages. Companies have trouble sourcing materials of almost every kind and often experience difficulties in securing such basic services as bunkering, communications, medicine and security. The fourth obstacle is the constantly shifting regulatory and legal environment. Quite simply, the ground rules change with maddening frequency, as do the nature and locus of governmental authority. The Russian federal government and local authorities continually amend old levies and add new ones, leaving Russia's tax and fee structures unstable. International lenders thus view Russia warily and are unwilling to grant loans without the protection of guarantees and insurance from foreign investors' governments. The fifth is high inflation. Russia's inflation in 1993 was in the order of 20 per cent per month. These five formidable obstacles have both prevented many foreign investors from plunging in and have forced many others to pull out along the way.

More specifically, in addition to general problems with Russian joint ventures, the Korean partners have faced major problems in formalising and managing shipping joint ventures and joint operations, which are outlined as follows:

Lack of a capital management philosophy

Until recently, in Russia 'market and profit' and 'the free competition principle' have had very negative connotations. The concept of market economics has been widely associated with the chaos and social injustice which Russian partners have often faced since the mid-1980s. The issue is further complicated by the fact that an illegal parallel economy is the only continued experience of a market which exists at present. Therefore, although the 'market and profit' and 'com-petition principle' are now considered to be goals to strive for, the attitudes of Russian partners are still influenced by former ideology and by distortions in the previous system. However, Korean partners understand that since Russia has recently made the switch to capitalism, considerable patience is often required. In addition, Russian partners also have little knowledge of capitalistic and management philosophy in the management of joint ventures, for example, the notion of profit and cost centres.

Obscure relationships regarding responsibility and authority

In the former Soviet system, power in any organisation was concentrated in the CEO's hands, with little influence in the decision-making process on the part of middle level managers. Attempts to decentralise responsibility and authority amongst Russian managers of a joint venture often failed because, although many have now accepted that the organisation of firms is not necessarily different to that of the former shipping operation system, there is still an unabridged gap between the acceptance of responsibility and the implementation of authority. Other problems continue to discourage Korean partners. Russia's decision-making structure remains haphazard, without clear legal protection for investments and contracts. Often there is no clear delineation of responsibility and authority between departments within a joint venture, or between the parent company and the joint venture authority.

Incongruencies in the goals of joint ventures

Korean partners have often considered their Russian counterparts simply as a 'connection' which would help establish business, provide useful contacts and supply ships with a cheap rate of charterage. Meanwhile, Russian partners have expected to be provided with capital, equipment and management training, leaving all other responsibilities in the hands of their partners. In particular,

FESCO tried to utilise a joint venture arrangement in order to claim the right to load container cargoes in Pusan and transport them to third countries through the joint venture Transorient.(See Table 10.1) This is an extreme example of the problem and despite many maritime talks between the two countries, it is still the biggest stumbling block for the establishment of a passenger shipping joint venture between the two countries. Moreover, this supports the assertion that impediments to efficient implementation and management can also arise out of either incongruencies in the goals of the venture, or the differences in perception regarding the strategic importance of a joint venture project.

Lack of managerial manpower

Proper management is crucial to success in a shipping joint venture. The sad truth is that there are probably few managers in Russian shipping companies who know how to even comprehend financial statements. Many Korean interviewees complain that their Russian partners, though often dedicated and competent in operating ships, have virtually no usable concepts of marketing, business strategy, or managerial and financial accounting systems.

Absence of a generally accepted accounting system

Successful business planning is based on sound and consistent managerial and financial accounting data. Historical, and to some degree current, accounting statements from Russian shipping companies are very unreliable due to volatile price swings, uncertainties about inflation, translation errors, arbitrary assignments of asset values and a lack of true independence for former state-run agencies. Moreover, Korean partners could not make even a short term management decision on the basis of the extremely short term data provided by FESCO. In 1993 it introduced a European accounting system in the process of its privatisation.

Misunderstanding cultural differences

Joint venture failures are often the result of difficulties in managing major cultural differences between two business environments. Recent research concerning a Korean-Russian joint venture suggested that cultural barriers were a major cause of misunderstanding and conflict and, consequently, mis-understanding cultural differences often resulted in not keeping container operating schedules published.[6] Because of these 'intangible' problems it is more difficult to find solutions which are acceptable to both partners.

Along with cultural differences, existing differences in management styles of both partners constituted a major impediment to effective implementation. Various administrative factors play an important role in determining the extent to which performance expectations in a venture can eventually be realised. For example, incompatible administrative systems of parent companies can prove to be a serious impediment to the effective implementation of the venture. Incompatibility makes the choices of appropriate accounting, planning and control systems doubly difficult, with each company naturally favouring the system they use themselves.

Problems in the management of a joint venture can also stem from incompatible organisational policies and strategies. Russian partners had very different notions of the appropriate advertising policy, the analysis of the markets served, crew management, the introduction of an incentive policy for employees, the invest-ment required for management information systems and the quality control standards to be adopted,[7] all of which often generated dysfunctional and damaging conflicts. Unless these differences are reconciled or equitable mechan-isms are developed to resolve the resulting deadlocks, they can be extremely detrimental to the overall performance of the joint venture. Moreover, resulting inefficiencies can easily erode many of the potential economic benefits initially offered by the joint venture.

Successful factors and some recommendations

Many of the problems and misunderstandings in maritime joint ventures have their roots in cultural differences and the diversity of management styles that exist at both national and organisational levels.[8] Although definite solutions regarding the dilemmas, as discussed in the previous section, are impossible, this section is devoted to proposing some tentative guidelines and recommendations, based on the literature survey and the author's academic and consultative experiences.

The effective management of a joint venture also requires well defined reporting relationships and communication channels to be established as early as possible. However, it may not be an easy task - in joint ventures generally, optimisation in both means of operation and organisational structure are seldom, if ever, found. Most successful joint ventures, therefore, use a mix of organisational participation and control. In this study it can be generally suggested that the following are factors and mechanisms commonly used and considered for the successful management of joint ventures:

- Define the goals and objectives of the joint venture and devise a win-win basis[9] for co-operation.
- Recognise the limits of the joint venture.

171

- Allocate accountability and responsibility within a joint venture company.
- Parent company executives should make frequent informal visits.
- Initiate staff exchange programmes and formal planning systems.
- Implement an effective information retrieval process.
- Enhance career prospects and incentives for joint venture employees.
- Monitor progress of the joint venture through regular reporting and financial and management audits.
- Measure and review staff and business operation performances.
- Review and revise joint venture agreements based on regular post-audits.

More specifically, the successful factors of joint ventures will be drawn from case studies in this study as follows:

Bridge cultural differences and develop a relationship before signing a contract

The most successful joint venture in this study has understood from the outset that the development of a trusting relationship across barriers of language, culture and education requires a generous investment of time and attention. In one case, the author introduced a Korean shipping businessman to his eventual Russian general manager in Yakusk. They liked each other immediately, continued to meet, talked business by the hour, and progressed through phases of mutual testing through to a relationship of friendship and trust. Towards the end of this process, the Korean invited the Russian to Korea to visit his company and business. The Korean general managing director brought Russian staff to his headquarters to establish extensive formal and informal relationships. Most of their time was devoted to building personal relationships between their own top managers and the Russians. All engaged in an ongoing, reiterative process of discussion and probing that ranged back and forth from casual social discussions to concentrated dialogues on strategic business issues. The Korean introduced them to friends and associates and gave the Russian a chance to wander through his business premises and ask questions. The Russian began to disclose step by step what their company needed and to ask him for his advice. The next time the Korean was in Russia, the two men began developing a specific joint venture plan. Repeated visits and discussions on business have kept the relationship healthy. Finally, they have established a second type of joint venture as discussed in a previous section in this paper, and have developed further trading business, mainly for consumer goods.

Choose a reliable interpreter

A Korean general director employed a Korean-Russian as an interpreter in Vladivostok in order to formalise a joint venture. Although the interpreter had no knowledge of maritime jargon, he was satisfied with his fluent Korean. The interpreter was invited to all the business discussions as well as dinner parties with the Russian partner. The Korean partner was very confident that he could succeed in establishing a joint venture in due course, however, negative signs from Russia gradually came to him. The Russian partner requested him to change some terms and conditions involved in establishing the joint venture. Ultimately, the Korean partner came to realise that the interpreter had passed confidential information to his competitor who in turn had suggested a better offer to the Russian partner. It took considerable time and incurred additional costs to revert the mind of his partner back to the establishment of the original joint venture.

Try to identify what the partner's individual needs are through the joint venture

Ideally an international joint venture should be supported by a partnership philosophy. It can be easily noted though, that joint ventures are so varied in their objectives as to make generalisations difficult. However, it was found that a Russian party tried to meet their own private needs through a joint venture, although they are not relevant to the overall objectives and goals of the core business. A good example of this is from a joint venture between a Korean party and AMUR, as can be seen in Table 10.1.

From a general perspective, a joint venture is implicit in every bareboat charter, the participants being the shipowner with his capital investment and the charterer with his cargo and/or operational expertise. In the case of the joint venture in the study though, we have observed something new about the use of bareboat charters; here, several changes to the traditional relationship of the two parties are apparent, due to the 'needs' of certain individuals within the Russian party. AMUR wanted the ships to fly their own national flag and to secure the employment of seafarers of their own nationality. The last two considerations can potentially produce very peculiar arrangements if limited by the traditional bareboat charter structure. In addition, the Russian party requested that the Korean party include a peculiar clause of off-hire which allowed them, on four occasions annually, to utilise vessels already chartered to the Korean party, at the owner's expense of bunker supplies. On these occasions, therefore, the Korean party had to secure an additional ship during the week-long off-hire period in order to both keep a planned operational schedule and to meet such special needs. At a later stage, the Korean side came to realise that the Russian party deployed off-hired vessels to carry consumer goods, second-hand cars and electric goods that their top executives had purchased in the Korean market. This implies that Russian managers of the joint ventures are often more 'business' than 'company' oriented with related short term and windfall profit expectations. This attitude is difficult to counter since managers of joint ventures consider that they only want to meet their own needs and they operate this practice within a contract-oriented concern.

It is obvious that a structure such as the one described above is an unusual case. Therefore, generally speaking, Korean parties must understand that Russian perspectives on opportunities afforded by joint ventures will not necessarily match their own. Consequently, there is a need for flexibility during business negotiations in order to fulfil particular Russian 'needs', and thus prevent the loss of potential business through the non-establishment of a joint venture.

Be familiar with Russian negotiation styles; coping with the developing legal, economic and political environment in Russia

In many countries negotiating a joint venture agreement is a long and arduous process.[10] In Russia, such negotiations are further complicated by cultural, legal, and bureaucratic factors which sometimes bring prospective foreign participants to the point of despair. It is imperative that one should familiarise oneself with the Russian negotiation style or solicit professional help to do so, and one must be prepared to spend a substantial amount of time consulting with experts before a formal negotiation regarding a potential joint venture begins. We should look closely at some critical changes in the Soviet law and policy since *perestroika* began. No meaningful discussion of business strategy can be undertaken without an understanding of the economic landscape. For example, 'privatisation' means, in effect, passing the control of property down deeper and deeper into civil society and ultimately onto stockholders.[11] For any joint venture then, the new legal climate presents a most complicated business problem; namely, how to negotiate not only with the Russian government but also with the municipalities and enterprises. Intractable problems can often be turned to advantage. The key to every joint venture success, therefore, is the capacity for extraordinarily rapid, adaptive responses to problems of economic turbulence and social change.

Conclusion

The findings in this chapter emphasise that there are complexities in formalising and managing international shipping joint ventures and joint operations, and that the most complex aspects are more related to their management rather than their formalisation. They can be contrasted with the emphasis placed on financing collaboration, exchange of technology and legal aspects in much of the recent literature. The collection of tentative solutions and recommendations outlined here will be helpful for those contemplating such joint venture participation with companies in newly liberalising economies such as China, Eastern Europe, the former Soviet Union or Vietnam.

Notes and references

1   Abhyankar, J. and Bijwadia, S. I. (ed) (1994), *Maritime Joint Ventures*, ICC Publishing SA, Paris. Lloyd's of London Press (1984), *Maritime Joint Ventures*, Proceedings of a two day conference organised by the

International Chamber of Commerce and Lloyd's of London Press, 17-18 May, London. International Chamber of Commerce (1985), *Symposium on Maritime Ventures*, 25 March, Seoul, Korea.

2   Weber, M. (1949), *The Methodology of the Social Sciences*, The Free Press, Glencoe, Illinois.

3   Rosten, K. (1991), 'Soviet-US Joint Ventures: Pioneers on a New Frontier', *California Management Review*, Vol. 33, No. 2, p. 89.

4   Korea signed a fisheries agreement with the USSR in September 1991. This accord allows Korean vessels to fish in Russian waters in the north-west Pacific and calls for bilateral co-operation, including the development of Soviet-Korean joint operations in fish processing.

5   Lee, T-W. (1992), 'Study on the Emergence of Private Shipping Enterprises in Far East Russia and Their Impact on Korean Shortsea Shipping', *Journal of the Korean Institute of Navigation*, Vol. 16, No. 3, pp. 43-53.

6   Lee, T-W. (1994), op. cit., p. 203.

7   Ibid., pp. 203-4.

8   Moreby, D. H., 'Cross-cultural Issues in Maritime Joint Ventures, in Abhyankar, J. and Bijwadia, S.I. (eds.) (1994), op. cit., pp. 73-88; and Jackson, T. (ed.) (1995), *Cross-Cultural Management*, Butterworth-Heinemann Limited, London.

9   Newman, W. H. (1992), 'Launching a Viable Joint Venture', *California Management Review*, Vol. 35, No. 1, p. 77.

10   Pekar, P. P. (1986), 'Joint Venture: a New Information System is Born', *Planning Review*, pp.15-9, July.

11   On the privatisation process, see Chapter 9 of this book.

11 A quality management system for shipping companies

Introduction

The search for cost-effective or cost-saving options has always been in the forefront of the shipowners' and ship managers' minds, particularly in bulk and low freight trades. The economics of running a merchant ship are closely related to the employment of qualified crews at a low cost. In addition to this, the concept of the shipowner's responsibility for seaworthiness has been extended in case law and by implication to include not only the quality of the crew on board, but also those shore management systems that have an effect on the quality of ship-board operations.[1] Therefore, the concept of quality management is rapidly becoming a vital element in the shipping industry.

The purpose of this chapter is to suggest a conceptual prototype for a quality management system to ensure quality assurance of seafaring labour, which would itself be a sub-system of the total quality management system in a shipping company. This prototype will be based on the *'International Management Code for the Safe Operation of Ships and for Pollution Prevention'* (International Safety Management Code, ISM Code) by the International Maritime Organisation, *'International Ship Managers' Association Code of Ship Management Standards'* (ISMA Code), and the quality management guidelines by various classification societies, such as Lloyd's Register of Shipping, Det Norske Veritas, and the Bureau Veritas. Therefore, this chapter also reviews briefly the ISM and ISMA Codes and quality management guidelines, together with the effects of the successful introduction of a quality management system into the shipping industry.

The necessity for a quality management system in Korean shipping companies

In this section various reasons are given to explain why the Korean shipping industry urgently needs to develop and adopt quality management systems.

Since the late 1980s it has been very difficult for Korean shipowners to recruit qualified seamen at the required time, owing to their deterioration in overall quality and the decreasing number of applicants for training at maritime schools. As far as the rating classes are concerned, Korea is rapidly changing from a supply to a demand country. As a consequence, from 1991 onwards Korean shipowners have been employing Korean-Chinese ratings to overcome the shortage of seafaring labour and to save crew costs. In the period between 1991 and 1994 they have recruited approximately 800 seamen, who came mainly from the Province of Jilin in China. However, owing to the supply of unqualified seamen, cultural conflict between Korean and Chinese crews, the latter's lower labour productivity, a lack of cost consciousness caused by the Chinese socio-economic system, and high crew turnover, a recent survey showed that the effects of crew cost-saving measures were less significant than most Korean shipowners had expected.[2]

Meanwhile, the marine accidents and incidents which have occurred in recent years have served to focus attention on the quality of seamen in Korea. The problems associated with poor levels of communication, the consumption of alcohol, as well as inadequate training, have all been identified as the major causes of marine casualties. The rapidly increasing rate of ship losses by Korean crews has caused Korean shipowners to pay additional insurance premiums, not to mention suffer operational losses. As a consequence, this has resulted in an increase in total shipping costs and the deterioration of their international competitive edge. Furthermore, it is certain that the shipowners are suffering from an over-taxed system compared to that of their competitors, and very limited accessibility to foreign capital markets with favourable financing terms.[3]

In these circumstances, Korean shipowners will have to find other alternatives to improve international competitive power. Flagging options[4] aside, the quality management systems has been considered positively since 1993. By the introduction of a quality management system, in association with foreign classification societies, the initiative is being forced upon, rather than taken by, major Korean shipping companies, e.g. Hyundai, Yukong, Hanjin and Korea. However, interviews carried out by the author with top executives and the quality management system task-force teams from Korean shipping companies revealed the following problems associated with the development of a quality management system.

- Most owners were reluctant to become involved in developing the system, as it is described in the ISM Code, because of the time required to oversee its evolution and implementation.
- Without adequate understanding of its impacts and implications, they regarded the certificates of the quality management system as a license to undertake business in the international shipping market.

- Expecting the slimming effect, as outlined by Spruyt[5], they tried to utilise the quality management system as an opportunity to restructure, or re-engineer, their organisations.
- They understood that the quality management system would merely generate costs with few short term benefits.[6]
- They had the misconception that if they acquired some so-called 'manuals', distributed them around offices and ships, everything would be fine, 'it is a paper exercise anyway'.
- The quality management system is not related to sales and general administration departments but mainly to marine and technical areas.
- If the ISM Code had not been adopted, they would not have seriously considered the development of the quality management system as they are now.
- Effective company-wide communication systems were not established.
- Conflicts between shore-side management and ship-board management teams existed.

The above findings are the most common causes of problems associated with the installation of a quality management system and they must be resolved in order to overcome the adverse current climate in the Korean shipping industry.

A brief review of quality management in the shipping industry

There are many documents available to assist organisations in the design and implementation of a quality management system. These include: the ISM and the ISMA Codes, ISO 9000, ISO 9002, ISO 9004, ISO 9004-2; *'Guidelines on the Application of the IMO Code'*, developed by the International Chamber of Shipping and the International Shipping Federation; *'Guidelines for Administration on the Implementation of the ISM Code'*, by the International Maritime Organisation; the quality management guidelines of various classification societies, such as Lloyd's Register, Det Norske Veritas and the Bureau Veritas,[7] and other shipping organisations, such as the International Shipping Federation and the International Chamber of Shipping.

The purpose of the ISM Code is to provide an international standard for the safe management and operation of ships, for pollution prevention, and to establish a framework to improve the implementation and enforcement of international standards and regulations. The code requires a company to include in its policy defined specific standards of safety and environmental protection and to ensure compliance with mandatory rules and regulations. It also requires the company to include safety management objectives that continuously improve the safety management skills of personnel ashore and onboard, and to prepare for emergencies relating to both safety and environmental protection. In other words, the ISM Code is designed to serve two purposes; one being to improve compliance and provide for more effective flag state enforcement; the second being to support the development of a safety culture in the shipping industry. However, the code is often criticised for being too generalised and non-specific. Furthermore, owing to its lack of detailed prescriptive requirements, it can cause a less than stringent attitude in its implementation.

The ISMA Code was developed by the Group of Five leading ship managers (e.g. Barber, Columbia, Denholm, Hanseatic and Wallem) in co-operation with representatives from classification societies such as Lloyd's Register, Det Norske Veritas and Germanischer Lloyd. Not only does the code include those items which would be a part of ISO 9002 or the IMO Resolution 680 provision, but it also covers the subjects of safety and pollution prevention and the environment, and includes a description of a quality management system. In addition, it addresses all aspects of the services which ship managers are required to provide. Furthermore, it seems that the code and the methods of audit are the most practical and realistic.

Introduced in 1987, ISO 9000 is a series of international standards for quality control and quality assurance and it includes three models or specifications for the quality assurance system. It is a result of developments in the manufacturing industry and actually consists of five documents, numbered ISO 9000 to ISO 9004.

ISO 9002 (*Quality System - Model for Quality Assurance in Production and Installation*), together with ISO 9004 *(Quality Management and Quality System Elements - Guidelines)*, have been adopted by shipping companies such as J O Tankers, Sealink-Stena, Shell Tankers and Acomarit.

The understanding of, and the familiarisation with, the ISM and the ISMA Codes, ISO 9002 and ISO 9004 are recommended to the Korean shipping industry for a variety of reasons. Compared with the others, they are much more involved in ship management, the safer operation of ships and pollution prevention. (See Table 11.1.) In addition, they are closely interrelated in a variety of ways with the notion of profit by quality as put forward by Moir[8] and Parker[9], amongst others, and inevitably enhance international competitive power.

(continued over)

Table 11.1

Major contents of the ISM and ISMA Codes and ISO 9002

ISM Code
1. Introduction
2. Application
3. Basic International Instruments
4. Management: safety and environmental policy; designated person; ashore operation; documentation; accident reporting; suitably qualified seafarers; other company responsibilities.
5. Master
6. Crew
7. Emergency Drills

ISMA Code
1. General
2. Business Ethics
3. Organisation: shore based management; ship-board management.
4. Personnel: selection; recruitment; training; administration of personnel; drug and alcohol policy.
5. Safety: company safety policy; safety of personnel; safe ship operation; safety of cargo; monitoring of safety.
6. Environmental Protection
7. Contingency Planning
8. Operational Capability
9. Cost Efficiency/Purchasing/Contracting
10. Maintenance/Maintenance Standard
11. Technical Support
12. Insurance
13. Accounting
14. Certification and Compliance with Rules and Regulations
15. Cargo Handling and Cargo Care
16. Communication Procedures
17. Management Agreement
18. Records
19. Auditing Body
20. Quality System
21. Document Control
22. Internal Quality Audits

ISO 9002
1. Management Responsibility
2. Quality System
3. Contract Review
4. Document and Data Control
5. Purchasing
6. Control Customer Supplied Product
7. Product Identification and Traceability
8. Process Control
9. Inspection and Testing
10. Control of Inspection, Measuring and Test Equipment
11. Inspection and Test Status
12. Control of Non-conforming Product
13. Corrective and Preventive Action
14. Handling, Storage, Packaging, Preservation and Delivery
15. Control of Quality Records
16. Internal Quality Audits
17. Training
18. Servicing
19. Statistical Techniques

Sources: ISM Code, ISMA Code and ISO 9002.

Effects of the successful introduction of a quality management system into a shipping company

The shipping industry, in common with the manufacturing industry, seems to be obsessed with the issue of quality. Quality management has become the primary issue for the 1990s as the problem of low standards of operational control are addressed. There are two primary incentives for developing a quality Management System; firstly, there is the competitive advantage which the quality operator will gain over his competitor; and secondly, the impact on the industry of major items of international and national legislation, particularly concerning liability, is profound - it is a major reason for the desire by shipping companies to be seen to be quality operators.

Currently, there is a better understanding in the shipping industry of what quality management can offer ship operating companies in terms of greater management control and customer service. It is therefore quite natural that some companies can take a relatively short period of time (six to twelve months) to establish and have running a quality management system while others will take much longer, perhaps several years.

The most important resources of a shipowning company is its personnel and its ships. A successful balance between a vessel managed safety programme and fleet managed safety programme consolidates the personal desire to avoid injury with the company's desired risk profile. In this context, for example, the prime quality objectives for a competitive tanker company should be:

- to create and maintain an environment for office employees and sea-going staff that encourages teamwork and co-operation in solving any problem, facilitating quick decision making, and always striving for continuous improvement;
- to implement, review and improve systems and procedures, and to ensure consistency of work and services performed throughout the fleet, at all levels and worldwide;
- to establish and promote a philosophy, through onshore and ship-board management, which is focused on a charterer's satisfaction;
- to fulfil the company's contractual and other agreed obligations, and respond properly to the needs of its clients within the spirit of goodwill and understanding;
- to achieve and maintain a quality certification (ISM Code or ISO 9002).

The above objectives can be achieved through a quality management system and the resulting balance can be improved by quality control. (See Figure 11.1.) The achievement of company objectives demands co-operation and good interactions between onshore and ship-board quality management organisations. The two organisations require well established communications in order to ensure a successful introduction and implementation of the quality management system within the company.

The statement that the 'human factor' is the most significant factor involved in marine casualties is strongly supported by the West of England P&I Club. In 1993 the Club completed an extensive analysis of major claims incurred during the six year period from 1987 to February 1993.

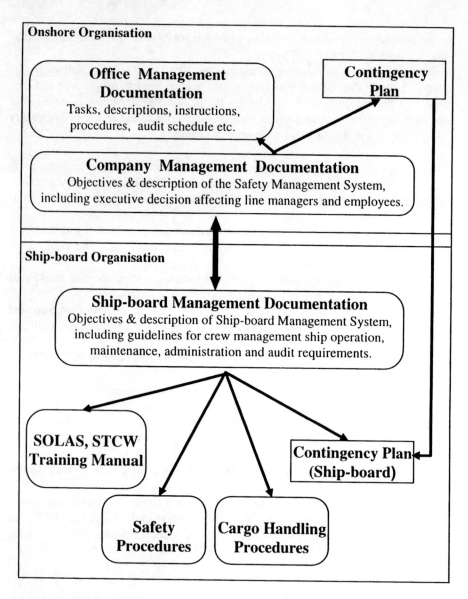

Note: *ICS/ISF Guidelines were slightly modified.*

Figure 11.1 Quality control between onshore and ship-board organisations

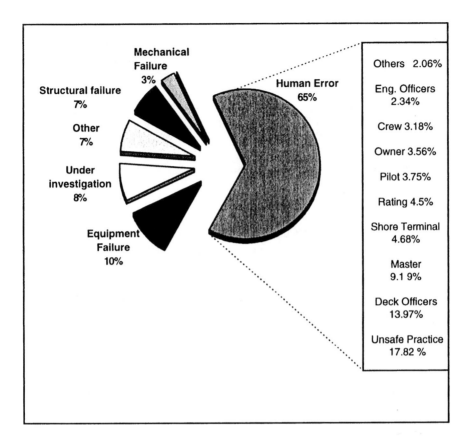

Figure 11.2 Primary causes in maritime casualties (1987-93)

As shown in Figure 11.2, the overall human factor was found to have caused 65 per cent of claims. The most substantial share of claims involving the human factor belonged to the category of 'unsafe practice'. The predominance of 'unsafe practice' claims indicates that crew quality and operational standards are inadequate. Therefore, the shipping company needs to obtain trained seafarers who have the necessary qualifications through a quality management system, which will be influenced by:

- existing regulations;
- the division and organisation of work;
- the ship's technological level;
- the crew's educational and training level;
- features relative to work and recreational areas;
- psychological aspects;
- influences of environmental conditions.

The benefits of using a quality management system are: firstly, the ship's safety organisation can be developed and practised; secondly, response time to emergencies is greatly improved; thirdly, the company can build a common quality control system on all of its vessels; and, as a consequence, finally, it can avoid direct and indirect costs caused by maritime accidents.

Quality will not, however, happen, unless people 'do' certain things. 'Doing' things requires time and time costs money, therefore, in this sense, quality has a cost. However, Crosby[10] argues that the real cost of quality is the cost of doing things wrong, the cost of waste. In contrast, the cost of doing things right is not a cost at all, but an investment. The following evidence could considerably support this argument.

Since 1990, the Det Norske Veritas has been issuing the Ship-board and Environment / Ship-board Management Certificate, which is equivalent to the ISM's Safety Management Certificate. Over the last four years statistical data from companies with safety management systems facilitated and certificated by the Det Norske Veritas, indicated that the effects of the systems were as follows: 10 per cent reduction in company liabilities insurance; 6-8 per cent reduction in P&I insurance; 37 per cent reduction in lost man-hours; 22 per cent reduction in hospitalised personnel; 40 per cent reduction in medical sign-offs; and a considerable reduction in fines from pollution and claims in connection with damaged containers.[11]

A prototype of the system for the quality assurance of seafaring labour

In this section a prototype for the quality management system of seafaring labour in the Korean shipping industry will be suggested on the basis of the ISM Code, the ISMA Code, ISO 9002, and other quality management guidelines as discussed above.

Major items enumerated in the two codes above and ISO 9002 (see Table 11.1) need to be taken into consideration in designing the Total quality management system. To satisfy the requirements of quality management, a useful approach for understanding the training process is to consider the process as a system whose boundaries interact with the remaining business operations. Training needs and requirements are identified, training is provided to meet them, the output is compared with the requirements and any necessary changes are made to the system to obtain the desired output. While this approach helps crew managers to understand how training processes operate, it must be emphasised that it should be considered within the boundary of the Total quality management system, so that training is an integral part of the overall system.[12]

A common approach to the evaluation of training is to assume that the relationship between training investment and improved organisational effectiveness is a straightforward case of linear cause and effect. However, in the vast majority of instances, training must be considered in relation to its role as a causal agent in the process of generating a quality culture. In this respect a quality trainer must have a wider outlook than a linear model allows, and seek to influence not only the individual performance, but also the development of improved communications and teamwork.[13] (See Figure 11.3.) This figure illustrates the basic concept of the quality loop of seafaring labour and was taken originally from ISO 9004 and modified for this study. Starting with market needs, the International Maritime Organisation and other quality requirements, constitute the activities essential to the quality of seafaring labour.

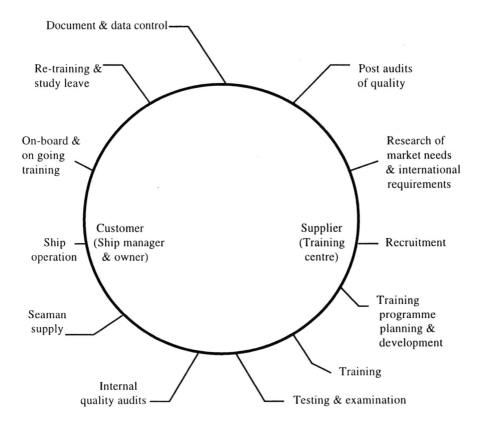

Figure 11.3   Quality loop of seafaring labour

The combination of the above figure and a modified quality system of ISO 9002 can be suggested as a prototype for the quality control and the quality assurance of seafaring labour. The box on the left in Figure 11.4 includes five requirements which concern management of a formal quality system. These requirements are closely related to the ISM and ISMA Codes, ISO 9002. Not only do assessors need evidence that all system control requirements are met, but they also need to understand that the system cannot work for any given time without the mechanisms covered in this part of the international training standards. The middle box in Figure 11.4 indicates nine requirements which relate to the training process. This is closely related to the conceptual model of the quality loop in Figure 11.3.

Each requirement is titled according to the quality management guidelines. Anyone planning this system should read the relevant information published and is also advised to consult any available interpretation document for the shipping industry. The box to the right in Figure 11.4 concerns support activities carried out to enable the training process to work effectively. As shown in the figure, these include those relating to the provision of key resources and those concerned with data arising from the operation of quality assurance.

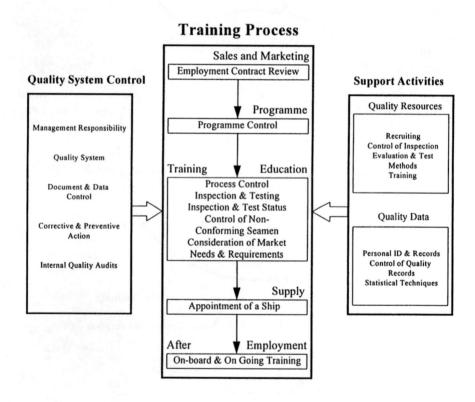

Figure 11.4 A prototype for a quality management system for seafaring labour

Although developed to match the requirements of international legislation, it is important to note that a quality management system has to be dedicated to its own organisation and must meet the quality assurance needs of seafarer qualifications and ship operation. For example, the system utilised by a liner shipping company[14] is likely to be different from that of a passenger shipping company. Moreover, systems of crew practice of the former type will probably be different in detail from one vessel to another because working conditions and cargoes are likely to be different.

Conclusion

As Korean shipping companies endeavour to compete strongly by utilising cheaper crew combinations and flagging out arrangements, there is the risk that quality control aspects of ship operations may be disregarded. Paradoxically, the provision of cheaper crews from developing countries increases the need for greater control and performance monitoring. Following the brief review of quality management codes and guidelines, and benefits of the introduction of quality management systems into shipping companies, a prototype for a quality Management System has been designed for the quality control and quality assurance of seafaring labour from both Korea and developing countries. This prototype is based upon the ISM and ISMA Codes, ISO 9002, ISO 9004 and other quality management guidelines. In this chapter it has also been argued that the quality management system, as a sub-system of a Total quality management system, is essential for the survival of the Korean shipping industry. It will contribute to the assuring the quality of seamen and, consequently, to increasing the international competitive edge of shipping companies in Korea.

To establish a continuous competitive edge, Korean shipping companies will have to commit resources to a quality management system that results in reliable quality control and quality assurance regardless of crew combinations or other factors.

Notes and References

1   Spruyt, J. (1994), *Ship Management*, Lloyd's of London Press Limited, London.

2   Oh, M. S., et al. (1994), 'A Survey on the Performance and Job Attitude of Korean-Chinese Ratings on Korean Ships', a working paper, Korea Maritime University, Pusan, Korea.

3   See Chapter 13 of this book.

4   Ibid.

5   Spruyt, J. (1994), op. cit.

6   Groocock, J. M. (1974), *The Cost of Quality*, Pitman Publishing, London.

7   American Bureau of Shipping (1995), *Management and Vessel
       Operation Guidelines*; Eriksen, H. (1994), 'The ISM Code',
       *Proceedings of the 5th International Ship Management Conference,
       Cyprus*, Lloyd's of London Press, London; and Fritzner, O. H. (1991),
       'Selecting Standards', *Proceedings of Quality Control in Shipping
       Operations*, Cambridge Academy of Transport, Cambridge.

8   Moir, P. W. (1988), *Profit by Quality*, Ellis Horwood Limited,
       Chichester.

9   Parker, L. (1994), 'Profit from a Ship Manager's Experiences',
       *Proceedings of the 5th International Ship Management Conference,
       Cyprus*, Lloyd's of London Press, London.

10   Crosby, P. B. (1979), *Quality is Free*, New American Library, New York.

11   Eriksen, H. (1994), op. cit.

12   Willis, M. (1994), 'Managing the Training Process', *Journal of
       European Industrial Training*, Vol.18, pp. 4-28.

13   Thomas, B. (1992), *Total Quality Training: The Quality Culture and
       Quality Trainer*, McGraw-Hill, London.

14   Frankel, E. G. (1993), 'Total Quality Management in Liner Shipping,
       Marine Policy, Vol. 17, pp. 58-63.

12 Development of Asian cruise and ferry markets

Introduction

Occupying close to one third of the eastern hemisphere the Asian market area offers unparalleled opportunities for passenger shipping. It is home to more than five of the world's busiest ports, several of the largest shipbuilding and repair centres and some of the most powerful shipping concerns. It is an area whose lifeblood is water commerce and contains a number of the world's most important domestic and international shipping routes. Truly well endowed as a destination, Asia is an excellent source of tourism revenue. The Asian cruise market has doubled its revenue from US $220 million to $496 million over the last five years. In 1992 the citizens of Singapore, Japan, Taiwan, Korea, Malaysia, Indonesia, Thailand, The Philippines, Australia and New Zealand spent more than US $48 billion on tourism abroad. This split was 55.8 per cent for Japan, 11.8 per cent for Taiwan, 8.3 per cent for Australia, 7.9 per cent for Korea, 4.9 per cent for Singapore, 3.6 per cent for Malaysia, 3.3 per cent for Thailand, 2.4 per cent for Indonesia, 2.0 per cent for New Zealand and 0.2 per cent for The Philippines. Hong Kong expenditures are excluded due to lack of data. However, between January and November 1993, according to figures from the Hong Kong Tourist Board, there were 1,622,807 departures to the Asia Pacific region, 189,717 to Europe, 263,982 to the Americas, 133,611 to Australia and New Zealand, and 42,854 to other areas excluding China and Macao. As a result, since the beginning of the 1990s the region has been recognised as being on the verge of expansion, much like the Caribbean in the 1960s.

This chapter examines the Asian cruise and ferry markets in the process of tourism development as well as regional economic development and co-operation from a macro and micro viewpoint. The macro viewpoint looks at the characteristics and the causes of growth in the markets, their market segments and development stages in three areas; the Far East, Southeast Asia and the South Pacific. The micro viewpoint examines the operators, the fleets and the market structure of the ferry services between Korea, China and Far East Russia; the potential prospects for the ferry lines in the region; and investigates the possibilities of co-operation with more advanced operators in the ferry business.

Characteristics and causes of growth in the cruise and ferry markets

When looking at the Asian passenger shipping market from the Western viewpoint one tends to regard it as a destination for well experienced, rather rich, North American and European cruisers. The majority of berths have been supplied by transient ships on world and Pacific cruises and a small number of pioneering ships such as the Pearl, the ill-fated Prinsendam and Club Med 2 which are based there all year round. There are also a number of Japanese registered ships catering to the Japanese market. Until 1993 this was mostly true.

The advent of Star Cruises, based in Singapore and Hong Kong, has changed the perception of local cruising by bringing the first quality 'state of the art' ships into the market. This is not to say that Fairstar, Andaman Princess, Empress, Leisure World and Coral Princess are not well maintained and operated, high quality ships serving both their owners and guest well, but that they are all ships from other markets where they had become non-competitive and were modified for their present markets and brought into the region rather late in their lives. However, these other ships carried out the important function of proving the concept that locally based cruising in Asia works. Star Cruises' ships were also built for other markets, but were acquired very early in their lives while they were still on the 'cutting edge' of current ship design.[1] The late 1994 entry of Lines International's Nautican, the former Cunard Crown Crown Monarch, has also contributed to changing the perception of local market based cruising. These events have changed the playing field and how the Asian market can be viewed. It is opportune firstly to briefly review the characteristics and causes of growth in this market and then to return to the scene of the Asian market as a prime candidate for multi-tier development.

Geography, one driver of market segmentation

Looking at the geography one can divide the area into three main regions: the Far East, consisting of the waters surrounding Japan, Korea, China, north of Hong Kong and Taiwan; Southeast Asia, consisting of the waters bordering China, south of Hong Kong, Vietnam, Thailand, Malaysia, Brunei, Singapore, Indonesia and the Philippines; and the South Pacific consisting of Australia, New Zealand, New Guinea, Micronesia and Polynesia. One of the most striking characteristics of these regions is the distances involved. The maps and tables in the appendices to this chapter show the major ports within the regions and give the distances between them. When reading the distances one should keep in mind that at 15 knots a ship covers 360 nautical miles (n.m.) a day, 480 n.m. at 20 knots and 600 n.m. at 25 knots with a big increase in costs for each 5 knots. The distance tables in the appendices are provided to put the distances in a European perspective.

The distances involved tend to push the market towards either short cruises or long cruises with their market specific software and hardware. Both the distances and the fact that most of the region is water have led to the development of the area's extensive maritime infrastructure. However, this infrastructure has developed mostly to support container and other freight operations. Looking through Lloyd's and Fairplay's port directories one finds relatively few dedicated cruise or non-ferry passenger terminals, e.g. Singapore, Hong Kong, Pusan, Shanghai, Tianjin, Kaohsiung, Yokohama, Tokyo, Kobe, Osaka, Nagasaki, Sydney, Fremantle, Auckland and a number of ports in Indonesia and Malaysia. In most of the other destination ports a cruise ship must either share a dual purpose facility with container ships or make do with a temporary arrangement. The ports which would be of interest for cruise operations are required to have berths of sufficient length, adequate channel and pier side depth and large enough turning basins.

Economic powerhouse and rising populations for the markets

Another characteristic of these regions is their economic dynamism. According to an article by Reginald Dale of the International Herald Tribune, World Bank projections place six of the biggest 15 economies by the year 2020 in this area, China, Japan, Indonesia, Korea, Thailand and Taiwan. From 1965 to 1990 the annual average rate of G.N.P. growth per capita was over 5 per cent for the economies of Japan; the 'Four Tigers', i.e. Hong Kong, Korea, Singapore and Taiwan; and the three newly industrialising economies of Southeast Asia, Indonesia, Malaysia and Thailand. These eight nations had a total population greater than 467 million people in 1994. In addition to this, the South Pacific, Australia and New Zealand had an estimated 1994 population of 21 million plus.

The population age distribution of the above countries, based on their latest census, indicated that all these countries have a fair proportion of their populations in the primary cruising group target age of 45 years plus. But one should also look at the groups 15-29 and 30-44 as sources of potential guests for short, activity intensive cruises, 'a quick getaway'.[2] They may have less money than the older groups but may also have far fewer obligations. The development of this market should pay rich dividends. One should also not ignore China, where the 1994 estimated population of the coastal urban centres of Shanghai, Beijing and Tianjin totalled over 33.5 million. The population of the Guangdong province with its capital city Guangzhou (Canton) was even greater with a 1993 estimate of 65 million plus. In China in 1992 the top 40 per cent of households controlled 53.1 per cent of the income, split fourth quintile 22.3 per cent and the fifth quintile 30.8 per cent. Though there is a great difference in the levels of income, this distribution compares favourably with Japan. There, the figures were 54.4 per cent, split 23.1 per cent and 31.3 per cent respectively. As economic prosperity increases and the government travel restrictions are relaxed, these areas should also provide substantial potential markets.

Regional economic co-operation

The Yellow Sea Economic Rim Area covers the north eastern coastal provinces of China, the Bohai major economic zone in the broad sense, the western coastal area of South and North Korea, and the Kyushu area of Japan. The coastal regions of the Bohai Sea consist of 17 major cities and prefectures, i.e. Liaoning, Hebei and Shandong provinces and Beijing and Tianjin municipalities, including Dalian, Qinhuangdao, Tianjin, Yantai, Weihai and Qingdao. Most of them are situated along the coastline of the Yellow Sea with seaports and a vast hinterland.

The above-mentioned cities have been linked to Pusan and Incheon by container and ferry services. The Yellow Sea has several distinctive advantages:

- geographical contiguity and historical relations for centuries
- a complex network of land-sea-air communications
- unique and abundant tourist resources
- opening of the Economical and Technological Development Zone (ETDZ), for example in Shanghai, Tianjin and Dalian
- abundant and low cost labour forces
- rich mineral resources

Let us pay further attention to the tourist resources and the land-sea-air transport in the region. As far as the tourist resources are concerned, the coastal cities such as Dandong, Dalian, Qinhuangdao, Yantai, Weihai, and Qingdao are situated close enough to link with tourist routes of other areas and form a complete tourist network. For example, these cities can be easily linked to: a tour to the Great Wall, which starts at Shan-haiguan Pass in the east and ends at Jiayuguan in the west; a tour to the Yellow River; a tour to the imperial residences of the Ming and Qing Dynasties; and a tour to trace the ancient states of Qi and Lu for the exploration of their cultures. Finally, such coastal cities can join air and sea routes for tours to both the Province of Jilin in north-eastern China, where approximately 250 million Korean-Chinese people live, and the regions that border with North Korea, where the Yalu River, the Tumen River and the volcanic Mount Paektu, Korea's highest mountain, are situated. They are attractive places for the tourists from South Korea.[3]

Apart from the major ports, transportation by railroad and air is easily linked to ferry services. For example, the main railroads Beijing-Tianjin and Shenyang-Dalian are linked to the coastal region of the Bohai Sea. As far as air transportation is concerned, the cities of Tianjin, Dalian, Qingdao and Yantai are comparatively large for China and are available for passenger transport. Tianjin Airport is now part of the international passenger transport of Beijing Airport.

Therefore, modern transport systems available in the region obviously play a powerful role in the supply of ferry transport in tourist markets.

Now let us look at the East Sea Rim Economic Area. Gorbachev's Vladivostok address and the break-up of the USSR played crucial roles in promoting and accelerating economic co-operation in the area. In particular, under the auspices of the UNDP, the Tumen River Project has been actively discussed since 1990 by the US, Russia, China, Japan, South and North Korea, and Mongolia as mentioned in Chapter 7. It covers the Chinese, North Korean and Russian border areas; the so-called 'Golden Triangle', which is divided into two triangles. The smaller one is formed by the Port of Rajin, the City of Hunchun, and the Port of Possiet, and the bigger one by the Port of Chongjin, the City of Yanji, and the Port of Vladivostok. Except for Russia, all the countries concerned with the project prefer the smaller one because the feasibility and practicability of the project there is higher.

As a part of their open-door policy, the Chinese government has also paid great attention to developing their rail, road and port infrastructure sufficiently to keep pace with the development of foreign trade in the smaller triangle. Equally, it is clear why the Province of Jilin views the transport networks as an integral part of its efforts to accelerate the container cargo and passenger traffic in the area.

Since 1991 three organisations have been established in order to promote and develop economic co-operation between Korea and Russia: Pusan-Vladivostok Friendship Association[4], Korea-Russia Far East Siberia Association, and Korea-Russia/CIS Economic Association. The Pusan-Vladivostok Friendship Association contributed to the opening of passenger services between the two cities in 1993.

Post-war Japan has emerged as the centre of economic gravity for the countries of the western Pacific and has become one of the most important factors for economic development in the region. Leaving international politics aside, Japan has made a lot of effort in promoting economic co-operation and cultural exchanges with China, Far East Russia and North Korea, at both national and international levels. The Japanese government has designated the City of Niigata in the north-west of Japan as a main centre for this. Consequently, a regional trading bloc has been seriously discussed and apparently one is emerging in the East Sea Rim area. It has strong impact on the ferry and container services, generating the highest levels of both intra- and inter-regional trade volumes.

The intra-regional shipping operations in East-Southeast Asia are now carrying a significant volume of passenger and container traffic within a number of sub-systems to and from the Kobe, Pusan, Kaohsiung, Hong Kong and Singapore hubs, as well as to and from the regional ports. It is the way in which the region's ports are now linked into the shipping networks - and, effectively, into port shipping systems - which is of particular importance in the East Asian area.

Cruise market segments by target passenger group[5]

Within each cruising product category, there is a series of different styles of cruising which can range from the inexpensive to the expensive, and use large or small vessels. Most operators tend to focus on specific styles, concentrating on a few geographical locations.

The actual and projected traveller numbers are equally impressive on the basis of the following figures given at the Seatrade Asia Pacific Cruise Convention in Singapore in December 1994:

- NYK Cruise Company Limited - 80,000 outbound passengers travelling on or outside Japanese waters in 1993; 32,000 on foreign registered ships; 47,000 on Japanese registered ships.
- World Express Group, Singapore - 20 million outbound travellers generated by the Asia/Pacific region in 1990. 60 million in 1993. Forecasted to grow to 120 million by the year 2000. Forty five per cent of Singapore's population make at least one outbound trip a year.
- The Australian Tourist Commission - tourism to Australia has increased by an average of 12.7 per cent over the past ten years. From Asia alone it is expected to increase at a rate of 12.8 per cent, from 900,000 in 1994 to 2.6 million in the year 2000.

From the cruise industry's perspective their share of the above figures can be divided into several categories or market segments.

The largest segment is the Japanese market. In 1993 Japan generated 12 million outbound travellers and this is expected to grow to 24 million in the year 2000. This is against a 1994 estimated population of 124 million plus, projected to reach 127 million plus by the year 2000. From discussions at the Asia Pacific Cruise Conference and the 1993 Yokohama Cruise Forum, Japanese passengers are primarily looking for a product that allows them to travel in a Japanese ambience. Of the 47,000 people travelling on Japanese ships in 1993, almost three-quarters were on seminar cruises sponsored by their companies. This would help to account for the very high proportion of short cruises within the Japanese market. The target group for pleasure cruisers, according to NYK, is Japanese in the middle to upper age bracket with middle to upper bracket incomes. They like to travel in groups and without children. They are also highly quality sensitive. This group has the time and the money for longer cruises within the Pacific, around the world and to other areas.

The next traditionally largest segment is formed by North American/European passengers. According to Mr Michael Hewitt, Director, Far East Cunard Line Limited, again coming from the middle to upper age bracket and high middle to upper income groups, this type of passenger wants to experience several different countries and cultures during his visit. In his view, this passenger is looking for cruises of 10 to 11 days' duration with a wide range of ports. The more elderly passengers from Australia and New Zealand coming into the Far East and Southeast Asia regions also fit into this category. The people in this category are more experienced and want to visit new places in a non-adventurous and comfortable style. As the 'baby-boomers' enter this market category, unprecedented opportunities should exist for new markets and destinations. According to Mr Tan Chee Chye of the World Express, shore excursions for this segment should try to capture the distinctive essence of each destination. They have both time and money and normally travel without children, independently or in small groups. They are also relatively recession proof and have high brand loyalties, however also want value for money. A broader category of this type of passenger which includes the upper end of the contemporary market is being targeted by the Royal Caribbean Cruises Limited for their year-round service operating out of Hong Kong and Singapore that is due to start in December 1995.

There is also a segment formed by people who have both time and money, seek more adventurous experiences and want to see out-of-the-way places. They are catered for by a small air/sea niche market operating small luxury ships both full and part time in these regions.

What is the profile of the typical non-Japanese Asian passenger? There is not one all-encompassing profile; there are similarities but also important differences in cultures, currencies, food likes/dislikes, languages, buying habits/preferences. According to Mr Daniel Chui, Managing Director, Cruise Lines International, operators of the Nautican, three onboard facilities have a major impact on passenger satisfaction - food and beverages, casino operations and gift shops. Some common desires of this segment are:

- They are looking for a cruise product shorter than seven days. According to Mr Hewitt of Cunard, three days is about right for the Hong Kong, Singapore or Bombay market.
- They like to travel with families.
- According to Mr Tan, the Asian passengers have sufficient disposable income to be selective in their purchases, look for value for money, and are changing from price to quality sensitive.
- They look for variety and action in the form of diverse itineraries and land-based activities, enjoyable entertainment, place high priority on 'good' eating and want sufficient port time in order to indulge in shopping.

Mr Tan further describes the passengers in this segment as coming from the higher income groups and being middle aged or retired. They are experienced travellers and will take their families on a cruise. Though recession resistant they are more prone to go on either cruise-only or land-only vacations. Mr Hewitt sees a part of the people in this segment as young, working and wanting short/busy holidays. Asian travellers make their decision to travel much closer to their departure date than their European/North American counterparts. The nearly explosive growth in the passenger numbers for the Asian regions has come mostly from this passenger group. Based on figures from the Port of Singapore Authority, the number of ships calling at Singapore rose from 32 in 1990 to 49 in 1994, while the number of calls rose from 143 to 986, and passengers from 62,585 to 703,377; 75.9 per cent of the 1994 passengers were from the ASEAN countries.

The permanent South Pacific market seems to remain fairly stable. This market can be divided into an Australian component and a Tahitian component. The Australian component has supported the Fairstar, first under the Sitmar then P&O house flags, the first Oriana and later Sea Princess for a number of years in the 1970s and 1980s. With a reference point of the line voyages from England and the distances between destinations, most of these cruises were for 10 to 19 days. Then as now, they were marketed mainly for Australians and New Zealanders, although they offered a unique opportunity to North Americans and Europeans to meet the local inhabitants on vacation. The Tahitian component, consisting of Club Med 2 and Wind Song, is targeted at the Japanese, European and North American passengers on air/sea package tours. The capacity figures in the Australian component have been boosted by an influx of one or two Russian/Ukrainian ships catering for a more budget-minded clientele. The figures for both these components grew between 1991 and 1993 by the deployment of Sea Princess and Royal Viking Sea to both areas to serve the local and the European/North American air/sea market. The major contributor to the increase in capacity is the increase in ships entering the region on world cruises and South Pacific winter deployments.

In Far and Southeast Asia the capacity figures showed modest growth, rising about 30 per cent from a capacity of 8,774 in 1990 to that of 11,425 in 1994. The Japanese component remained at just under 5,000, after the introduction of a number of new ships in 1990-92 and the retirement of some of the older ones. A number of companies such as Victoria Cruises, with six vessels, and Regal China Cruises, also with six vessels, started cruising on the Yangtze and other rivers in China in 1993 and 1994. In 1990-91 the permanent Southeast Asia fleet remained stable with ships sailing out of Hong Kong and Bangkok to serve the local market. The air/sea market out of Japan, North America and Europe was served by the Ocean Pearl and Song of Flower. In 1992 capacity in the local market increased with the introduction of Shangri-La World, Royal Pacific and Coral Princess into Singapore on short cruises. In 1994 and 1995 a new market had been developing with the introduction of Star Cruises, Lines International, Empress Cruises and Renaissance Cruises. These lines catered for a mixture of local passengers and the more cosmopolitan Japanese, European and North American passengers. It was this market that was responsible for the high growth in the passenger capacity and traffic experienced in those years. At the same time there was an increase in the number of small ships targeting the European and North American adventure/expedition markets.

The development stages of the cruise market and their ships

The cruise market in Asia can be classified into four stages.

Stage 1 - the embryonic stage wherein there exist strong cultural resistance and misconceptions to cruising, but a few have cruising experience abroad.

Stage 2 - the introductory stage comprising low product awareness, limited supply /choice and cultural resistance.

Stage 3 - the expansion stage wherein there exists an increasing awareness of the product, cultural acceptance, expansion and supply, efficiency and scale advantages with some price reduction.

Stage 4 - the mature stage wherein mature market growth is evident depending upon price and income. It is at this stage that the concept of marginal utility may begin to apply. In addition, both spending ceilings and time constraints will effect the level of demand.

All four stages exist simultaneously within the Asian market regions. Each stage depends on the line, its target market and area of operations. Each stage is discussed in further detail below.

Stage 1: Embryonic stage

At this stage, on the local level there are problems with product awareness, misconceptions of the idea of cruising, fear of the sea or loss of face from seasickness and there also exists strong cultural resistance and misconceptions to cruising. However, a few may have cruising experience abroad. For example, as will be discussed at the expansion stage, it has been found that Korean and Taiwanese tourists have 1 to 4 day cruises out of Kuala Lumpur. These cruises were combined with a variety of land options to form attractive air/sea packages. This may open up an untapped market in Korea and Taiwan.

Stage 2: Introductory stage

This stage would apply in the case of Siam Cruise's Andaman Princess based in Bangkok. Operating seven day cruises since 1990, this ship has helped introduce cruising in the Thai waters for the local population. The smaller Seatran Princess, another locally operated ship, operates on two, three and four day itineraries within Thailand. Andaman Princess is rated three stars by Douglas Ward's *1995 Berlitz Complete Guide to Cruising and Cruise Ships*. This is consistent with certain ships at Stage 3, such as the ships serving the Chinese market and the Russian/Ukrainian ships, targeting the local market, operating full and part time out of both Australia and Singapore.

Stage 3: Expansion stage

At this stage, there is a wide mix of ships and markets. The ships, under charter to German operators, making increased visits to the regions, tend to be four star or above. Two of the ships serving the expanding UK market, Canberra and Sea Princess are rated three stars plus and four stars plus, respectively. The Russian/Ukrainian ships serving an expanding budget-minded European market are rated between two and three stars. The smaller ships in this stage, such as Pearl, Club Med 2, Wind Song, Sea Goddess, Bali Sea Dancer, also carry a four star plus rating. Their target market is passengers seeking a port intensive itinerary to unique places. Bali Sea Dancer, Wind Song and Club Med 2 afford their passengers the opportunity to see some of the most beautiful places in the world from the sea as they should be seen. P&O Spice Island Cruises also operates the smaller Island Explorer and Spice Island, which can enter ports within Indonesia which are inaccessible to larger ships. Most of this market's passengers come from North America, Europe and Japan.

Within Stage 3 the length of the cruises vary. It tends to be shorter for permanently based ships, as short as a week or several days in combination with a land package. While for transient ships the cruise lengths tend to be 10, 11 days or longer. Some are cruises originating and terminating within the area while others are segments of 'around the world' or 'circle Pacific' cruises. Rated solely on their levels of comfort they would fall into Stage 3, but because of their deployment in market expansion of traditional markets they fall into Stage 4.

In comparison the Stage 3 market concentrates on one, two, three and four day cruises. These companies are aggressively pushing increased awareness and market expansion through competitive pricing and increased media/advertising awareness. The four main companies are Singapore-based Star Cruises, New Century Tours and Lines International and Kuala Lumpur-based Empress Cruise Lines.

Star Cruises, established in 1993, has the StarShips Langkapuri Star Aquarius and Star Pisces operating on 1 to 4 day cruises out of Singapore and Hong Kong, respectively. These are targeted at first time, local cruisers with young families. Their facilities make family cruising fun. The two ships are very new former Baltic Sea ferries and are rated at four stars. Although the ships are sister ships, there are subtle variations to better serve the ethnic contrasts between Singapore and Hong Kong. Star Cruises' main competition in this segment is the New Century Tours' Leisure World. Sailing a similar 1-4 day schedule Leisure World is rated at three stars. The Langkapuri Star Aquarius is competitively priced starting at approximately US $120 per person in a quad cabin for three days and two nights, up to US $490 for a single cabin. Leisure World charged from US $140 to $940 for a suite for the same time period.

The Star also has two smaller ships; Megastar Aries and Megastar Taurus. These recently acquired four star plus ships are targeted at the corporate market and sold on an 'invitation only' basis. Star's competition in this segment comes from Renaissance Cruises, with Renaissance IV and Renaissance VI and the Indocam Investments Pte. Limited's Lido Star, the former Columbus Caravelle.

According to press reports Star Cruises intends to continue to expand and broaden its passenger base to include Taiwan and South Korea. It eventually hopes to attract cruisers from the Australian and European markets.

Superstar Gemini may also offer some competition to the Royal Caribbean Cruises Limited's Viking Sun. However, the Royal Caribbean is targeting the experienced cruisers within their traditional North American and European markets. They have been marketing within Asia for a number of years and are probably hoping to draw on that market also. Royal Caribbean's market entry in December 1995 represents the first attempt to expand North American/European passenger based contemporary market cruising in this area. They will offer year round 13 and 14 night itineraries concentrating on China, the Far East and Southeast Asia. Fares run from US $2,999 to $5,699 in value season to US $3,199 to $5,899 in peak season.

Empress Cruise Lines, established in 1994, operates The Empress on 1 to 4 day cruises out of Kuala Lumpur. These cruises may also be combined with a variety of land options to form attractive air/sea packages. The Lines' target market is the new cruiser within Malaysia and the surrounding region and tourists from Korea, Taiwan, Hong Kong and China, who are visiting Malaysia. Offering Empress Class and First Class service, fares start at approximately US $170 per person for three days and two nights. The company intends to expand as suitable tonnage becomes available. As the only line in the region with a special sensitivity to the needs of Moslem passengers, it is well placed for expansion.

The activity in this segment is mostly the result of local entrepreneurs creating uniquely Asian products and selling them on the local market. However, the Royal Caribbean's venture may also open up an untapped market segment for the Asian regions.

Stage 4: Mature stage

By contrast Stage 4 ships, serving markets such as the Japanese and luxury North American and European segments, belong to well established companies with strong brand loyalties. These ships are all in the four star or more categories. As these companies enlarge their markets in their other operating areas, they will also enhance their Asian operations as their experienced cruisers seek new itineraries and destinations. Some of these ships are Asuka, Fuji Maru, Nippon Maru, Orient Venus, Crystal Harmony, Statendam, Sagafjord, Golden Princess, Pacific Princess and Island Princess. Itineraries in this category tend to be long with varying port-intensiveness and a tendency towards lengthier sea passages. Their per diem rates are consistent with their high standards of luxury and service. Though Fairsea is only rated three stars, she serves a well established market that would require the right tonnage with the right price sensitivity to grow. Therefore, Fairstar's market is placed in Stage 4.

The car ferry market in the Far East

Broadly speaking, the car ferry routes operating in the region of Korea, China and Far East Russia are long-haul ones, involving more than 14 hours at sea. (See Table 12.1 and Appendix 12.1.) These routes dominate the industry and operate across the Yellow Sea and the East Sea. The route structure of the ferry industry can be analysed by origin and destination of port. Incheon is a busy port in terms of passengers handled, and is the origin of three car ferry routes; to Weihai, Qingdao, and Tianjin. Pusan originates two routes; to Yantai and Vladivostok.

Weidong Ferry Company Limited (Weidong), Tianjin-Incheon Shipping Company Limited (Jincheon), Yellow Sea Ferry Lines (Yellow Ferry) and FESCO are operating on ferry lines between Korea, China and Far East Russia.

Table 12.1
Long haul ferry routes and operators (1995)

Korean Port	Destination	Hours	Operator	Service Frequency
Incheon	Weihai	14	Weidong	2 per week
Incheon	Qingdao	19	Weidong	1 per week
Incheon	Tianjin	29	Jincheon	6 per month
Pusan	Yantai	36	Yellow Ferry	6 per month
Pusan	Vladivostok	43	FESCO	5 per month

Source: Weidong, Jincheon, Yellow Ferry and FESCO (1995).

On one hand, the first three are joint ventures established on the basis of a series of maritime talks between the Korean and Chinese governments. (See Table 12.2.) Thus, they have agreements about services so that there is nothing to force them to make the operation of one ferry service more attractive than the other. The investment ratio in setting up the Weidong and Jincheon joint ventures was 50:50 between the Korean and Chinese parties, while that of Yellow Ferry was 5 to 95 per cent. On the other hand, FESCO[6] is operating on the Pusan-Vladivostok route without a Korean partner.

Generally speaking, the company size of the Korean parties on the Chinese routes is no bigger than the average in Korea. However, they have run the car ferry business with enthusiasm and entrepreneurship.

Table 12.2
Joint venture companies and fleets operated on China-Korea car ferry routes

	Weidong	Jinchon	Yellow Ferry[+]
Established	14 August 1990	9 December 1991	29 August 1994
HQ Location	Weihai	Seoul	Yantai
Contract parties	*Korean party:* Dongnama Shipping Co. Yukong Line & 5 other companies	*Korean party:* Dae-A Shipping Co.	*Korean party:* Zinsung Corp.
	Chinese party: Weihai Shipping Co.	*Chinese party:* Tianjin Shipping Co.	*Chinese party:* Shandong Prov. Yantai Marine Shipping Co.
Equity ratio (Korea:China)	50:50	50:50	5:95 (25:75)[++]
Type of ship	car ferry	car ferry	car ferry
Ship name	New Golden Bridge	Tien In	Yellow Sea (Ziyulan)[++]
Gross tonnage	9,978	6,870	8,475(16,071)[++]
No. of passengers	631	631	300(392)[++]
Teu	100	100	80(293)[++]
Ship age(year)	15	19	18(1)[++]
Sea speed(knots)	16	18	18(20)[++] ts

Notes: [+] *This company was taken over by C&K Ferry Lines in October 1995. (See Table 7.7)*

[++] *Figures in parentheses indicate information of the car ferry operated by C&K Ferry Lines.*

Sources: Korean Foreign Trade Association (1993), Dongnama Shipping Company (1994) and Zinsung Corporation (1996).

In particular, it is interesting to note that, trying to follow a diversification policy, the Zinsung Corporation, i.e. the Korean party of Yellow Ferry that opened the Pusan-Yantai route in September 1994, owns an international travel agency as well as a shipping agency.

The first ferry route between China and Korea was opened in 1990 by Weidong. The company serves two routes; Incheon-Weihai and Incheon-Qingdao, with one car ferry; M.V. New Golden Bridge, carrying 631 passengers with 105 teu capacity. The car ferries deployed on Chinese routes are on the whole old. Field surveys carried out by the author confirmed that the ones which used to be employed on the coastal routes in Japan are neither suitable nor convenient for passengers and containers on long haul routes.

The volume of passenger arrivals and departures by sea at Korean ports increased from 100,000 in 1992 to 117,000 in 1993. This represents a 16 per cent annual growth rate. Departures for China accounted for 47 per cent of the total in 1992. In 1993, the departures rose by a further 8 per cent to 55 per cent.

The upward trend in passenger traffic is due to a general increase in demand for foreign travel, but particular factors have come into play in recent years, one of these being the striking and consistent rise in the number of Korean-Chinese tourists, mainly from the Province of Jilin, in north-eastern China with a population of approximately 250 million. They migrated to the region to seek freedom, thus avoiding Japanese colonial rule in the first half of the 20th century. Another factor is that there was no direct liner service by air until 1994 when Korea and China signed a bilateral agreement on air transport. Finally, as mentioned earlier, the development of the ETDZ, with the increase of foreign direct investment and the expansion of economic co-operation in the coastal cities of the Bohai region, has generated considerable passenger and container traffic.

Ferries offer a complex variety of fares on each route, depending on such basic factors as the season, the time of crossing, the age of passengers and, in the case of passengers with cars, the length of vehicle. This complexity increases when the fares on different routes are considered. The traveller departing from (and returning to) any particular point in a country must consider the difference in the cost of travel to the port of departure and from the port of arrival to the ultimate destination before choosing the ideal ferry route. Therefore, compared to those in the UK for example, the fare structure and ferry routes in Korea are relatively simple. The consideration of economic factors such as accommodation class and market prices, are not reflected to a great level of detail, within these structures. Although policies differ between companies, the classes can be simply summarised in a consistent way for comparison. (See Table 12.3.)

The value of cross Yellow Sea ferry market was thought to be between US $100 million and $150 million in 1992, including container freight. However, these figures must be taken as broad estimates because they were roughly calculated based on the current fares and container cargo freight rates.

Table 12.3
Current fares by class and ferry company (1995)

	Weidong	Jinchon	Yellow Ferry
VIP class	220 - 300	210 - 250	330 - 450
Special class	180	210	250
1st class	140	145 - 170	150 - 190
2nd class	110	110 - 135	120

(unit: US $)
Sources: Weidong, Jinchon and Yellow Ferry (1995).

Cross East Sea ferry services have been developed in an entirely different way from cross Yellow Sea ones. As economic and political relations between Korea and Russia have been considerably improved since 1990, the demand for passenger traffic has sharply increased in Far East Russia. Despite a series of shipping conferences between Korea and Russia, including the last conference in February 1995, the issue, among other things, of whether Russian carriers have a right to book container cargoes in the Korean market and transport them to a third country, has not yet been settled. Therefore, the two governments have not reached an agreement to establish a joint venture company for passenger services on the Pusan-Vladivostok route. However, the latest conference hinted that this is expected to be settled by the end of 1996. (The agreement was made in May 1996. As a result, the KORUS Shipping Company Limited, which was jointly established by Sungwon Shipping Company and FESCO, began to deploy M.V. Olga Sadovskaya on the route from 20 July 1996.)

Henceforth, the only means for a Russian shipping company to legitimately enter ferry services on the route between Pusan and Vladivostok within the scope of the Korean shipping regulations, is to operate passenger ships on either a tramp or voyage charter basis. FESCO, which had eight passenger ships with accommodation for 2,084 passengers and spaces for 300 cars as of present in 1994, began a voyage charter service in 1993. After trial operations, it operated a so-called 'quasi-liner' service on the route, first with M.V. Mariya Savina from January 1994 and then by alternating five others vessels. (See Table 12.4.)

Although each of the passenger ships thus employed can accommodate approximately 200 passengers with a cargo capacity of 300 cubic metres, the ship 'Rus' is more modern and luxurious when compared to the others. Except for Rus, the other vessels have an average sea speed of 14.5 knots and their ages range from 17 to 20 years. They called in at the Port of Pusan on average five times per month, totalling 60 calls into Pusan from January to November 1994. They utilised, on average, 65 per cent of the passenger and 90 per cent of the cargo capacities during the same year.

Table 12.4
FESCO passenger ships called into Pusan between
January and November 1994

Ship name	Gross tonnage	Call sign	No. of calls	Built year
Mariya Savina	4,251	UHJZ	18	1974
Olga Sadovskaya	3,924	UKCW	23	1976
Antonina Nezdanova	3,942	ESWY	7	1978
Olga Androvskaya	4,258	EOFW	5	1977
Lyubov Orlova	3,941	UNSC	5	1975
Rus	12,798	UVBB	2	1985

Source: collected by the author (1995).

It is necessary here to briefly outline the reasons why Russian tourists visit Korea.[7] Their trips are mainly organised by tourist companies. These companies charter a passenger ship from FESCO and sell tickets to either their customers or to other tourist companies. They provide tourists with transportation and accommodation only.

The Korean market offers various kinds of goods to the Russian tourists, from clothes to second-hand automobiles and used tyres. The most popular goods are foodstuffs, clothes, footwear and electronic goods. Most of these goods are of high quality and are, on average, half the price of those in the Russian market. They can also be purchased within one city in Korea. Moreover, the distance between Pusan and Vladivostok is relatively short and cheap sea transportation allows bulky cargoes to be carried. All the above factors make their business easier and more profitable. However, a survey showed that cargo and cabin spaces on FESCO ships could not hold all the cargoes and personal luggage of the passengers.[8] As a result, wholesale traders with a group of peddlers chartered a scientific research vessel on the basis of voyage or time charter for the route Vladivostok-Pusan, and slightly modified her into a passenger ship at the expense of her charterer and shipowner, who are mainly based in the Primorsk region. She can accommodate approximately 30 passengers with a cargo capacity of 300-400 cubic metres. (See Table 12.5.) Ships of this kind called into Pusan a total of 64 times from January to November in 1994, and it is estimated that they transported 1,600 round-trip passengers.

Owing to the flood of Russian shoppers, Pusan is currently enjoying an unexpected boom, following years of decline in the apparel and shoe industries. Nearly 80 clothing and shoe manufacturing companies, which were faced with shutdown, have bounced back to life because of the 'Russian demand'. Some special trade and shopping areas have been established for Russian tourists in Seoul as well as in Pusan.

Table 12.5
Other Russian ships deployed on Pusan-Vladivostok route,
January - November 1994

Ship name	Gross tonnage	Ship type	No. of calls into Pusan
Akademik Shokalskiy	1,753	Convential passenger	6
Akademik Kalorov	5,497	Convential passenger	1
Akademik Oparin	2,441	Convential passenger	5
Akademik Kalorov	5,804	Convential passenger	12
Akademik Shrishov	5,754	Convential passenger	12
Priboy	3,270	Convential passenger	14
Ocean	3,143	Convential passenger	14

Source: collected by the author (1995).

The fares of FESCO ships on the Pusan-Vladivostok route started at a level of US $500 per person in January 1993 and, owing to the high demand for the service, increased to US $800 in 1994 for a return ticket. A round trip takes eight days, including two or three days for shopping in Korea. The fares cover meals at sea and accommodation on board in the Port of Pusan and up to 100 kg. of personal luggage. The fares of the modified ships on the same route were US $500 in 1994 on equivalent terms.

During the period from January to November 1994, all Russian passenger ships made approximately 140 voyages on cross East Sea ferry routes and transported approximately 13,000 round-trip passengers from Far East Russia. The estimated value of the Pusan-Vladivostok ferry market amounted to US $6 million in terms of fares and cargo traffic in 1994. As this calculation was mainly based on information acquired by interviews, consisting of very fragmentary evidence, the reader should be warned against placing too much reliance on it.

Prospects for cruise and ferry markets in Asia

Links between large cities in Asia are important factors in the development of cruise and ferry routes. They have their own relatively uncontested traffic, in particular in Far East Asia, both in passengers and cargo. The traffic is well connected to the hinterland and cities with sufficient tourist resources in the region. In this section much more emphasis is made on the markets in Far East Asia because the cruise market is an embryonic stage.

It would seem that both the introductory stage of the cruise market and the approach of more modernised car or fast ferries into the Asian area are expected. An outline of the major causal factors and future prospects follow:

- An infinite number of highly desirable destinations, both famous and not so famous.
- Superb maritime infrastructure and government interest in a number of countries to improve cruise facilities.
- Well established tourism infrastructure and organisation in major ports.
- Excellent air connections and capacity from various turn-around ports.
- Support from tourist and trade organisations.
- Growing regional economic power, affluence and population.
- An untapped market of potential passengers in Taiwan and Korea, where local capital and entrepreneurs are entering the market.
- Good climate that allows rotation of ships through the area to take advantage of the best weather, i.e. Royal Caribbean's Far East and Southeast Asian itineraries suggest Southeast Asia and South Pacific rotation.
- Incomes in Korea are, on the whole, rising so that not only is the number of tourists from Korea increasing but also their demand for high quality services is increasing rapidly.
- Owing to low-skilled labour and over aged, outmoded loading and discharging equipment at Chinese ports[9], modernised ro-ro ships are urgently required.[10]
- The Chinese government's policy towards State-owned shipping companies gives them the authority to negotiate contracts with their foreign partners and to make flexible management decisions by themselves.
- Two more car ferry routes, i.e. Incheon-Dalian and Pusan-Shanghai, are due to open soon. Each route will be operated by a Chinese company in association with a consortium in Korea. They are looking for second-hand ships for the routes. For example, a family controlled company is looking for a second-hand ship, which should be less than 15 years old, 7,000-10,000 grt., 300 to 500 passenger, 200 teu, and with a sea speed of 20 knots. She is intended for upmarket car ferry services. M.V. Ziyulan was purchased and deployed on Pusan-Kunsan-Yantai route in June 1996. (See Table 12.2 and Appendix 12.1.)
- FESCO is striving to seek new customers with the aim of maximising hard currency inflow.
- Plans to increase the carriage of goods for foreign affreighters, expanding the geographic areas of operation.
- Plans to renew cargo and passenger tonnages with the capital from foreign capital markets or through joint ventures.
- Plans to open the route Vladivostok-Pusan-Shanghai in order to increase the rate of utilisation of passenger ships.
- Furthermore, FESCO is planning to decommission the passenger ships of the Maria Ermolova type beginning from the year 2001, and to expand the fleet of the FESCO by five new passenger ships with 400 to 500-passenger

capacity under the State Programme of Revitalisation of Russian Merchant Fleet and Ports.[11]

However, the area also has a number of challenges to make the cruise and ferry markets efficient and to make the voyage more interesting:

- On the local level - problems with product awareness, misconceptions of the idea of cruising, fear of the sea or loss of face from seasickness.
- Increased safety demand for cruising services.[12]
- Regional/ethnic preferences, customs and backgrounds force the development of very 'market specific' ships, tend to make economies of scale difficult, and work against the demand for new buildings.
- Time and Money! The cost of the cruise, the cost of getting there. Short Asian vacations versus long North American and even longer European vacations.
- For the Japanese, North American and European cruise markets, long flight times might cause a problem, i.e. from FRA to NRT 11 hours, to HKG 12 hours, to SIN 12 hours, to SYD 21 hours; from SFO to NRT 11 hours, to HKG 12 hours, to SIN 18.5 hours, to SYD 14.5 hours; from NRT to SIN 7 hours, to SYD 9 hours, to PAP 10.5 hours.[13]
- The political situation in the Philippines, the pirates in the South China Sea, terrorist threats - one incident can ruin an entire season.
- As the number of ships increases problems with congestion at the facilities may increase along with conflicts between transient and area based ships.
- To develop a total revenue management technique[14] and to assure total quality management services at a cruising company.

Since 1994, air transport has been available on the routes Seoul-Beijing, Seoul-Tianjin and Seoul-Shanghai in the form of liner services and Seoul-Vladivostok on the basis of voyage charter. It generally means that car ferry services may be facing competition from air transport. However, for the time being, it is not likely that competition between the two is going to be severe. The reasons for this are; firstly, traffic is generated mainly from China and Far East Russia and their incomes, on the whole, are lower; secondly, the coverage of regional air services is currently inadequate between the respective hinterlands of the competing ferry ports; thirdly, tourists on cross East Sea and Yellow Sea ferry routes have a high demand for cargo space to transport bulk goods which they have purchased and, thus, they prefer the sea to the air.

New niche markets in Far East Asia?

The Asia Pacific cruise market has long been considered to have great growth potential but has not always lived up to the expectations of its operators. Table

12.6, in which the historic figures for capacity in terms of passenger-days (or bed-days) are set out, illustrates that, while the market had been gradually developing, growth had been erratic with a high in 1987 of 1.1 million passenger-days followed by a low of 691,000 in 1990. Since 1991, growth was modest in Far East Asia until 1994. In spite of this uneven growth pattern, there are indications that the region has massive potential in cruising and that the embryonic stage in the cruise market may well develop into an introductory one. For example, in 1994 the inauguration of a significant new river cruising operation in China was made by Victoria Cruises, which is based in New York. It deployed the first two vessels entering service, Victoria I and II, which operate five-day cruises.[15]

Table 12.6
Growth of Asia Pacific market 1985-94 ('000s passenger-days)

Year	Far East	Southeast Asia	South Pacific	Trans Pacific	Total
1985	164	249	86	29	528
1986	274	168	508	78	1,028
1987	466	273	353	18	1,110
1988	280	173	317	69	839
1989	239	207	383	114	943
1990	149	185	303	54	691
1991	169	121	407	2	699
1992	189	165	402	11	767
1993	252	227	378	15	872
1994	305	283	764	51	1,403
% change 1985/94	+ 86	+ 14	+ 788	+ 76	+ 166

Source: Lloyd's Ship Manager, *Cruise and Ferry Review* (1994), Oct/Nov, p. 8.

Referring to the above-mentioned current situation and the prospects for ferry lines in the East Sea and Yellow Sea areas, the ferry conversion, refit and second-hand markets are expected to flourish over the years to come. The upward market for conversion and refit may be, above all, attributed to the existence of the possibility of converting ships which were previously research ships, but are now used as passenger ships. In addition, this market is also likely to be fuelled by the replacement of older vessels by younger ones and thereafter by undertaking upgrades and modifications to suit trading routes and car ferry requirements. Moreover, because new building prices have risen sharply in recent years and ferry companies in the region are in a financially weak situation; upgrades and conversions are seen as being a cost effective alternative.

Furthermore, the other alternative can be found in co-operation with advanced ferry operators. As mentioned in the above section, second-hand car ferries purchased from Japan, where they had been deployed on coastal routes, are not considered to be efficient on long haul routes. Thus, advanced countries will be able to sell their ferries, which are comparatively modern and comfortable, cheaper than locally built new ships. If the business is combined with favourable foreign financing, it will be helpful for the ferry industry operating on ferry routes between Korea, China and Far East Russia. Consequently, a busy second-hand market profitable to both parties will come into existence.

To remain competitive in a more demanding market, the ferry companies will have to operate competitive and cost efficient ships and to maintain a high profile in the new markets in the Yellow and East Sea areas. Therefore, experienced management teams are required for the ferry industry in the region. Advanced specialist operators will help the industry to solve covert and overt problems in their ferry operations and management, shorten the ferry business learning curve, earn the benefits of know-how, e.g. crew training, casino[16] and duty free shop operations on board, and to promote the business.

As far as the acquisition of passenger ships is concerned, according to FESCO, the main question of financing the construction of new ships, the purchase of second-hand ships or the conversion of its existing passenger ships, may be solved by the investments from foreign partners in mutually profitable joint operations.

It is also worthwhile mentioning the prospects for the ferry business of SASCO. It began to enter the tramp ferry service on the Pusan-Korsakov route with sister car ferries, accommodating 100 passengers in addition to about 300 cubic metres of cargo capacity in 1994. They operated, on average, one voyage per month on the route, carrying on average 70 passengers per voyage from January to November 1994. The SASCO car ferry fleet called into the Port of Pusan in the same period, nine times in total. Although the volume of passenger and cargo traffic it transported was small in 1994, it is expected to grow steadily in the years to come.

Three reasons for this are, firstly, 800,000 Korean-Russians, who were forced to migrate by Japan during the Second World War, live in Sakhalin; secondly, Korea is a suitable country for their shopping requirements; finally, the transportation cost per container teu on the direct route Pusan-Korsakov is much cheaper than the indirect routes via Vladivostok or Vanino. Furthermore, it is important to note that at the maritime talks held in Seoul in February 1996 between the Korean and Russian governments, it was agreed to open a container liner service on the direct route. They also have plans to use the Port of Possiet for the transfer of passengers on the route from Sokcho to Hunchun, which is due to be opened in the near future. (See Appendix 12.1.)

In these circumstances, it can be suggested that there are three possible ways to participate in the cruise and ferry business in the region; firstly, to go into partnership with a Russian company; secondly, to have a business relationship with a Korean company; finally, to have a business link with a Chinese company. It is very difficult to judge which alternative is the best. It may depend on the co-operative business sector, the foreign investor's company structure, know-how and business culture. It seems that the first two ways are more likely to be suitable for western operators. The reasons for this are that, firstly, there may be more room and a higher chance for them to be involved and co-operate in the sale and purchase of second-hand cruisers and car ferries, their modification or conversion and refit projects, and the transfer of advanced management and operation know-how. Secondly, as far as business communications and history of cruise and ferry businesses are concerned, they have a more competitive edge and may co-operate with their partners in more favourable environments which result from socio-economic systems.

Conclusions

Of particular interest is the growing economic integration of Asia which has already been reflected in the rapid development of cruise and ferry networks.[17] The interface between intra- and inter-regional transport systems is not only the catalyst for economic development but also one of the principal stepping stones to economic co-operation within the region. Inter-regional passenger shipping operations are now carrying significant traffic within the region, where the ports are now linked into shipping and ferry services.

It has been found here that all four stages of the cruise market, i.e. the embryonic, introductory, expansion and mature stage, exist simultaneously within Asian market regions; that each stage depends on the line, its target market and area of operations; that a niche cruise market is evolving with high potential in Far East Asia; and the possibilities of joint venturing or co-operation with advanced operators in the cruise and ferry services are high in the region.

In spite of challenges the Asian ferry and cruise markets have great potential for further development at all tiers. If a company wishes to build or buy a new ship for the cruise market, it is required to decide what country and which nationality is to be focused upon as the market target. It is also necessary to have a very thorough knowledge in customs, fashion, laws and regulations in order to obtain the full support and satisfaction of its customers targeted in the market concerned. Therefore, it appears that the companies involved in expanding Asian markets have taken this into account and are acting accordingly.

Car ferry services are a crucial and flexible means of transporting tourists and the potential is considerable in Far East Asia. In addition, providing the two Koreas are reunified in the near future, the tourist resources at Mt. Keum-Kang in North Korea may be another important factor to attract tourists and to accelerate the cruise and ferry markets in the region. Rising disposable income, increased leisure time and a thirst for travel are valid stimuli to inspire growth in cruise and ferry markets in Asia. We should hear much more about these markets in the region during the next century.

Notes and References

1 Lloyd's Ship Manager (1995), 'Star Rises in Asia', *Cruise and Ferry Review*, March/April, pp. 28-29.

2 Schule, M.J. (1980), *An Analysis of the North American Cruise Industry: Executive Summary*, p. 5, US Department of Commerce Maritime Administration, Washington D.C.

3 Lee, T-W. and Song, D-W. (1995), 'Current situation and prospects for ferry lines between Korea, China and Far East Russia', in *Cruise & Ferry '95*, Vol. 1, Business Meetings Ltd., London.

4 On further information on the association, see Chapter 7 of this book.

5 Coggins Jnr., A. (1995), 'Asian Cruise Market - a candidate for multi-tier development?', in *Cruise & Ferry '95*, Vol. 1, Business Meetings Ltd., London.

6 According to the privatisation programme, FESCO, as one of the State-owned shipping companies of the former USSR, became a joint stock company in Vladivostok. On the privatisation process and business performances of FESCO, see Chapter 9 of this book.

7 Lee, T-W. and Yatsenko, A. (1993), 'A Survey and Short Study on the Russian Peddler in Pusan', unpublished paper, Postgraduate School of Maritime Industrial Studies, Korea Maritime University.

8 *Ibid.*

9 On the current bottlenecks at Chinese ports, see Chapter 7 of this book.

10 On the role of ro-ro ships, see Boyce, J., et al., (1980), *Ro-Ro Ships and Their Market Role*, Fairplay Publications Ltd., London.

11 On recommendations for Russian water transport, see Holt, J. (1993), *Transport Strategies for the Russian Federation*, The World Bank, Ch. 7, Washington D.C.

12   Parker, C.J. (1993), 'Aspects of Passenger Ship Safety', in *Cruise & Ferry '87*, Business Meetings Ltd., London.   Drewry Shipping Consultants (1993), *Cruise Ship and Ferry Costs in the 1990s: The Economic Impact of Increased Safety Demand*, London.

13   Doy, G. (1985), *The Quality of Service Index and Passenger Attitudes to Airline Service Levels*, working papers no. 6, Department of Shipping and Transport, University of Plymouth, Plymouth.

14   Zayas, B. (1995), *Revenue Management: Does it receive enough attention in the cruise/ferry industry?*, Revenue Technology Services Corporation, Texas.

15   Lloyd's Ship Manager (1994), *Cruise and Ferry Review*, April/May, p. 2.

16   Rahn, H.J. (1987), 'Effective Ship-board Casino Operations' in *Cruise & Ferry '87*, Business Meetings Ltd., London.

17   On container transport in Far East Asia, see Chapter 7 of this book.

Appendix 12.1
Ferry routes between Korea, China and Far East Russia

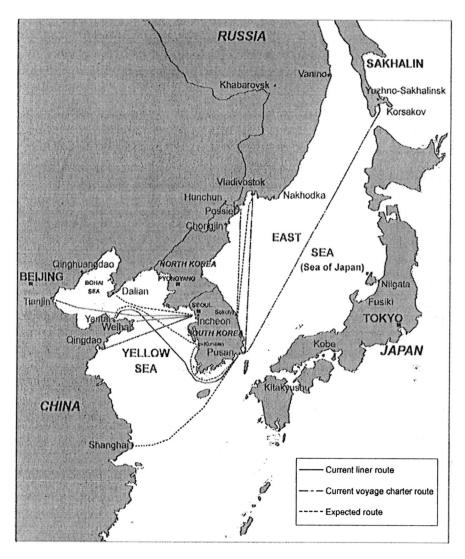

Appendix 12.2
Major cruise ports in Far East and Southeast Asia regions

Far East region

Destination	Sea Miles	Origin	Sea Miles	Destination
Kure (KRE)	515	Yokohama	528	Hakodate (HKD)
Nagasaki (NGS)	683	(YOK)	357	Osaka (OSA)
Shanghai (SHA)	1036		659	Pusan (PUS)
Tianjin(TSN)	1250		1584	Hong Kong (HKG)
Manila (MNL)	1758		2892	Singapore (SIN)
Bangkok (BKK)	2979		4330	Sydney (SYD)
Tianjin (TSN)	1360	Hong Kong	1140	Pusan (PUS)
Shanghai (SHA)	824	(HKG)	471	Keelung (KEL)
Quangzhou (QZJ)	410	northbound	342	Kaohsiung (KHH)
Xiamen (XMN)	340		210	Shantou (SWA)

Southeast Asia region

Destination	Sea Miles	Origin	Sea Miles	Destination
Macau (MAC)	60	Hong Kong	300	Hainan (HAK)
Manila (MNL)	632	(HKG)	803	Haiphong (HPH)
Ho Chi Minh City (SGN)	927	southbound	1460	Singapore (SIN)
Bangkok (BKK)	1489		4480	Sydney (SYD)
Hong Kong (HKG)	1460	Singapore	1341	Manila (MNL)
Haiphong (HPH)	1322	(SIN)	1031	Danang (TOU)
Ho Chi Minh City (SGN)	646		831	Bangkok (BKK)
Port Kelang (PKL)	210		430	Penang (PNG)
Langkawi (LGK)	520		640	Phuket (HKT)
Jakarta (JKT)	525		1000	Bali (BOA)
Sydney (SYD)	4275		3012	Cairns (CNS)
Singapore (SIN)	210	Port Kelang	310	Langkawi (LGK)
Penang (PNG)	220	(PKL)	430	Phuket (HKT)

Major cruise ports in Far East and Southeast Asia regions

South Pacific region

Destination	Sea Miles	Origin	Sea Miles	Destination
Auckland (AKL)	1275	Sydney	1275	Sydney (SYD)
Wellington (WLG)	1236	(SYD)	561	Wellington (WLG)
Suva (SUV)	1735		950	Suva (SUV)
Papeete (PPT)	3306	Auckland	2120	Papeete (PPT)
Cairns (CNS)	1277	(AKL)	2120	Cairns (CNS)

Appendix 12.3
Major Asian cruise market regions

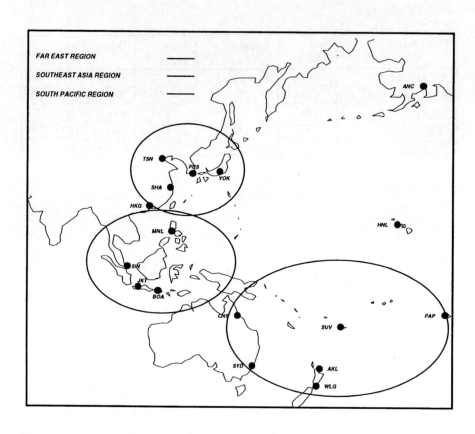

Appendix 12.4
Major cruise ports and distance tables in the Mediterranean

Destination	Sea Miles	Origin	Sea Miles	Destination
Beirut (BEY)	132	Limassol	643	Beirut (BEY)
Alexandria (ALY)	271	(LMS)	593	Port Said (PSD)
Aqaba (AQJ)	595	Piraeus	352	Istanbul (IST)
Piraeus (PIR)	530	(PIR)	729	Tunis (TUN)
Tunis (TUN)	309	Naples	1071	Limassol (LMS)
Marseilles (MRS)	457	(NAP)	1189	Beirut (BEY)

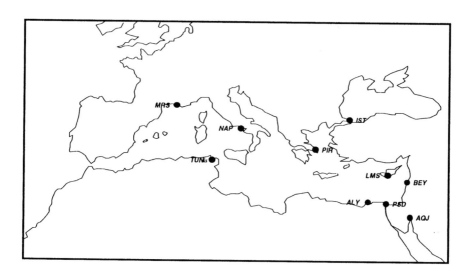

Appendix 12.5
Major cruise ports in Far East and Southeast Asia regions

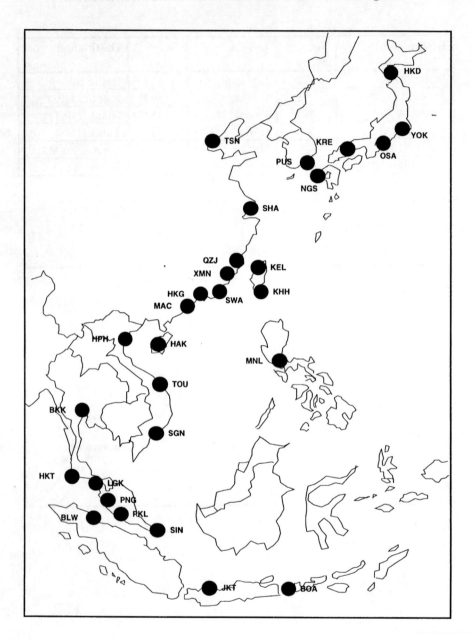

13   Flagging options for the future: A turning point in Korean shipping policy?

Introduction

Debates with regard to the introduction of, firstly, a second register and, secondly, professional ship management methods, have been increasingly prominent during the last five years in Korea. The level of concern has been accelerated by an unfavourable shipping environment and the deterioration of the competitive edge, as well as by the inherent complexity and changing nature of the shipping industry and its structure. Those who have vested interests in these issues may be broadly classified into two groups: the Korea Shipowners' Association (KSA) and the Korea Ship Management Companies' Association (KSMCA).

Members of the former group may turn to open or second registers and ship managers in order to help them survive and eventually flourish throughout and beyond the current decade, specifically: (i) to cut operating costs, (ii) to flag out to established second ship or flag of convenience (FOC) registers, (iii) to acquire access to alternative sources of manpower, and (iv) to avoid the disadvantageous fiscal policies suffered currently by Korean shipping companies. The latter group has concentrated predominantly on crew manning management for the last three decades, but the number of vessels which it has manned is sharply decreasing annually, due to both the deteriorating quality of Korean seafarers and the increasing in their labour costs. The KSMCA wants to expand its business portfolio by entering both national and international markets of ship management and by introducing the Korean International Ship Register (KIS).[1]

The purpose of this paper is to outline the current shipping situation in Korea and to suggest flagging options so that both Korean owners and managers can optimally face that situation, exploring the advantages and disadvantages of each solution. Because ship management is closely interrelated to flagging strategies, the paper also discusses areas of co-operation between Korean shipping or ship management companies and advanced foreign ship management companies.

221

The current situation in Korean shipping

With the downward trend in shipping markets during the early 1990s, the freight earnings in most segments of the international ocean transport industry were considerably below the break-even levels which reflect the minimum charter rates or freight tariffs to cover all shipping costs.[2] The search for cost-effective or cost-saving options has always been in the forefront of shipowners' and ship managers' minds, particularly in the bulk and low freight trades. Selecting the flag of a vessel is a crucial issue in a successful shipping business, as the economics of running a merchant ship are closely related to her registration.

This section is devoted to highlighting the major negative factors of the current situation in Korean shipping which shipowners are facing under Korean ship registration.

Rising crew costs and difficulties in the recruitment of qualified crew

Increased crew costs for Korean shipping companies were inevitable with the rapid improvement in wages and working conditions for shore-based occupations within Korea since the mid-1980s, when movements in democratisation in Korea were accelerated. Over the years this has been closely coupled with the increase of bargaining power for seamen. Korean seafarer's unions claimed that both their average rate of wage increase and working conditions must be equal to those of shore labour. As a result, Korean seamen were able to push up their wages and demand better contract terms including increased fringe benefits such as paid holiday leave. This has become a critical factor in the struggle to keep Korean shipping competitive.

The KSA calculated that annual manning costs for Panamax bulk carrier crewed by Korean officers and ratings exceeded US $800,000 in 1994. If the vessel were crewed by Filipino officers and ratings, all paid at the ITF approved rates, the annual cost would be reduced to just over US $350,000. In the light of figures such as these, it is not difficult to understand the attraction to a Korean shipowner of flagging his or her ship out to an open registry. However, in recent years, Korean shipowners have tried to cut crew costs through employing Korean-Chinese ratings. In the period between 1991 and 1994, 20 shipping companies employed a total of 868 ratings to man their fleet, drawing mainly from the Jilin Province in China.[3] Generally speaking, shipowners are demanding a greater continuity of personnel to match their own commitment to the continuity of their operations. Two important benefits of continuity of personnel are its contribution to both safety and efficiency, for example as mentioned in the quotation below:[4]

> People inevitably develop a sense of belonging. They come to know exactly what is expected of them. They have time to get to know the ships and the PSMS operational style. They come to value our programmes, designed to raise safety awareness.

222

The higher the turnover of seafarers, the more expensive it is, in recruitment and training costs, to run a manning operation.

A recent survey illustrated that most shipowners were not satisfied with their crew's performance and job attitude, that the effect of cost-saving was not largely due to low productivity, and that the continuity of ratings employment was less than two years.[5] Meanwhile, both the quality of new entrants in maritime schools and the passing rate of licence examinations in Korea have gradually decreased. It has been therefore very difficult for the Korean shipping industry to recruit them as it had planned since 1990. It can be stated that as far as the rating class is concerned, Korea is gradually changing from a supply country to a demand one.

High insurance cost caused by a high rate of marine casualties

It is thought that the good reputation earned by Korean crews for their aptitude and attitude during the 1970s has been eroded since the latter half of the 1980s and, consequently, in terms of crew costs and job performances Korean crews held no advantages over Filipino or Indian ones in the labour market.[6]

To make matters worse, the world statistics of total losses of ships by registration between 1989 and 1992 showed that Korea was one of the foremost countries in terms of gross tonnage of total losses of nationally manned ships.[7] This has caused Korean shipowners to pay additional insurance premiums which consequently has resulted in increasing shipping costs.[8]

The shipping industry in an adverse taxation climate

Taxation issues are highly complex and the amount of effort expended in a typical shipping enterprise in order to both legally minimise taxes and to accurately report their activities under various tax statutes is considerable. In general, the shipping industry is taxed in the same manner as any other industry in Korea. The kinds of tax imposed on a Korean shipping company can be classified into three groups:

(a)   National tax: corporation tax, income tax, withholding tax on the income of bareboat chartered vessels, and tax on capital gains.

(b)   Customs duties: on the amount of repairs and maintenance abroad, on the price of the imported ships, and on the amount of imported equipment and materials.

(c)   Local tax: registration tax, acquisition tax on the ships, property tax, special tax for the promotion of education equivalent to 20 per cent of registration tax, inhabitants' (poll) tax, and common facility tax.

Although international tax comparisons are difficult to make precisely and may often be misleading, it is worthwhile to search for a more objective yardstick in order to make comparisons of tax cost country by country.

Table 13.1
A comparison of tax burdens on shipowners by major country

Tax Item	Korea	Japan	Norway	Liberia
Regional tax	8,527	191,700	63	3,107
Annual total tax	448,100	4,142	10,650	24,225
Grand total	456,627	195,842	10,713	27,332
Index (Korea = 100)	100	42.9	2.3	6.0

(unit: US $)

Source: The Korea Maritime Institute (1991), *Haewoon Sanup Kalyeon Seijeieui Gaeseon Banghyang*, [*The Proposal for Improving Tax System related to the Shipping Industry*], p. 73.

Table 13.1 illustrates the relative burden of taxation on shipping in different countries based on the following assumptions: ship size - 78,000 gross tons, 50,000 net registered tons; ship price - US $35.5 million; exchange rates - US $1 equivalent to 716.4 Korean Won and 5.9075 krone at the end of 1990, respectively. With this simple comparison it is possible to conclude that Korean taxation is totally unfavourable towards shipowners and contributes to the declining competitive power of shipping in Korea.

Table 13.2
A comparison of annual taxation by register

Register	Annual fees (US $)
Korea	448,100
Liberia and Panama	4,550
Malta	3,488
Bermuda and Cyprus	2,500
Bahamas	1,769

Source: Lloyd's of London Press (1992), 'Flagging Strategies', Proceedings of 2nd International Ship Management Conference, pp. 59-68.

Table 13.2 highlights the adverse taxation situation further, showing the annual fees payable in established open registers and compared with the Korean register.

Furthermore, a comparison between the Korean air industry and the shipping industry serves to illustrate a lack of parity in the government's treatment of its transport sectors. Although both industries have quite similar business characteristics, there exists unequal taxation between the two industries within Korea as can be seen in Table 13.3.

The air industry enjoys freedom from customs duties on imported aircraft, repairs and maintenance carried out abroad, and equipment and materials imported. However, the shipping companies must pay customs duties on imported vessels, on repairs and maintenance, and equipment and materials imported for the ship. To make matters worse, a ship purchased by bareboat chartered with purchase option financial arrangements[9] is regarded as an imported one and a customs duty, i.e. 2.5 per cent of the purchase price of the ship, is imposed on her even before she is registered in Korea.

Table 13.3
Comparison of taxation between air and shipping industries

Tax item	Tax for the total price or cost on the following items:	Shipping industry	Air industry
Customs duties	The importation of craft	2.5%	none
	Repairs and maintenance undertaken abroad	2.5%	none
	Imported equipment and materials	13%[+]	none
	% of ship's price for BBC/PO[++]	2.5%	n/a
Registration tax	Purchase price of craft	0.02%	0.1%
Acquisition tax	Purchase price of craft	2%	None[+++]
Property tax	Market price of craft	0.3%	0.15%

Notes:
[+] The rate is average value. For shipbuilding ocean-going vessels with the equipment and materials which are not produced in Korea, 90 per cent of the rate is exempted.
[++] A bareboat chartered with purchase option.
[+++] The rate is exempted until end of 1997.

Sources: The Korea Maritime Institute and the Hanjin Group Logistics Research Centre (1995).

While the taxation system and government regulations are, as ever, unfavourable towards shipping companies, it is very difficult for them to increase the share of the international shipping market.

The total revenue of a shipping company comes largely from two major business activities: (i) freight and chartering earnings from ship operations, and (ii) capital gains from the sale and purchase of ships. The former may be referred to as the operational function and the latter as the commercial function. Successful owners must properly combine the two functions efficiently to maximise their total revenue. Generally speaking, in the long term, the portion of the total revenue earned through capital gains tends to be higher than that of freight earnings. Thus, the strategy for ship sales and purchases is regarded as a very important factor in the whole spectrum of shipping company strategies.

One very significant factor which seriously affects the shipowner's choice of purchases or new orders is the availability and cost of capital. Further, it must be stressed that timing is of paramount importance for the purchase of a second-hand vessel. Unfortunately, these two factors are not freely available to Korean shipowners due to government regulation. In other words, they are often not able to access favourable foreign markets to raise the required funds for the purchase of second-hand vessels, due to limitations regarding the introduction of total foreign currency into Korea. Even if funds could be raised, they could only be utilised for a limited range of vessels due to the control regulations on importing second-hand vessels. This means that the opportunity to gain revenue through the commercial function is very limited for Korean shipowners and has caused Korean shipping companies to achieve only low levels of profitability over the past four years.

New transitional era in Korean shipping

Profit seeking is a principal objective in a market economy. Shipowners must operate economically and efficiently in order to even survive in the world's commercial bulk cargo trades, the most competitive segment of the entire shipping industry. To register ships under FOC or second national registers is one of the ways to achieve a comparative advantage through cost minimisation. For example, Norwegian and American-controlled ships were registered abroad as a way of meeting the international competition on equal terms and conditions. This might not be possible under their own registries because of comparatively higher operating costs and unfavourable tax systems. This is one of the reasons why FOC and second registers appeared in the world shipping arena. Many shipowners in the traditional advanced maritime countries such as UK, Japan, Norway, and Greece, have utilised this strategy. Even in less developed maritime nations, with their generally lower cost structures, the advantages gained by flagging out are proving to be attractive, as is illustrated by the case of India.

In light of both the recent trend for flagging out vessels and the current situation in Korean shipping, the question of where to register vessels has to be confronted by Korean shipping enterprises. It must be queried as to whether patriotic sentiments can continuously prevent shipowners from entering ships in an open register rather than under the Korean flag when both options are available. Probably NOT. Eventually Korean shipowners may consider the following two scenarios to overcome the current situation in shipping.

The first scenario

The Korean International Ship Register (KIS) will be instituted following the example of established second registers such as the NIS, GIS, and DIS. Korean flagged ships will be registered under the KIS to make Korean shipping more competitive through, for example, tax benefits and flexible crew and financing arrangements.

The second scenario

Korean-flagged ships will flag out to open registers in order to enjoy the advantages outlined above to facilitate an increase in competitive power.

Under the two scenarios, Korean shipowners can expect to experience advantages and disadvantages as illustrated in the check list, Table 13.4. Some obstacles exist to the implementation of the first scenario.

Firstly, it may take a long time, probably at least two years, and complicated procedures will be necessary to complete the so-called KIS Act. This is because it must be approved by the Council of Ministers and then be put before the National Assembly for final approval. Secondly, because most maritime matters are inter-related between various Ministries, which have bureaucratic characteristics, a stumbling block to their solution may be the vested power of each Ministry. Finally, the negotiations on the KIS between seafarers' unions and shipowners are likely to continue for a considerable time without any clearly defined agreement.

Under the second scenario it is likely that in the early stage of flagging out, Korean shipowners register bulk carriers, notably older carriers, in open registries in order to have more cost-effective savings. It is believed that 'flagging out' may have a substantial impact both on shipping policy and on the structure of the shipping industry in Korea.

Table 13.4
Applicability of advantages and disadvantages by flag

Check Item	Korean reg.	KIS	Open reg.
Advantages			
• Subsidies and financial support from government	O[+]	O	X[++]
• Flexible crew arrangements	X	O	O
• Crew cost savings	X	O	O
• Free access to national cargoes	O	Δ[+++]	X
• Free access to foreign capital markets	X	Δ	O
• Flexible management decision-making (e.g., ship sale and purchase)	X	Δ	O
• Ease in the establishment of a ship management company	X	Δ	O
• Possibility of rationalising organisational structure of a shipping company	X	Δ	O
Disadvantages			
• Commitment to Korea in a war or national emergency	O	O	X
• Taxation	O	Δ	X
• Shipowner's payment on social security and fringe benefits	O	Δ	X
• Lifetime employment contracts	O	Δ	X
• Restrictions on foreign exchange	O	Δ	X
• Government regulation	O	Δ	X
• Labour disputes with Korean crews	O	Δ	X

Notes: [+]   *O means 'applicable'.*
       [++]   *X means 'not applicable'.*
       [+++]   Δ *indicates possible applicability.*

Source: compiled by the author.

Possible area for co-operation in ship management

Assuming that the second scenario is implemented, attention can now be focused upon ship management, a possible solution to alleviate the current situation facing Korean shipping. Partial ship management, or the delegation of one or several Korean shipowners' functions to ship management companies, both national and international, may initially be conceived as the early stages of flagging out. The desired initial role of ship management is not likely to extend further than to that of crew management. As Sletmo describes it:[10]

> the transnationalisation of shipping through flagging out and a greatly increased dependence upon manpower from the developing countries.

Korean ship management companies would potentially provide Korean shipping companies with crew management services when they are able to supply low-cost crews to the owners. To be able to do this ship managers must have a reservoir of crews from developing countries at the time of request. However, it does not seem that most of the management companies have sufficient resources of either manpower or training centres for the education of safety and environmental protection. Here there exists an opportunity for co-operation through a joint venture between Korean and foreign ship management companies.

As flagging out accelerates, the role of ship management may be expanded from crew manning to technical management. According to recent research,[11] in this circumstance, only a few Korean ship managers have the capability to deal with technical management. Without resorting to foreign ship management companies, a Korean shipping company may set up an in-house management company for ships under its control. They may anticipate the following benefits:

(a) The slicing effect - the separation of functions with the shipping company.[12]

(b) The reduction of the progressive accumulation of crew pension costs.

(c) The changing of crew employment contract from a life time to an one-year base for newly recruited crew.

(d) The avoidance of labour disputes.

There is contention, though, as to whether Korean institutions are proficient enough to facilitate these benefits. The KSA maintains that the KSMCA has insufficient capability to provide a technical management service to the standard of international organisations.[13] Conversely, the KSMCA with the licence of ship management chartered from the Korea Maritime and Port Administration, maintains that they have legal rights to deal with such ship management services, that owners should not also be managers, and that the licence should not be issued to the shipping companies. They each strive to attain a position of hegemony, or restrained dominance, in order to capture an optimum market share of the Korean ship management business.

The research above showed that in March 1991, five out of 35 ship management companies were suitable for carrying out technical management in terms of personnel, expertise, and organisational scale. It seems that this situation has changed little until now. Here there is obviously room for foreign ship managers to enter the new market of ship management in Korea, in association with either shipowners or ship managers. Outlined here are potential areas for co-operation in the field of ship management between Korea and foreign countries.

Field surveys and interviews with managers from 20 ship management companies in the UK, Hong Kong, and Singapore, which were carried out by the author from August 1992 onwards, showed that co-operation on ship management may be made in the following fields:

(a) Crew manning management:
   • cost-effective recruitment of crews from developing countries, in particular from the Philippines, China, and Myanmar;
   • operation and establishment of training centres in the Philippines and China;
   • personnel management for cross cultural manning;
   • establishment of efficient shipboard organisation;
   • establishment of efficient communication channel systems between shore and offshore;
   • safety and pollution prevention training.

(b) Technical management:
   • establishment of a network of repair and maintenance facilities in China, Korea, Hong Kong, Singapore, Taiwan and Japan;
   • search for new ship scrap yards in China and North Korea;
   • the employment of a technical superintendent;
   • supplying ship stores;
   • surveys on ships' hulls, holds and machinery;
   • shore management teams and backup systems;
   • quality control system.

(c) Commercial management:
   • financing and legal advice related to ship sales and purchases;
   • dealing with foreign exchanges;
   • cost accounting related to repairs and maintenance;
   • agency and chartering;
   • selection of alternative flags;
   • insurance claims;
   • computerisation.

The above areas were mainly listed in the light of the demand from Korean owners and managers for ship management services. Further expansion of these areas depends on consultation and discussions between both parties and the initial progress of the Korean ship management market. This co-operation may, firstly, aid the development of ship management in Korea and, secondly, through the subsequent improvements to competitiveness, help to overcome the unfavourable climate which the industry faces at present.

Conclusion

It is evident then, that Korean shipowners and the shipping industry as a whole are facing formidable problems. These are caused by:

(a)   rising crew costs and difficulties in the recruitment of qualified crews;

(b)   high insurance costs caused by the high rate of marine casualties;

(c)   an adverse taxation system;

(d)   very limited access to foreign capital markets with favourable financing terms; and

(e)   an inflexible government regulatory environment.

It is unlikely that the Korean government would be in a position to solve these problems for the shipowners and the industry as it had until the early 1980s.[14] In these circumstances, two methods were suggested to Korean shipowners to acquire the greater international competitive power not possible under the Korean flag registration: to establish a second register and to flag out. It was found that the latter would be the most preferable way because of the time and effort required to establish the second register the so-called KIS. However, before a ship register is selected, the KSA must carefully evaluate the advantages and disadvantages drawn from it. The choice of flag must be linked to the maximisation of the required favourable effects.

The selection of an open registry and ship management are closely inter-related and, therefore, as flagging out begins to develop, Korean shipping companies may increase their demands for ship management to make them increasingly cost-effective. Considering that Korean ship management companies are in an early stage of development in terms of manpower, know-how, and business network compared to those of advanced ship management companies and that the Korean market for ship management will be open to everyone, there may be considerable potential for co-operation in the field of ship management services. In these circumstances, the KSMCA may have two major competitors, namely: in-house management companies established by Korean owners, and foreign ship management companies. Therefore, the KSMCA must be capable of satisfying client needs in terms of cost and quality as soon as possible, in order to secure shares of the Korean market and to survive in the 1990s and beyond.

Flagging out to either the KIS or an open registry, will not only be a turning point in the recent history of Korean shipping, but will also act as a catalyst for the further development and co-operation in this sphere of the shipping world. The point to be emphasised here is that by responding to an emerging free world trade system like the World Trade Organization launched in 1995, the Korea Maritime and Port Administration visibly endorses both the acceleration of the deregulation process and the introduction of free competition principles in shipping policy formulation, in order to improve the competitive edge of the Korean shipping sector.

Notes and references

1   Park, Y-S, et al. (1991), *A Feasibility Study on the Introduction of International Ship Register into Korea*, Korea Marine Policy and Foundation, Pusan, Korea.

2   Peters, H. J. (1993), *The International Ocean Transport Industry in Crisis*, p. 21, The World Bank, Washington, D.C.

3   Korea Shipowners' Association (1993), *Maritime Statistics*, KSA No. 93-5.

4   Lloyd's Ship Manager (1990), *Ship Management*, p. 36, Lloyd's List International, London.

5   Oh, M. S. and Lee, T-W. (1994), 'A Survey on the Performance and Job Attitude of Korean-Chinese Ratings on Korean Ships', working paper, Korea Maritime University, Pusan, Korea.

6   Ibid.

7   Lloyd's Register (1994), *World Casualty Statistics*, p. 13.

8   Consolidated profit and loss statements in the period 1989-1992 showed that the insurance cost had increased from 2.7 per cent to 3.0 per cent of the total costs. Korea Shipowners' Association (1993), op. cit.

9   Lee, T-W. (1993), 'Some Reflections on the Causes of Growth of Korean Shipping', in Gwilliam, K. M. (ed.), *Current Issues in Maritime Economics*, p. 8-21, Kluwer Academic Publishers, Amsterdam.

10   Sletmo, G. K. (1989), 'Shipping's fourth wave: ship management and Vernon's trade cycles, *Maritime Policy and Management*, Vol.16, No. 4, pp. 293-303.

11   See Park, Y-S. et al. (1991), *Some Proposals for the Development of Crew Manning Management Companies*, KSMCA, Pusan, Korea.

12   Spruyt, J. (1994), *Ship Management*, p. 5, Lloyd's of London Press Limited, London.

13   Ibid., pp. 103-8.

14   Lee, T-W. (1990), 'Korean Shipping Policy: The Role of Government', *Marine Policy*, Vol. 14, No. 5, pp. 421-437.

Index

238

Vladivostok 134, 195, 202, 205
Vostochny 111, 124, 125, 126

waiver system 49, 57, 61, 104
Weber, Max 9, 86, 164

wigs 55
World Trade Organisation 232

Yellow Sea Economic Zone 116 - 7,
129 - 30